DIRTY WORDS

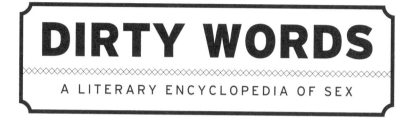

DIRTY WORDS

A LITERARY ENCYCLOPEDIA OF SEX

EDITED BY
ELLEN SUSSMAN

BLOOMSBURY

Published by Bloomsbury USA, New York
Distributed to the trade by Macmillan

All papers used by Bloomsbury USA are natural, recyclable products made from wood
grown in well-managed forests. The manufacturing processes conform to the environmental
regulations of the country of origin.

Library of Congress Cataloging-in-Publication Data

Dirty words : a literary encyclopedia of sex / Ellen Sussman.—1st U.S. ed.
p. cm.
ISBN-13: 978-1-59691-474-2
ISBN-10: 1-59691-474-2
1. Sex—Dictionaries. 2. Sex—Slang—Dictionaries. 3. Sex—Humor.
I. Sussman, Ellen, 1954–

HQ9.D58 2008
818'.5402—dc22
2008001460

First U.S. Edition 2008

1 3 5 7 9 10 8 6 4 2

Typeset by Westchester Book Group
Printed in the United States of America by Quebecor World Fairfield

To Neal, with love, the word I've saved for you

CONTENTS

CONTENTS

viii

CONTENTS

DIRTY WORDS

INTRODUCTION

ELLEN SUSSMAN

When my brother was eleven years old, my father invited him for a car ride.

"Where are we going?" my brother asked.

"Nowhere," my father said. "We're just going to drive around."

"I wanna go!" I wailed, ten years old and desperate for my father's attention.

"Boys only," my father said.

My brother flashed me a triumphant grin, and the two of them marched out of the house and into my dad's Rambler station wagon.

About an hour later, they returned. I was waiting on the front steps, imagining what wonderful adventures they were having without me.

They got out of the car and walked up the path. My brother avoided me. He had a smug, secretive look on his face, and I was ready to kill him for it. They strode right past me and into the house.

I might have used torture; it wasn't beneath me. Somehow in the next few days I twisted an arm and extracted this information: they did really just drive around. But during that time, my father told my brother that he was going to tell him the Facts of Life.

"What's that?" I asked.

"I don't know," my brother said. "Dad told me I could tell him all the dirty words I knew, and he would tell me what they meant."

"Did you?"

"Yep."

"And he told you?" I asked.

"Yep." And my brother sauntered away.

This is my revenge. Instead of a car ride with Dad, swapping curse words for stories, I got a lousy pamphlet: *Your Changing Body*. No spicy language there—no *fuck*, no *blow job*, no *slut*. Who cares about fallopian tubes? Give me an orgy of dirty words.

This is my orgy of dirty words. You might learn the Facts of Life in these pages; you might learn the Mysteries of Life. I gave my contributors this assignment: pick a sexual word or term. Let it be your madeleine—let it summon up memory. Or take that word and toss it around, juggle it, work it through your teeth. I invited these remarkable writers to create stories or essays, rants or riffs, poems or persuasions. And they delivered the goods: a sexual literary feast.

This book is not porn or erotica, but tucked between these covers is some of the most erotic writing I have ever read. This book is not a social science textbook, but on these pages the sexual temperature of our culture is recorded—feel its heat. This book is not a dictionary, but in these essays and stories and poems, sexual terminology gets defined through bedtime romps, through wordplay and etymology and historical reference, through whimsy and happenstance.

I asked my contributors to offer up their musings in short pieces that would range from 250 to 1,000 words. I wanted them to boil down their material until they could offer us the essence of experience or thought. I wanted the heady rush of so much flavor—a taste that explodes in your mouth. I want the impact of that literary experience to linger, so that long after the book has been placed back on the shelf, the reader might still savor that rich concoction.

I gave my contributors the freedom to pursue their definitions in the format of their choice: fiction or nonfiction, poetry or play. This stylistic range seems fitting for the wildly different ways in which sex moves us, affects us, shakes us up, feeds us.

My contributors range in age: they're twenty-four years old and they're elder statesmen. I've learned that dirty words change with each generation. A year from now there will be new words and sexual curiosities to explore. If I've missed some words, let me know. I'll collect new words and missing words on my Web site: www.ellensussman.com. This isn't a complete list—it's an offering, a smorgasbord. And I've chosen to include words that aren't dirty at all: *kissing*, *monogamy*, *virginity*, for example. In fact, in my mind, no words are dirty: that's part of my intention here. Let's put it all on the table and talk about it. Something surprising happens: the words are mere words. It's what they represent that so intrigues us.

Why did I choose to gather literary essays about sex? I think that in writing about sex, writers get a chance to tap into unexplored territory. They push below the surface of relationships, of passion, of our urges and needs and dreams. They reveal truth about human behavior and about our society. Sometimes they even get closer to that illusive concept: love.

Pick a word. Any word.

69

ELLEN SUSSMAN

DEFINITION: simultaneous and mutual oral sex.

The term, originating in the French soixante-neuf, *suggests the shape of bodies engaged in cunnilingus and fellatio.*

6 and 9 swim with the help of their fine tails, they flip with those perfect circles tucked inside them, they somersault in a wild circus act of tumbles.

6 is 9, 9 is 6.

I remember sitting on the floor in my yellow nursery-school classroom writing a perfect 6. Bravo, Miss D'Quilla says. 9! 6, I say, my lips quivering. I had worked so hard! 6! she says, turning the paper upside down. I look at my 6. It's 9. It's 6. It's my eyes that swim, that nudge tail over circle, set the number spinning, and no matter where it settles, the number is 6 or 9.

Later I find out I'm dyslexic. 6 and 9 unmoor me. I can't catch them, can't make them stick.

I'm in bed with a man. His body flips and suddenly his head is gone, tucked somewhere below the covers, and his penis appears where his face once was. His mouth seems to have found my other mouth, and we've taken each other in, and in a quick instance I've lost my bearings. Is that him or me? I can't concentrate. If I think about what I'm doing, then I can't think about what he's doing. If I give in to what he's doing, then I can't keep doing what I'm doing.

I push away.

I'm confused, I say.

Don't think, he says.

He dives back under the covers.

I stop thinking. All my life I've wrangled to keep the 6 and 9 in order, and suddenly I'm told, give it up. There is no order. A 6 is a 9 is a 6. Let it go.

So I do. 69. I give up years of struggling to hang on, to make sense of numbers and letters that swim before my eyes. I'm not doing it to him, he's not doing it to me. It's a whirlwind, a wild storm, we're in this together.

The 6 and the 9 come together. Oh! O. O. It works no matter how you flip it. I can barely catch my breath. O!

ADULTERY

DONOVAN BRIGHT

DEFINITION: voluntary sexual intercourse between a married person and someone other than his or her partner.

One man's folly is often another man's wife.

—HELEN ROWLAND, 1875-1950, AMERICAN JOURNALIST

Here's a word to the wise: if you're an adulterer, you're not in it for the sex. I'm serious. Hey, I'm not denying there's a decent whack of it, with all the bells and whistles, fresh partners, and so on—but adultery isn't about the sex at all. I'm not pulling your chain. If it's regular sex you want, sort it out at home. Who in his right mind would sweat bullets for three and a half weeks trying to organize a measly half hour on a rainy Tuesday morning in a shitty Hampton Inn at the wrong end of Newark? That's a rough planning-toexecution ratio. Plus, six months in and who's to tell whom you're horny for anymore? I've known guys to cheat on their girlfriend with their wife. Done it myself. No, it's not about the sex, fledgling adulterers, nota bene. Get on a different bus if that's your ride.

You don't wanna hear it. You're still all about the ecstasy, the soft pillows, the wild humping, rah rah rah. I'm telling you—look at the evidence. This ain't no pleasure dome, this. The sooner you admit it the better. This is a life of secrets. You'd better have a thing for them: better keep mum. Are you ready for clandestine ops? Got stamina? Got a tight mouth and a penchant for loneliness? You'll need it. You get a lot of time to yourself. It's kinda spooky in the Land of Cheats. It's always night and the streetlamps are out. Whom can you trust? Who's on your side? Where did all your friends go? You can't know. Shadows everywhere. Don't trust 'em. All you wanted was a bit of fun and someone to adore you, right? Aw, you fell in love, you sweet-hearted li'l rose? It don't make a crow of difference: you just murdered company with a serrated knife. Breathe deep. You're on your own now.

Hey, I understand the draw of it: who wouldn't want to bend space and time up in knots? You were there when you were here, you were talking to him while you were fucking her, you were on the train but you were in the cab. What are you now, Stephen Hawking? Gotta tell you, physicists would kill for your talent. If it weren't corrupt as hell, your data would make some textbook. So you're a liar. All right, man the ramparts. Lying is your standard. Now we're getting somewhere. We're admitting to something! You tell more lies than you have sex, by a long way, huh? So lying is part of the kick, right? Don't get all coy on me now. A good liar is hard to find. Governments jump for 'em.

Get where I'm going with this? Come on. Confess. What's really turning you on here? Blow jobs in the back of a Jetta? I don't believe it. Think about it, toots. Here's one life, an ox's burden, work work work and never a word of thanks, a bunch of yapping relatives and boring kids and college accounts bleeding you dead. You're booked from morn till moon and she can quote everything from the color of your jockeys to the cut of your mulligatawny. But wait a moment. Just when you thought you were done, schmuck of the decade, old toast in the old garbage can, here's another life, a second life, one you pull out of the ether one randy afternoon and look . . . look, you can make a paradise out of it. Nobody can tell you whom or what. Nobody even knows who you are. You'll never share it with a soul. It's a private island with an airstrip for lovers, it's ocelots in the trees and red meat on the fire, it's endless merlots and droit du seigneur. It's beautiful here. Wreaths and servants. Executive power. Absolute monarchy. Eureka.

No, it's not about the sex. You've slipped the surly bonds of sex. This is about something bigger, and much better. This is about the kingdom you've built. It's about the country you rule. No checks, no balance. No resistance. Go on. Admit it. You're Zeus. You're Thor. You're the boss of all bosses. On planet Adultery, you're unaccountable at last. Now tell me that's not better than sex.

AFFAIR

JESSICA ANYA BLAU

DEFINITION: a sexual relationship, especially a secret one.

Conservative estimates are that 60 percent of men and 40 percent of women will have an extramarital affair. These figures are even more significant when we consider the total number of marriages involved—since it's unlikely that all the men and women having affairs happen to be married to each other. If even half of the women having affairs (or 20 percent) are married to men not included in the 60 percent having affairs, then at least one partner will have an affair in approximately 80 percent of all marriages.

—ADAPTED FROM *THE MONOGAMY MYTH* BY PEGGY VAUGHAN

AFFAIR: A SHORT STORY

An affair is what your father is having when he never shows up at home, even when your younger brother, who is a fifteen-year-old drug addict, punches a hole in every door in the house (twelve, including closet doors) when your mother won't let him leave to meet his dealer. An affair is what your father is still having when that same brother takes a handful of your mother's Valium and drinks what's left in the vodka bottle as he tries to kill himself. Your father won't even talk about his not visiting your brother when he was in the hospital for attempted suicide. He likes to pretend it was just an accidental overdose.

An affair can also be what your mother is having when she walks around the house alternately so happy that she seems giddy and drunk or so short-tempered that you're afraid to ask her for anything—to sign a field-trip permission slip or pick you up from the movies. When you come home from school, you feel jittery and ill because you're never sure which Mom you'll get: the singing, smiling, affectionate one, or the one with that far-off look that grows to a frown when you interrupt her thoughts. Your brother is happy when your mother is having an affair because it takes the focus off him and leaves him free to do drugs.

When you're fully grown and your now sober brother has an affair, he'll bring his lover to your house where you are raising two daughters and not having an affair. He might have loud sex with his lover in the blue, frilly bedroom of one daughter (the one out on a sleepover), and you might burst into that room in the night dark and say outrageous things that make you sound like a puritanical old woman, like, How dare you do *that* in my child's bed! Really, what neither you nor your brother understand just then is that what you are angry about is not his affair, but the ones your mother and father had years earlier.

When your husband has an affair, you feel as if you've gone crazy. This is because what you see and know is specifically contradicted by what your husband is telling you. When you find the e-mail on his office computer that says, *I miss you sooooooo much!!!!!! Can't wait to see you again!!!!! Love ya!!!!!* and he insists that the e-mail is from a really friendly colleague to whom he has ABSOLUTELY NO ATTRACTION, your brain cannot reconcile the use of so many eager adolescent exclamation points and the semi-retarded use of the word *ya* with what your husband claims is a somewhat dull, overly friendly woman he is working with. Eventually, you allow yourself to believe your husband, but not because the idea of the affair is so painful (although it is). Rather, you believe him because the idea that you may have married someone as charming and sneaky as your father is too much to bear.

Your affair is different. Unlike others, you're not simply repeating some bad family pattern. Your affair is based on true love with someone who is truly lovable, not some Lee-press-on-nails-wearing trollop (like your father's lover) or some overly bearded poet (like your mother's lover) or some body-hair-less woman-child (like your brother's lover). Oh, no, your lover is better than all those people, and so are you, because you have no choice in this affair. It is more compelling than anything that has come before it. You now understand the strength of frustrated desires, the force that propelled your brother to punch holes in the doors. In fact, you often think of punching holes in the doors, such as when your daughter interrupts your thoughts at nine o'clock at night (during the affair, your mind becomes your full-time home and reality is like a time-share in Reno where you resent having to show up) to tell you that she needs forty Powerpuff Girl valentines for school the next day. But you don't punch holes in the doors, you're not that kind of person (besides, you know how much time, money, and effort it takes to replace twelve doors). Instead, you get in the car, click off the radio so you can think about your lover, and drive to the Rite Aid down the street. At a red light you turn your rearview mirror toward yourself and look at your clavicles, which are jutting out like drumsticks implanted below your neck. You have lost ten pounds since your affair started, but you insist to your friends that you don't know why or how.

You know the affair is over when you gain the weight back. Sometimes you regret the affair; you can't believe you actually risked your marriage to be with some ponytail dude who turned out to be no better than the Lee-press-on trollop, the overly bearded poet, or the body-hair-less woman-child. In an effort to erase the affair, you roll over your brain to make it new again, the brain of someone who is totally committed to marriage, the brain of someone who is utterly dissimilar to her parents or her brother. But sometimes you miss the affair, the way it solidified every thought, anxiety, desire, and disappointment into one absolute, central focus that made you feel utterly contained—as if your body had previously been land-mined to bits, scattered from your hometown in Santa Barbara to your current home in Baltimore. You might miss the affair so much that you gather yourself up, take a Pilates class, buy new bras, actually go to a Shakespeare in the Park performance where you continually scan the crowd, holding your heart open for the next affair.

ANAL SEX

STEPHEN MCCAULEY

DEFINITION: anal sex is stimulation of the anus during
sexual activity. It can be done in several different ways:
manually, orally, or by anal intercourse.

*For the first time, during the mid-Ming period, sodomy was criminalized. A
pre-1526 amendment to the Ming Code compared anal penetration to forcing garbage into someone's mouth, and punished sodomy with 100 bamboo
cane strokes. The same scale of punishments applied to homosexual and heterosexual offences.*

—WWW.GLBTQ.COM/

At first, Brian was hesitant. True, it was what he wanted, the main
reason he'd driven in from the suburbs to meet someone he'd
only talked with online, but he was married, he hadn't done it in
over a year, he and Thomas were essentially strangers, he pointed
out, and he was concerned about Thomas's size.

Thomas, who prided himself on knowing how to manage a
situation like this, told Brian it was up to him. If he wanted to
leave, that was fine. If he wanted to go through with it, he only
had to do exactly what he was told, and there would be no problems. "I promise you," Thomas said.

It was a Sunday afternoon, one of those hot, breezy September days that feel like midsummer, minus the intense sunlight and
the oppressive humidity. A day when the air caresses the skin and
stirs all the senses. The windows were open to the street below,
and a real estate agent was holding an open house in a neighboring apartment. Thomas could hear people coming out of the elevator in the hallway of his building: "I don't much like the color
of this carpet."

He wondered what excuse Brian had given for coming to the

city on such a perfect afternoon, how many children he had, what his real name was. Naturally, he asked no questions.

There was something eager and pleading in Brian's eyes, and Thomas could see that he wanted to be pressured. "I'll bet you arranged your whole day around this," Thomas said. "I'll bet you thought about it all last night."

Brian confessed that he had. As Thomas had suspected, Brian seemed to enjoy confessing.

"Some men just need it," Thomas said. He was most comfortable with the need being the other person's, since this was the best way to short-circuit any question of his own. "You can tell me. You can tell me anything."

Brian trembled as he pulled off his clothes, and then again when he knelt before Thomas to undo the rest of his. Brian was obedient, as married men usually are, and although probably not under forty, his body was flexible and firm. He had an odd combination of timidity and hungry abandon, and Thomas could see that there would be no turning back.

"Stop holding your breath," Thomas told him. "That will make it easier." Once Brian did, Thomas felt his resistance dissolving, and then it was as if Brian had let go of the dock and was being carried out to sea on a current he had no desire to fight. He arched his head back and began to make a loud, panting sound.

Thomas nodded toward the hallway and said, "If you want me to keep going, you'll have to be more quiet."

"I'm sorry. I will be. Please."

Thomas kept adjusting Brian's legs, his arms, the curve of his spine. Brian was on his back staring into Thomas's eyes when his body began to shudder and spasm, without either of them touching Brian's cock. A few seconds later, he gazed up at Thomas nervously and said, "It feels like I'm still coming."

Thomas could feel a strong, rhythmic pulse inside Brian. If he moved, the pulsing came faster, so he kept still until, gradually, it faded. Brian shut his eyes with gratitude and exhaustion. A prospective buyer in the hallway coughed and commented on a lighting fixture.

"Does that always happen to you?" Thomas asked.

Brian shook his head, apologized once more for the noise, and began to gather up his clothes.

"If you need it again," Thomas told him, "you know where I am."

He usually came in the late afternoon. The time had to do with his work schedule or maybe the after-school activities of his kids or his wife's job. Thomas never thought it was important to know why. Brian would call and say, "I need it today. I really have to have it," and they would make a plan. He became more and more sensitive, so that eventually he would start to flush and shiver just from being touched there. "Sometimes I dream about it," he confessed. "Sometimes when I'm driving home, my whole body starts to shake again. I'm afraid I'm getting addicted."

"You are," Thomas said. On this matter, as with need, he preferred to keep himself out of it.

What Brian wanted was predictable, almost to the point of cliché—to be in the bedroom what he never was elsewhere. Sub-servient, submissive, controlled, needy. And so it was easy to ig-nore that he set the agenda, he defined the terms, he made the calls.

After almost a year, Brian began to feel the heavy burden of guilt, and with it, a powerful sense of shame. His children, his job, his vows. Sometimes he became angry at Thomas: "You did this to me."

Eventually, his calls stopped. Thomas concluded that Brian was not, apparently, as addicted as he had feared himself to be. When Thomas was ready, finally, to lay claim to his own needs, he discovered that Brian had blocked Thomas's number on his cell phone. There was nothing he could do about it. Thomas didn't know where he lived. He couldn't be certain he knew his real name. And so, despite what Thomas had consistently done to Brian for so many months, he ended up feeling as if he was the one who'd been fucked.

APHRODISIACS

MICHELLE WILDGEN

DEFINITION: anything that increases or tends
to increase sexual passion or power.

It's sad how our effort to promote the survival of our species through copious copulation has run other species to the brink of extinction. Rhino horn, prized by some as an alleged aphrodisiac, offers no such sexual power; and its (illegal) use in Chinese medicine for other ailments is questionable. The horns look a little like an erect penis, and in traditional medicine that's sometimes enough to mean that grinding them up and eating them will make one's own penis erect. At best, they contain nutrients, such as phosphorus, which gave our nutrient-poor ancestors a little more energy.

—WWW.LIVESCIENCE.COM

The word derives from Aphrodite, the Greek goddess of love and sex. And as with many potential aphrodisiacs, her origins prove disturbing on second glance. Conventional wisdom says she simply appeared in the ocean waves on a roomy scallop shell, but Hesiod's *Theogony* reveals a gorier birth: the goddess of sexual desire was born where the severed testicles of the god Uranus were hurled into the sea. Uranus suffered this loss during a heated coupling with his rebellious wife, Gaea, who had exhorted their son Cronus to ambush his father with a sickle. After years of bobbing in the sea water and generating much white foam, the testicles were gone forever but the goddess swam ashore.

Now consider the famed Spanish fly, or cantharides, an erotic treat derived from the pulverized bodies of the North African blister beetle. As the Marquis de Sade and his unlucky prostitute cohorts discovered, Spanish fly can deliver more than a strategically placed rush of blood: it is an inflammatory agent, the effects of which include irritation, vomiting, and kidney damage. Spanish fly literally creates an itch one has to scratch. Frankly, when you think about it that way, you can buy a cream for that.

Humans have contributed other shortcuts to bliss, but they're often just as graceless, even crude, whereas nature's gentler aphrodisiacs are merely direct. Man-made Viagra and other "ED" treatments go right to the source and engorge it; the commercials are all smug silver-fox boardroom types, waltzing or suggestively hurtling a football through the placid hole of a tire swing. We've also come up with pornography, of course, which walks a fine line between ridiculous and effective. A few shutters in the brain must close before a dirty film can work its magic, and the effort required to overlook the mullets and simian dialogue disqualifies porn as a transporting sex-enhancer.

Other so-called aphrodisiacs abound, it's true, but I am sorry to tell you that you probably know them all: time and vacation and doors that lock, a little wine, a few tokes of good weed, but not a stuporous amount of either, a fig and a square of chocolate but not a bellyful. You want that first flush of heat, the hibiscus-flowering of blood vessels. You want the throb that fills the eardrums and everything else. And you can have it, but it's a bit like when your mother told you Santa Claus is a spirit of generosity that lives in all our hearts. It's not what we were hoping to hear.

Therefore, I suggest less time on the pharmaceutical and the order of Coleoptera and more on the culinary. Here the effect is not so much the medicinal magic and overriding urgency promised by a true aphrodisiac. It's more suggestion. You present your companion with a reminder, silent but absolutely clear, of what else you might be doing. Consider the classics: The plump, glistening salinity of a little oval oyster seems like something Prince might have sung about back in the days of songs like "Head" and "Soft and Wet." A spear of asparagus is suggestively elegant, but disqualified by its disheartening tendency to droop. Some suggest carrots. Where's the sensuous nuance in a woody, pointed stalk? Forget the carrots. Look to the fig, which everyone agrees is so overtly sexual the Italians use the word for *fig* as slang for *vagina*. And wisely so: rounded at the hip, meltingly soft, velvety outside with a juicy flare of rich pink within; the tanginess of actual sex is here made textural in the tender pop of a fig's soft-skinned seeds. It's as frank as eye contact, so clearly a call to action that it's enough to leave you speechless.

Just as bold but less commonly mentioned is the scent of crab apple trees. They lined the streets of the neighborhood I grew up in, and each spring they flowered and released a tangy, humid, musky scent, enough to paralyze me beneath their branches, head surrounded by blossoms and feet by petals that had swooned to the dirt. The air was pollen-drenched and hazy with a fragrance somewhere between baking bread and overripe fruit and sweat and smashed, tart berries. Mentally, I couldn't quite merge that scent's deliciousness with its slight unpleasantness, its too muchness, and the way it suggested an intense need for privacy—I could not define its allure back then. Now I can.

Nature can get away with such overt displays of sex and fertility. She probably *has* to: unaided, humans run around feeding each other dried beetles. Yet her most fetching overtures—and ours as well—are not pure sugar: think of chocolate's dark notes and the slow heat it needs to melt; think of the faint leather-belt backnote in a mouthful of red wine. The finest aphrodisiacs utilize a little yin with their yang, and those that try for mere sweetness are missing the point. Just as Aphrodite herself came from someplace much darker, even bloodier, than a scallop shell, an effective aphrodisiac has a little bite, is just a bit uncomfortable. Like sex itself, it is unseemly in the wrong context—too moist, too salty, too fecund.

But why all the striving in the first place? Mere consciousness has never quite been enough for us as a species—we alter it any way we can. Mere pleasure is never quite enough, either—we want the overpowering thrum, the surge all the way out to the edge, but we're always dismayed to find more than happiness out there. The ongoing search for aphrodisiacs is proof that when we hear a story like that of the god Uranus, no one thinks of the blood—just, with thrilling envy, of the pleasure of being so dazed and unwatchful with lust that it's impossible to imagine the sickle.

AUTOEROTIC ASPHYXIATION

THOMAS BELLER

DEFINITION: suffocating oneself via strangulation for sexual
stimulation, especially to increase the intensity of orgasm.
AKA: scarfing. A *rasper* is a person who engages in
autoerotic asphyxiation.

The age range spans from 9 to 80 years of age for male practitioners of AEA (Uva, 1995). Deceased victims of the practice are most often white, middle-class unmarried males (Lowery & Wetli, 1982). Although one might presume that practitioners of this bizarre and dangerous behavior suffer mental illness, this is usually not the case. The adolescent victims are usually well adjusted, non-depressed, high achievers (Uva, 1995).

—ANDREW P. JENKINS, "WHEN SELF-PLEASURING BECOMES SELF-
DESTRUCTION: AUTOEROTIC ASPHYXIATION PARAPHILIA," *INTERNATIONAL
ELECTRONIC JOURNAL OF HEALTH EDUCATION* 3, NO. 3 (2000): 208-16

1. A strange, solitary sex act in which the autoerotic asphyxiator deprives himself (it is often a he) of oxygen, while manually

bringing himself to a climax. The more dire the need for oxygen, the closer the climax. The tricky calculation is in getting off before passing out. Sometimes people miscalculate and die. This happens to all sorts of people, including those in the public eye, such as a British MP, Conservative, of course, which was a kind of last gasp, so to speak, of self-inflicted insult, because it seems like it is always the most moralistic and pious figures in society, the Moral Majoritarians, and, in this case, the "back to basics" contingent, who are found out to be masturbating while a hooker fondles herself on a bed, or to be snorting amphetamines and having sex with gay hustlers, or, in this case, to be masturbating in woman's clothes with an amphetamine-laced orange in your mouth and a noose around your neck while dangling from a rope hung above the dining room table. Which means that in addition to the insult of being found out, and of dying, there is the final insult of being rendered a cliché, which, while not nearly as bad as the wound itself, definitely qualifies as a big portion of salt.

Another alleged but unconfirmed victim was an Australian pop star, lead singer of a band called INXS (another annoying irony, if you think about it, but then after every premature death the world becomes a hall of mirrors in which every reflection is an annoying or excruciating irony, all of which are very difficult to articulate).

2. The less discussed meaning of *autoerotic asphyxiation* is much more common, especially among adults, though the tendency can develop very early. This version involves being in an intense state of desire. The desire is an end in itself. Having is not the goal. The autoerotic asphyxiator will gravitate to perilous and precarious situations in which the lover—man or woman—is within your grasp, then not; present, then not; havable, then not. The more tantalizing and impossible, the better. The lover, and the love affair, flit in and out of the realm of possibility. When the object of your

obsession is in your grasp, you know what to do with him or her. Immediately: have sex. Because the sense of deprivation is an incredible aphrodisiac. The sex ameliorates not just the deprivation, but the feeling of insult that this deprivation causes. The energy and force of the sex is representative of the drive to have and possess, which is stoked by not having, not possessing. The dynamic involves being saved from despair and loneliness and Can't Live Without You–ness, but it also relies on the deprivation, the rejection, the "you" not being there to live with. For those for whom autoerotic asphyxiation is the chosen method of achieving pleasure, the pleasure is always intense and always fleeting.

BAD TASTE

STEPHEN DUNN

DEFINITION: manner, with respect to what is not
pleasing, refined, or in accordance with good usage or style.

In the 1987 movie Bad Taste, *directed by Peter Jackson, the population of a small town disappears and is replaced by aliens that chase human flesh for their intergalactic fast-food chain.*

−WWW.IMDB.COM

BAD TASTE
Once in Utah, after I asked everyone to think
of a secret, one of those
dark secrets we mistakenly believe

peculiar to ourselves, a Mormon woman
 who had no secrets,
no shadow, no coffee, tea, or doubt,

said I was conducting the class
 in bad taste,
and might I consider the others present

who didn't share my views? I told her
 that in this room adultery,
quiet evenings at home, bestiality, religion—

no subject matter was out of bounds.
 She wouldn't be appeased.
Other members of the class asked her

if she remembered any desires for revenge,
 any unspoken ambitions,
or perhaps the lie she told her husband one night

when he wanted love and she just wanted
 some honest sleep.
She didn't have such thoughts, she said,

and the class proceeded to eat her alive,
 which seemed only right
in a class with bad taste, first her thighs

and the flesh on her upper arms, then
 the fine, often unnamed parts
tasteful poets would never mention.

It was a poor lesson, of course,
  for the better students.
I had hoped to teach them humility,

gracefulness, and just enough arrogance
  to get them through
the coming years of neglect.

The other Mormons were silent.
  They didn't want
to be eaten next. "The truth,"

I told them, "is always somewhat
  in bad taste,
if good taste is what's decided on

by a group." But I'd failed by then.
  One of their friends
had been eaten alive, and I'd forgotten

where I was. All of them clearly knew
  the likes of me
who'd proven them, once again, correct.

BASES

PETER MARKUS

DEFINITION: the game of baseball is often used
as a metaphor for physical intimacy, especially to describe the
level of intimacy achieved in intimate encounters or relationships.

*Other parts of the baseball metaphor include "striking out" (sexual frustra-
tion), "pitcher" (for the penetrating partner) and "catcher" (for the receiving*

partner) in male homosexual intercourse, and more obscure allusions such as
a "catcher's mitt" for a contraceptive sponge.

−ALVIN L. HALL AND THOMAS L. ALTHERR, "EROS AT THE BAT:
AMERICAN BASEBALL AND SEXUALITY IN HISTORICAL CONTEXT,"
THE COOPERSTOWN SYMPOSIUM ON BASEBALL AND AMERICAN CULTURE,
1998 (MCFARLAND & COMPANY, 2002), 157-82.

When I was a boy, I lived and ate and breathed baseball. Baseball from morning to night. Especially in the summer. So it was confusing, to say the least, when one summer the boys in my town started talking about getting to first base, then second base, and rounding third base, only to find out that they weren't actually talking about baseball. I myself had gotten to second base, a fumbling sort of a check-swing bunt, with a girl named Lori Hetzel, who was my friend Richie's little sister. We were in a field of scrub brush on the edge of the golf course where we used to go swimming for golf balls that had been shanked into the thirteenth-hole water hazard when she and I fell and fumbled into and onto each other and my hand, somehow—bless its bony heart—found its way up to Lori's second base. That was the same summer that I began to fantasize about getting to third base with other girls, such as Kristy McNichol of *Family* fame, or the girl who played Joanie on *Happy Days*, or Brooke Shields, who, the next summer—the summer we were both thirteen—whispered into the ears of American boys like me that nothing came between her and her Calvin's. That summer, at night, I was what came between me and blue jeans. And once I started coming like this, let me tell you, I could not stop. Eventually I doubled my way into second base in the basement of Shelly Longfellow's house one day when her mother was away at work. The end of that summer I tripled and found myself sliding headfirst, Charlie Hustle style, into third. It took me quite a few summers before I knocked one out of the park, though I kept swinging and kept on striking out. I must admit that when I did finally hit a home run, it wasn't quite as glorious as I imagined it might be. When the ball rose over the fence, is what I am saying, it just as quickly disappeared. And I was left to trot around the bases, careful to touch each corner without tripping myself up. When I finally reached home, I walked back into the dugout, wanting to feel more heroic than I did. The truth is, I ended up sitting by myself, back in the shadows of the dugout, where my eyes seemed to only want to stay staring down. I didn't know what to do with my hands. So I picked up a bat—they were all wood back then—held it tightly in my grip, and knocked the dirt out of my rubber cleats.

BDSM (*see also* TOP/BOTTOM)

STEPHEN ELLIOTT

DEFINITION: BDSM is Bondage Domination SadoMasochism—
in practical terms it means the utilization of restraint,
power exchange, and the giving and or receiving of
pain in the interests of sexual fulfillment.

Just as an aside here, before and during the war, kinky folks seeking to identify each other would sometimes defensively ask, "Do you play the mandolin or the saxophone?" to discover which of them was the masochist or the sadist by the first letter of these instruments.

−GUY BALDWIN, M.S., A LOS ANGELES PSYCHOTHERAPIST,
SERVED AS INTERNATIONAL MR. LEATHER AND
MR. NATIONAL LEATHER ASSOCIATION DURING 1989-90

My earliest fantasies revolved around being kidnapped by beautiful women and held hostage. I would be tied up, and the women would never be far away. They would whisper threats, their fingers resting on my chest. As puberty hit, the women wore tighter clothes, but the fantasies were essentially the same. I was tied up, they were sitting on me, smothering me, reminding me I had no control. The women in my fantasies were stronger than me. They overpowered me. And in some strange way I could not yet understand, they made me feel safe. Growing up I never felt safe.

Then I was thirteen and I ran away from home and slept on rooftops for a year and thought about other things. After that I was put in a series of group homes where masculinity was important. There were gangs and violence and I tried not to think about women dominating me, pulling me down the street on a leash, blindfolded and gagged. I didn't want to think about being humiliated, forced to wear women's clothes. But I did.

I met a lady in Amsterdam in a leather bar. She was old and stocky and sure of herself. She wore a leather dress. I was twenty-one years old and worked as a stripper when I was back in Chicago. I was so much prettier than she. She took me back to her hotel room where she slapped me across the face and told me to take my clothes off. She had a box full of tools, hoods, gags, needles, whips. She used these things on me, and when she was done, I left her sleeping and took the first train to Berlin.

I am not pro-BDSM, but I am anti-shame. You don't choose your desires, your desires choose you. And you have to find the best way to interact with those desires so you can lead a healthy, prosperous life and not do harm to other people. If you are a sadist, someone who likes inflicting pain, then you need to find someone who craves pain instead of taking it out on those who don't. And if you are a submissive, you need to find someone who enjoys controlling you rather than manipulating your lovers into a pattern of abuse. In fantasy there is no consent, but in real life we have to look out for each other. BDSM is a voluntary exchange of power.

I like to give up control. I have scars. I like to be cut and burned, but when someone cuts you with a knife or sticks needles through your body or puts a cigarette out on your chest, you will wake up the next day tired. In the world of BDSM we call it playing. If you play two or three times a week, you will walk around in a haze, flooded with endorphins. There was a time in my life where I felt like a junkie. Lying on my bed in the Mission District, stuck full of pins, bleeding, my girlfriend running her hand across my face saying, "I think you're amazing," I lifted up and floated away.

You have to play safe. You have to have safewords and you have to know who is tying you up, holding the knife blade against your throat. Will the person stop if asked? Do your friends know where you are?

BESTIALITY

KARIN COPE

DEFINITION: sexual relations between a human and an animal.

The God Zeus appeared to Leda in the form of a swan, producing her children Helen and Polydeuces. Zeus seduced Europa in the form of a bull, and carried off the youth Ganymede in the form of an eagle. The half-human/half-bull Minotaur was the offspring of a white bull and Queen Pasiphaë. King Peleus continued to seduce the nymph Thetis despite her transforming into a lion, a bird, and a snake, among other forms. The god Pan, who has goatlike features, is depicted having sex with a goat.

We are so close to the animals; it is inconceivable that we would not mingle with them. I sleep, for example, nearly every night, with a cat or two cradled in my body, and often a dog stretched out beside my lover. Over the years, we have had to acquire a larger bed.

The softness of fur, the tucking of one body into another, the scent of grassy paws, the rumbling of a cat's purr in and against my belly, these are primal, essential pleasures, sensuous treasures; much of what I know about how to be comfortable in my own body and skin I have learned from animals. Eagerness, joy, longing, hungers of every sort, the seeking after warmth, the direct pursuit of desires, the need for a walk, a run, a swim, the sorrow of being left behind, the joy of reencounter, the richness of touch and scent—these are a few of the sensations I forgot as I slipped from childhood to adulthood, and that I learned again from living with animals, from loving them.

We humans have not always been so distant from animals as many of us are now, particularly in the urbanized West. We are distant and we are ridiculously sentimental: we turn our animals into little people, when we might do better to bestialize ourselves. After all, secretly, many of us already do.

Who has not ridden a lover like a horse or imagined lovemaking as a kind of flying? We writhe and fishtail through the atmosphere, breathing noisily, showing off, breaching, spouting. Who has not sported feathers, leather, stones, a bit of fur?

In pursuit of love and sensuous pleasure we consume animal and mineral matter as nourishment and aphrodisiacs; we change our appearances—shave, dress up or down, bedeck ourselves; dance, parade, cover ourselves in oils, perfumes, silky materials. Some of us collect stuffed animals or imagine ourselves small or large furry creatures. We invent pet names for one another, for various body parts: my little cabbage, my bunny rabbit, my furry bear, my dandelion, my aspergusto, my most beloved.

The language of gender, with its separations and oppositions, its masculine and feminine designations, is not nearly as flexible and apt as our multiplied sensuous explorations and expressions of these other, more animal, vegetable, or mineral embodiments. The terms of gender are too narrowly cast; they cannot begin to account for the variety of experiences of body, surface, and transformation that every growing or striving being knows. I am never simply one thing, a unity, a clear identity, a sex, but wind and solidity and fluid and small or large cradled thing, I am muscular movement and tooth-gritted want, fingernail and scale and new-mown hay and fluttering wing and devouring maw.

We are bestial in the broadest and most lovely sense when we are thus alive: of, like, one with, one of, the animals. We play; we take pleasure in warmth, in sensation, in our appetites. We are tender and ferocious, all at once. We know this—and yet, *bestiality*, as a term that is somehow descriptive of our deepest desires, carries other judgments, other histories, most notably the stringent command to separate ourselves from other life-forms, in order to establish and maintain our place at the top of some "chain of being": to exercise dominion over the earth and its elements and creatures.

The word *bestiality* first appears in Western European languages as a negative coinage sometime in the late Middle Ages or early Renaissance, hard upon the heels of the popularity of medieval "bestiaries"—fanciful and moralized accounts of admixtures of birds, fish, stones, plants, and other animals real and imagined. As the Aberdeen Bestiary claims, the purpose of the illustrated bestiary was "to improve the minds of ordinary people[:] the soul will at least perceive physically things which it has difficulty grasping mentally."[1]

Interestingly, and perhaps unsurprisingly, the emergence of "bestiality" coincided, roughly, with the invention of the notion "human" and the birth of "humanism" in Europe. As a certain version of human was circumscribed, described, and elevated,

---

1. Aberdeen MS 24, f25v, cited in "Introduction" to the Aberdeen Bestiary Project, p. 1, www.abdn.ac.uk/bestiary/what.hti (consulted 6/28/07).

other versions of being were demoted, as if all beings might be arrayed in a single line, on a single vertical scale, with European "man" at the top.

Humanism and the Enlightenment were concerned with purifying methods and categories, doing away with hybridizations. Thus, although acts of interspecies congress have surely always been with us, "bestiality" has not. It marks out what we must exclude if we are to be human in the "modern" sense: we must not descend to "lower orders," to consorting with beasts, or engaging in "less than human" or "savagely cruel and wicked" behavior—including sexual acts with animals.

Ironically, science, that prince of Enlightenment arts, no longer confirms our difference from and superiority to the beasts. Genetically speaking, we are very little different from them; indeed, we carry, inscribed in our genes, the elements that also make up other orders. Thus, we share 60 percent of our genes with fruit flies, and with our near relatives, chimps, 98.77 percent.[2]

We are, perhaps, less masters of the universe than messy doodlers in the nursery of wisdom. Our project of dominion has gone hand in hand with stupefying destruction. As we begin to take the measure of our damaging footprint on the earth, it becomes apparent that we're not really so smart, we all-too-clever humans.

In elevating and purifying ourselves, we've also lost ourselves. Now, again, we must learn to be.

Let us begin then, not with male and female, not with gay or bi or trans or straight, but with breath and touch and skin and fur. Let us begin with what we already sense without knowing we do.

As Pablo Neruda writes in his *Extravagario*, his book of va-

2. See U.S. Department of Energy Human Genome Program, "Genomics and Its Impact on Science and Society: The Human Genome Project and Beyond," March 2003, http://ornl.gov/sci/techresources/Human_Genome/publicat/primer2001/index.shtml (consulted 5/7/2007).

garies, a child's foot does not know its own nature; it does not know it is a foot. It "wants," he says, "to be a butterfly or an apple."[3]

Who is to say it also is not or will not be?

Could bestiality be reinvented as a second innocence?

What the enlightened mind can no longer fathom, the soul yearns to learn through the body.

BISEXUALITY

MEREDITH MARAN

DEFINITION: a person who is sexually attracted to and engages in sensual or sexual relationships with people of either sex.
AKA: AC/DC, playing for both teams, switch-hitter, ambisexual, flexible, AM/FM, pansexual, omnisexual, bi-curious.

A bisexual is a person who reaches down the front of somebody's pants and is satisfied with whatever they find.

–DANA CARVEY AS THE CHURCH LADY, *SATURDAY NIGHT LIVE*

It's a sweltering Saturday night in August, six months after the birth of our second son. My husband and I are sitting in a darkened theater in downtown San Jose, out for the evening on our first date in years, waiting for the film to begin.

"What's the movie called?" S. whispers to me. He asks because, as in all matters marital, I have made all the decisions, plans, and reservations.

"The Story of O," I whisper back, betting these words will mean nothing to him.

S. rattles the bucket of popcorn in his lap. Even in the dark

---

3. Pablo Neruda, "To the Foot from Its Child," trans. Alastair Reid, in *A New Decade: Poems 1958–1967*, ed. Ben Belitt (New York: Grove Press, 1969), 17.

I know he's mining for the half-popped kernels at the bottom. Any minute now, I'll hear those kernels crunching between his teeth—as will everyone in the seats around us. I suppress a sigh. "What's it about?" he asks.

I think, it's about saving our marriage. It's about overcoming, so to speak, the eroticism-evaporating events that have sucked the passion out of our sex life like an aesthetician extracting zits: the two years of raising babies; the four years of infertility treatments that preceded their arrival. If we've made love anytime in the past few months, I don't remember it. Which kind of says it all.

I say, "Sex."

S. takes my hand. "Sex," he repeats, running a finger down the center of my palm. My body responds as it used to, time-traveling back to when we were young, childless, and in lust. "I remember sex," he says. He moves his hand to my thigh, his fingers spilling down between my legs.

The first image appears on the screen. A blindfolded woman is led into a room in a baroque medieval castle, her hands bound behind her back. Her breasts erupt from a corset of purple velvet, proffered to the one man and the three women in the room like giant pearls presented on the half shell. The man reaches into his pantaloons, watching the women swarm around the blindfolded one. A delicate female hand reaches out, caresses one nipple. A red-lipsticked mouth licks and nips at the other. The blindfolded woman swoons and moans. The man's hand moves more vigorously inside his pants.

S. grips my hand so hard it hurts. I don't appreciate the distraction. I'm busy watching the women's hands, the women's lips, the women's breasts. I'm memorizing it all, burning it into memory to be summoned another time—whenever S. and I make love again; sooner, probably, the next time I make love to myself.

The man is naked now, moving purposefully toward the

blindfolded woman. The women whose hands are all over her peel away, parting like the Red Sea. As the man enters the woman, I feel S. tensing excitedly. "Finally," he whispers, his eyes transfixed on the screen.

As the fucking begins, I grow impatient. I can see this anytime, I think. I can *do* this anytime. When are we getting back to the girls?

The lights come up in the theater. People rush for the exit doors, avoiding each other's eyes. I'm bowlegged, so aroused I can barely walk. My husband's tumescence is impossible to miss. He hurries me to the car. I can hear him calculating how long it'll take him to drive the babysitter home.

"Which scenes turned you on most?" S. asks hoarsely as soon as we're alone. He wants car-talk confessional. I'm struck dumb by the shock of what I have to confess.

"The women," I say.

My husband drives, saying nothing. "The women with the guy?" he asks finally. Hopefully.

"Yes, that. But mostly, the women with the women."

"But it's just a fantasy, right? You're not . . . bisexual or anything?"

I think, if it's just a fantasy, why am I already plotting how I can make it—and me—come true?

S. and I sit in silence at a red light, pondering the consequences of the unexpected situation in which we now find ourselves. "I've always worried you'd fall for some other guy," he says. "Now I have to worry about . . ."

Everyone, I realize. I see my life stretching out in front of me, a very different future from the one I'd planned. "Everyone," I say, knowing for the first time that this is true.

BLOW JOB (*see also* FELLATIO)

ANTONYA NELSON

DEFINITION: the sexual activity of moving the tongue across
or sucking the penis in order to give pleasure.
AKA: hummer, BJ, head, sucking dick, giving head,
fellatio, smoking a pipe.

*This term, now widespread in English-speaking countries, spread from the
USA in the 1960s. A puzzling misnomer to many, to* blow *in this context is
probably a euphemism for* ejaculate, *a usage occasionally recorded in the
1950s. This may itself be influenced by the* there she blows *of whaling
cliché. An alternative and equally plausible derivation of* blow job *is from
the black jazz musicians' hip-talk expression* blow, *meaning "play" (an instrument). This term probably caught on in Britain and Australia simply
because there was no well-known alternative in existence.*

–TONY THORNE,

THE DICTIONARY OF CONTEMPORARY SLANG (PANTHEON)

He was old enough to be my father, my mother reminded me,
worried. My father, whom she was divorcing for his conduct in
an extramarital affair with a much younger woman, had no comment. I was twenty-one; my boyfriend was fifty-two. He was my
professor, and we bonded when the famous visiting writer pulled
out a gun in our class. The two of us—professor and I—made
alarmed eye contact as the writer waved the pistol around. Alcohol
was in the air; I didn't think I'd get shot, but I *did* think that the
class would result in some sort of volatile combustion.

We took the writer out for drinks after his reading, a die-
hard group of young fans, plus the professor, who was his host
and friend. By the end of the evening, the famous writer was
so drunk he did not care that we saw him adjust his toupee or

not-so-surreptitiously spit phlegm into an ashtray held way too near his nose. At one point he explained that he had an issue with expectoration. Whatever. This was going to be the first night I had sex with my professor. For every piece of embarrassing misconduct the visiting writer performed, I got a little excited knee nudge under the table from my professor. He, too, was a writer—not famous, like our visitor, but also not losing his shit. Not drooling on the bar or threatening to shoot the jukebox or the bartender, whom he kept calling Skippy, as in "Skippy, get yer ass on toppa my Jack Daniel's, hasta pronto."

The professor and I had been doing this dance in class since the first week or so, me shy and attracted, him intense yet seemingly professional. We shared a disdain for my peers, his students; we understood the simultaneous gravitas and ludicrousness of our endeavor as workshoppers of their work. He wouldn't sleep with me until I was no longer his student, until he'd assigned a grade and ushered me out the official door and then through the unofficial one. Nonetheless, we lay together occasionally in his bed, clothed and close, chaste, waiting for Christmas, for the English Department party, the end of the semester.

The night of the visiting writer, we forsook our (his) vows of abstinence. We dropped the man at his hotel, escorted him up the walk, and suffered his embraces, tainted as they were with the smell of whiskey vomit and Old Spice. Through the revolving door he lurched, while we laughed weepingly in the front seat of the professor's car, clutching one another in spasms of superiority. We drove to his house by mutual agreement: something had changed. Off came the clothes, away went the rules. And although we made love many successful times later, that first time was no good. I was no good. Not drunk enough, not abstracted enough, not released from what had happened in the classroom or the barroom, the waving gun and outrageous declarations, the toupee and the ashtray, the fizzled ego and insanity, his unsteady lurch around the revolving door of the Holiday Inn. I'd admired that writer's fiction, before I met him in the flesh. He'd been on a pedestal before he was in the bag.

The pact that my professor and I had shared, glances passed over the head of our gonzo visitor, had seemed sexy enough, back there at the bar. But here, in the bedroom, at the moment of truth, it no longer held sway. Where was my true boyfriend? The correct one? Several years my elder, but still a member of my generation? Not holder of a mortgage and tenure, but drummer in a band, still paying student loans, or some other bright-eyed wannabe writer? I'd spent too much of the evening in the presence of has-beens and hadn't-beens. Was this my father's penis in my mouth? His liver-spotted hand on my head, pressing me against him?

I gagged. Spat. Rolled from bed with the excuse of tequila, toupees, waved weaponry. Behind the locked bathroom door I pleaded hangover instead of a purer nausea.

The source of that nausea? My own father's affair, no doubt, his position as professor, as lover to a younger woman who had been his student. My esteem for that writer who'd betrayed a trust—and who, simultaneously, owed his fans absolutely nothing, no moral superiority, no higher road. Perhaps I predicted my own flawed future, wherein I would again and again come to the threshold of that humiliation: waving a metaphorical gun, adjusting a symbolic hairpiece, drizzling what meager portion of talent I'd been assigned into an ashtray or highball, hoping some young thing would want to join me in my bed, slave to an ego insatiable, salved only—and only briefly—by the ministrations of adoring, adorable youth.

BLUE BALLS

ERIC GOODMAN

DEFINITION: a slang term referring to testicular aching that may occur when the blood that fills the vessels in a male's genital area during sexual arousal is not dissipated by orgasm.

RELATED TERM: *bluewalls*: the female equivalent of blue balls.

Men are not alone in experiencing the discomfort of unrelieved vasocongestion. Women's genitals also become engorged with blood during sexual arousal, and like their male counterparts, women can experience pelvic heaviness and aching if they do not reach orgasm.

−DISCOVERY HEALTH, HTTP://HEALTH.DISCOVERY.COM/CENTERS/
SEX/SEXPEDIA/BLUEBALLS.HTML

A SHORT STORY

We were sixteen, but she was born in April, a month before I was. And she would be a senior in September, while I was only a junior. So when we met at our parents' beach club and quickly became girlfriend and boyfriend, I expected great things, especially when after only a week, she left me feel her up under her bikini top. We'd walk four beaches down, slip through the fence that marked the beach club boundaries, spread a blanket, and make out. She had small, well, maybe medium-sized breasts—they were the first I'd seen bare, so I had nothing to compare them to—with dark brown nipples that seemed too large for her breasts. (But what did I know?)

I learned to tongue them, to slurp them, to tease them erect until they became bumpy little birds' beaks trying to take off. She'd get squirmy and whisper my name and seem not to mind when I placed my hand against her bikini bottom. Soon she'd be grinding her pubis against the bony knob where my hand met my wrist, and I could feel her getting *wet!* through the thin cloth, but as soon as I tried to slip my finger underneath (once I succeeded, feeling with a thrill I could not describe except as *Good, very good!* what it felt like to touch a pubic hair not my own, and that, *that* I thought but wasn't sure was the tip of her vagina, her pussy, her wet cunt), she'd push my hand away and say, "No, Jimmy, I can't."

But if she couldn't, she seemed to want to. As July crept toward August and the tan on my back grew toward burnt sienna, she began letting me slide my hand under her bikini bottom, though she never let me remove it. Sometimes it felt as if my wrist were breaking, but if I bent it just right and she arched her pelvis, I could slip my middle finger inside her, slide it in and out and in and out. She'd moan even more than before and press through the front of my trunks against the most insistent hard-on Breezy Point had ever known, a hard-on I relieved once and sometimes twice a day onto the truly unbelievable tits of Miss April 1969 behind the locked door of my bedroom, but which here on the beach Lisa would touch only through my suit and seemed to have no idea what to do with.

One overcast August afternoon, after I'd kissed her breasts for hours while moving my finger in and out of the wet chute of her vagina, she moved her hand from the outside of my Speedo, where it had played concertos against my erection as if it really were the skin flute my cousin Bobby called it, inside that very same Speedo, where it became only the second person's hand (this left out the probability that my mother or older sister, when changing my diaper, had touched me there, but thank God I couldn't recall that) to touch my penis.

"Like that?"

No, not like that. She was squeezing as if it were a loaf of bread, and it was starting to ache. But I didn't say anything; I'd been pestering her to do this for weeks. I kept fingering her, she kept kneading me, and when we got up ten or fifteen minutes later to begin the long walk back, something was really, really wrong and getting worse with every step.

Blue balls. I'd heard about this. There'd been rumors. And now, my testicles felt large and heavy as pool balls. I ached from just above my knees almost to my sternum, although there was no doubt that the locus of the pain was my balls, which were not only blue but very, very sad. Blue balls, and I couldn't tell Lisa or she would never put her hand down my pants again.

I couldn't wait to kiss her good-bye. I promised to call as I did every night, then hobbled, half boy, half creature from the Throbbing Blue Lagoon, to my family's cabana, where my mother was packing up.

"How was your day, Jimmy?"

"Fine."

"You don't look so good."

"I'm fine."

I followed her to the car, trying not to moan, and lay in the backseat in a fetal position, knees tucked to my stomach, hands between my knees, wondering how something that had felt so good could lead to this. At home, I told my mother I was too tired to eat and went up to my room, locked the door, and got out Miss April. My penis leapt to attention, but when I began to stroke it, I wasn't sure it was such a good idea. If anything, it hurt even worse. But I carried on—I adored Miss April—and when I was cleaning up after myself, I didn't feel any better, but I didn't feel any worse, because that wasn't possible. Achy, pukey, and for the first time in my life, sorry to have a dick.

A month later, two days before school would start, and a week after we'd broken up, Lisa called and said she'd been drinking, said she wasn't wearing a bra, said her parents were out. Said, why don't you come over?

I culled a condom from the box of twelve in my father's top drawer, tucked it in my wallet, and rode the bus to Lisa's house, where I'd only been once before. She led me to her parents' bed. In a moment, the lights were down and she was naked. Her mouth tasted of Southern Comfort. She explained she didn't want to start her senior year as a virgin. Together, we fumbled with the condom. It must have taken us two minutes to get it in place, while I remained inside her maybe thirty seconds.

No blue balls.

I never saw her again.

CELIBACY

AMELIA PERKINS

DEFINITION: abstinence from sexual intercourse, especially by reason of religious vows.
AKA: abstention, born-again virginity, chastity, continence, frigidity, impotence, maidenhood, nonogamy, purity, singleness, virginity, virtue.

NOTABLE CELIBATES

- *Stephen Fry, the British actor, comedian, writer, critic, novelist, and taxi driver, was the UK's most prominent and vocal celibate for several years, although he has since rediscovered the alleged joys of wanton carnality.*

- *Isaac Newton, the mathematician and scientist (said by some to be the greatest scientist ever), was a virgin all his life.*

- *Cliff Richard, singer, is one of the most vocal celibates of modern times.*

- *Simone Weil was one of the best-known European political thinkers of the twentieth century and, as far as anybody knows, a lifelong celibate.*

- *Also rumored to be a lifelong celibate was the Dutch philosopher and theologian Baruch Spinoza.*

- *Stevie Smith, poet and novelist, was celibate all her adult life, after sampling and rejecting romance and sex in her youth. She was fiercely critical of those who thought that her life must be emotionally impoverished by not having sexual relationships anymore, emphasizing the depth of her friendships, especially her bond with the aunt with whom she lived.*

- *Nikola Tesla, who developed the system of alternating electrical current that is the standard nowadays worldwide, was a self-proclaimed celibate.*

- *Carol Channing, the Broadway musical star of* Hello, Dolly! *fame, was celibate in her marriage to Charles Lowe for forty-one years.*

- *Benjamin N. Cardozo, former chief judge of the New York Court of Appeals and later associate justice of the Supreme Court of the United States, is believed to have been celibate for most if not all of his life.*

- *Antonio Gaudi, the Spanish architect most famous for the Sagrada Familia in Barcelona, is said to have never had sex.*

- *Sigmund Freud undertook a strict vow of celibacy from about the age of forty-one, which he maintained up to his death.*

—TIM RANDALL, "STAR MAN: STEPHEN FRY—'PEOPLE THINK I AM A GHASTLY POOF,'" SUNDAY MIRROR, NOVEMBER 23, 2003; AIMEE HUSMAN, PSYOGRAPHY: INTERNET SOURCE FOR BIOGRAPHIES OF PSYCHOLOGISTS, HTTP://FACULTY.FROSTBERG.EDU/MBRADLEY/PSYOGRAPHY/SIGMUNDFREUD1. HTML; JAMES GLEICK, *ISAAC NEWTON* (PANTHEON BOOKS, 2003); WENDY

HOLDEN, "WHY CLIFF RICHARD IS STILL ON TOP," *NEW STATESMAN*, DECEMBER 6, 1999; MEGAN GRESSOR, "THE POWER OF NONE," *SYDNEY MORNING HERALD*, JULY 23, 2005

In a monastery in the mountains of Greece, a priest-monk, believed to have purified his heart so completely that the Holy Spirit speaks through him without hindrance, told me that if I gave up the erotic for a time, I would understand my vocation.

"The erotic makes life a dream for you," he said. "You float down the river. You can either keep floating or you can turn the river back—like the Jordan."

I let out a small scream and then got sulky. I had hounded him for advice, but giving up the erotic was not what I wanted to hear. "What?" he responded, smiling. "I have not scolded you. I have only told you how to understand the treasure that you are."

When I told my mother that, after years of studying religion but believing little, I had fallen in love with a sisterhood of Eastern Orthodox nuns and would be heading off to a convent to give up the erotic for a year, she replied with a kind note and a long, raucously hot poem she'd just composed, entitled "Ode to Cunt." I was not raised to turn my back on the erotic.

But even after my renunciation, I was still left with myself: weeks of steamy nights in my monastic cot. I dreamt of making love to slick lesbian fish from other dimensions, and rubbing myself against everything: chairs, banisters, icons, giant nuns.

Celibacy is basic. But chastity, virginity, purity—this is the direction of the monastery. This includes more than bare physical actions and inactions. It involves the activity of the mind, a turning away from fantasy toward the joy of the real.

At first there was only loss. I was well steeped in the goopy deliciousness of relations, the endless pet names: love-cakes, muffin-breath, angel-pants.

The nuns told me chastity means whole-mindedness and is a

cure for fragmentation. It is a progression of freedom toward love without grasping. This is about the heart. And when your heart is pure, everything is pure.

One nun told a story about Maria, a woman beloved by the nuns, a woman who was meant to be their first abbess, but who died suddenly, very young.

"We were in the city, stuck in traffic, and it was blazing hot. I looked out the window and saw that beside us was a magazine stand filled with racks of pornography. Immediately I turned away. But then I noticed that Maria was staring toward the stand. The car didn't move for five minutes, and the whole time she stared and stared. Then, finally, when we began to move on, she said, 'That poor man without even an umbrella.' She was speaking of the owner of the stand. This is the difference between asceticism and holiness. I saw only the pornography and she saw only the person—a man getting baked in the sun."

I was told, when you are no longer sloppily merged and confused with things and bodies, you begin really to love. You can really help or love or serve or enjoy the people because you don't need anything from them. You don't need to hold that thing that is beautiful. You progress through freedom to a new dimension where you start to make love again—but totally differently.

One day, as a nun thrust a letter into an envelope, the abbot observed with a smile, "You have to make perfect sex with everything."

When you are in the presence of such a person, it's as though you stand before a deep well of honey. Not like me: jam spread out over everything.

Slowly it became clear there is another kind of eros, an antidote to the sweet dreaminess of habit. I attempted to gather honey, to exchange one sweetness for another.

I was familiar only with what I had read of late-medieval Western mystics, who relay visions of tasting, feeling, kissing God deeply. The Viennese nun Agnes Blannbekin, on taking the Eucharist, found she had received the circumcised foreskin of the baby Christ in her mouth, and it tasted ever so sweet. The French nun Marguerite of Oingt saw herself as a withered tree, which suddenly flowered when flooded by a great river of water representing Christ. Written on the flowering branches of her self, she saw the names of the five senses: sight, hearing, taste, smell, and touch.

But these Eastern Orthodox nuns shook their heads gently and told me, "You don't want to see anything. You must narrow yourself to fit through the keyhole. Reject all images. Even if an angel comes, send it away. If it is a real angel, it will understand. Let only the prayer exist: 'Lord Jesus Christ, have mercy on me.' Don't imagine anything. Because what you will find through the keyhole, you can't imagine. It must be given to you."

"The heart is a vast realm," one wild-haired monk with the bearing of a joyful outlaw told me as he passed through the monastery. "Enter it."

And the Elder reminded us, "Love without martyrdom is like a kiss without love."

Meanwhile, I continued to dream of rubbing myself against everything in the monastery. Until finally, a certain spaciousness. A traveler in a space without other bodies. A quiet that comes when there isn't a city in sight. And somewhere out there in the bright darkness, as yet unknown to me, is the fullness of eros.

There is a famous story of a Christian monk who gazed on the prostitute from the pagan temple riding her horse through the square. When his brother monks turned away in horror, he said to them, "Does her beauty not astound you?" And when they drew back, scandalized, he asked again, "Does her beauty not astound you?"

The Holy Spirit is everywhere present and filling all things. God's act of creation is erotic, fecund, says Saint Dionysius. An outpouring of love overflowing itself. This is not only about the soul's yearning for God, but God's own eros for all of creation.

Does her beauty not astound you?

CICISBEO

S. P. ELLEDGE

DEFINITION: a professed admirer of a married woman; a dangler about women (especially in Italy during the seventeenth and eighteenth centuries); an escort or lover of a married woman.
AKA: boy toy, cavalier servente, cornutor, gallant, harem, illicit lover, kept man, leman, male concubine, out-of-marriage lover, paramour, partner, spark, Sunday husband, toy boy, wittol.

Lord Byron was cicisbeo to Contessa Teresa Gamba Guiccioli. After his death, her second husband, Marquis de Boissy, was known to brag about the fact.

–BARBARA HODGSON, *ITALY OUT OF HAND:*
A CAPRICIOUS TOUR (CHRONICLE BOOKS, 2005)

"How perfectly scandalous!" exclaimed her wickedly eccentric uncle Yardley, who had, it was clear, both money *and* a past. "Your very own *cicisbeo*, Cecily, my dear little adventuress."

Cecily looked at him with wide, uncomprehending eyes, winding strands of Bakelite beads between her artfully ringed fingers: cameo, amethyst, and one small diamond. They were too late to be characters out of Browning or James, but this *was* Venice, after all; even in 1930 Uncle Yardley's inevitably drafty palazzo, the one he had won either from an heiress or in a game of chance, and where he preferred to paint philanthropists' fat families, still seemed to reverberate with the tubercular laughter of ancient grandees and ruined contessas.

"*Italian*, darling," Uncle Yardley informed his favorite, youngest, most impressionable niece; he frowned at his glass, doubting the Prosecco, before explaining, "Plural *cicisbei*. Lord, it's the trompe l'oeil of romantic relationships, you innocent girl. Possibly not quite what it seems. Something more or much less. Being the male companion of a wife who, with explicit approval of the elder stay-at-home husband, escorts her from *ristorante* to opera house or ballroom to bedroom. In the eyes of the world, he may be her lover or he may not. He may be paid or not. He may be interested in women or he decidedly may *not*."

Cecily knew all about old Uncle Yardley's shockingly young models and the rude red Horse Guardsman's jacket she had glimpsed in flagrante upon his watered-silk duvet. She snapped an amaretto *zaletto* between her sharp little incisors. Her mother had warned her not to visit this household unchaperoned, due to "bad influences," which she supposed would include the narghiles and Jesuit poets and occasional Guggenheims. "Lanford is hardly what you might call a *shee-sheese-bay-oh*, is it? Hardly that! He has his own income, and you must know my dear Peter tutored him at Balliol. Late British Romantics. Just because we're both doing the Continent this year—just because *my husband* has encouraged him to watch out for my welfare— doesn't mean there's the slightest trifle going on between us. Ha! Or ever *will* be." Narrowed, her eyes took on the gleeful malice of a civet cat's.

Uncle Yardley muttered something presumably Latin and held aloft his *cristallo* as if it were a chalice. In quaint half-spectacles, under the slanted and burnished light that fell from high up in the clerestory, he could pass for a cinquecento monsignor or doge, a patron of the arts. A Medici, even, but a merry one. He knew he was too late for Browning or James but was sorry to be no longer young and to be playing so small a part in this niece's racier, modernist novel. "All my friends see the two of you simply everywhere," he told her. "At the Ca' d'Oro drinking in the Tintorettos, lost among the folios of the Old Library, sharing *sigaretti* in some intimate corner of St. Mark's or a gondola in the moonlight . . . well, perhaps I made up that last part, but it's *still* the talk of this parish, my dear."

Cecily was not the sort to give an inch in these matters. "Oh," she said, worrying a wrinkle in the hem of last season's imitation Schiaparelli, as any underdeveloped ingenue might, "Peter would be *so* amused by such gossip. Rather *cicisbeo* than gigolo, he'd say! He absolutely adores his boy Lanford, and if I didn't know he has no latent homosexualist ten—oh, I am sorry for being so crassly Freudian, Uncle Yardley," and with that she knew she had deftly parried his thrust.

"Really, darling, I've *no* idea what you're implying, but you misconstrue what I'm saying. A *cicisbeo* is a position of honor, something the elderly or, pardon me, *impotent* husband is ever so grateful for and the woman is ever so glad for—the flowers, the fun, the flattery, the very properly placed public kiss and whisper. One goes about with a *cicisbeo* under full protection of Church and court, and if the lady's boudoir, quite far down the winding hall from her husband's chambers, should be a convenient and hospitable place to stop the night . . ."

Cecily shot up with a rattle of Bakelite and blown glass. "My, look at the time," she announced, although not so much as a sundial was in sight and the Campanile had not rung for seeming hours. "Dora Farley-Paddington is expecting me at the Rialto any minute and you know how absolutely beastly she gets. It's been delightful, Uncle Yardley, this 'tea'—and all your other teas. Please don't get up."

"A pity," Uncle Yardley said, getting up nevertheless, and taking her hand as he must, "to be estranged from your husband while he writes his book, for Peter could so *manfully* fend off these horrid engagements—and share all the beauty of this island with you, as well. A husband is the real thing, you know, Cecily, and you are lucky to have found true love in *your* own life. A *cicisbeo* is in the end just an illusion, isn't he, an artifice one has constructed oneself, or with help from society; and just as varnished and lacquered lips cannot kiss, he cannot *really* love you the way you might love him. Speaking purely as a matter of illustration, of course."

"Of course, an illustration, merely," she said, withdrawing her cameo and amethyst hand while testing her marcelled waves with the diamond other. "You must meet our Lanford and see he's not at *all* as you picture him. Ta!" And then she was gone, nothing left but the repetitive tattoo of high heels echoing and fading down the portrait gallery.

The amaretto-colored sunshine lingered. When he finished his latest masterpiece, her uncle thought, studying his pretty niece in his mind as if *she* were a Tintoretto, he should like to compile a list of foreign words and terms as lovely and venereally dangerous as *cicisbeo*: *cortejo*, *estrecho*, *petit maître*, *cavalier servente*, and so on, endlessly.

CLIMAX

MARIA DAHVANA HEADLEY

DEFINITION: the physical and emotional sensation
experienced at the peak of sexual excitation.

*Women who fail to orgasm during sex may be genetically programmed to
weed out unreliable men who are a flop between the sheets, according to new
research.*

*Scientists who have studied the ability of thousands of women to cli-
max say it is largely written in their genes—the most compelling evidence so
far that the female orgasm has a biological role. The findings suggest the failure of some women to orgasm regularly is not a dysfunction, but a sophisticated mate-selection strategy that evolved during prehistoric times.*

—DAVID ADAM, SCIENCE CORRESPONDENT, *GUARDIAN*, JUNE 8, 2005

An old song's lighting up the radio, someone asking their darling
to "come and go with me," and I'm thinking about the implica-
tions. I'm thinking about the way coming with someone stops
time and starts your life over. I've glanced at a clock after what felt
like seventeen hours, only to discover that no lifetime had passed
at all, but only twenty minutes, that we were still the same people
who had kissed and fallen together, but that somehow, everything
had changed. *Come with me*, possibly the best request most people ever receive. What can top it, this invitation to travel around
the earth and fall back, gasping, on the bed, still together?

I'm thinking about the time I was in college, and you were
an actor, and we met for the first time at a party and ended up in
a closet laughing as we came and couldn't stop laughing for sheer
delight until people started knocking on the door, and the time
you (another year, another you) fucked me so exuberantly on such
a soft bed that I catapulted onto the floor and had to be retrieved,
and the time you had a sketchbook and tried to draw what I

looked like with my head thrown back, complaining that I kept moving and then clarifying that you were actually not complaining. I'm thinking about the time both of us were girls and neither of us were much in the way of lesbians, and we couldn't quite figure out what to do or if we ought to be doing it, but that turned out not to matter as much as we'd thought it would. I'm thinking about the time you were my neighbor and your stubble rubbed my lips raw and your dog kept trying to sit on my head the whole time we were having sex, and the time I couldn't decide if I was in love with you or if it was just that you had just made me come ten times in ten minutes. I'm thinking about the time I was eight years old and learned how to have an orgasm from an exercise in an aerobics video involving Jane Fonda, then tried to teach a girl from my school how to do the exercise, too, thinking that no wonder adults loved aerobics. I'm thinking about the time you were a writer and got me out into a field claiming that we were going to look at the stars even though I knew it was about to rain, and the time we'd stayed up all night and you said *just talk to me, don't stop talking*, and I told you everything I'd ever thought as you moved inside me and even as I was moaning, you still whispered *keep talking*. I'm thinking about the time we were in the backseat of a taxi, and you put your hand up my skirt and I saw you grinning even in the darkness, or the time we accidentally woke the entire apartment building and became legendary, or the time you went down on me next to a hotel swimming pool in Florida at four in the morning, my ass squishing through the slats of the plastic chair so that later I looked like something grilled.

I'm thinking about the time you were the one for me, and I fell in love with you on our first night together, when at five in the morning I woke up with you touching me, and the time I got you off in broad daylight in a ferry line, while we waited in our car for our turn to drive on board, and the horn that honked at us just as you came in my mouth. I'm thinking about the time you tried to declare us platonic and lost the argument on the floor of your apartment. I'm thinking about the time I bought pasties in New Orleans and brought them home under my T-shirt and nearly put your eye out when I tried to spin them and then nearly tore my nipples off trying to remove them, because the glue was significantly stronger than I'd thought it would be, and still you loved me enough to make me come for two hours straight. I'm thinking about the time we weren't sure if we were going to stay together, and we cried the whole time, but because we were good even then, we both came. I'm thinking about the time you made me come behind a pull-curtain in the emergency room, successfully distracting me from my appendicitis for long enough that I forgot I was about to have surgery. I'm thinking about the time you tied me to the dining room table with red silk cords, forgetting to close the blinds, and our neighbors apparently had binoculars, because two years later, at our rehearsal dinner, one of them toasted that view. I'm thinking about the time at Crater Lake in the winter, when we stood up, and underneath us, the snow had melted down to green grass.

I'm thinking about the time our wedding guests walked through the hotel courtyard in the middle of the night trying to see the meteor shower, which was supposedly happening high above the storm clouds, and instead heard us consummating our marriage. I'm thinking about how they raised their wineglasses to us.

Come with me, I was thinking then, and am thinking still. *Come with me. Never leave.*

CLITORIS

ALIX OHLIN

DEFINITION: the erectile organ of the vulva,
homologous to the penis of the male.
AKA: clit, button, knob, the little man in a boat.

*The head or glans of the clitoris is a simple bundle of 8,000 nerve fibers, es-
timated to be twice the number found in the penis, making it particularly
well-suited for sexual stimulation.*

—NATALIE ANGIER, *WOMAN: AN INTIMATE GEOGRAPHY*
(ANCHOR BOOKS, 1999), 63.

THE CLITORIS QUIZ
Which clitoris personality are you? Take the quiz to find out!

1. Your early experiences with the clitoris can best be summa-
    rized as:
    a. Awkward but humorous struggles toward self-
       understanding, flowering eventually into womanhood.
    b. A painful junior high school incident involving the bal-
       ance beam and an ill-timed jump.
    c. Nothing you'd care to discuss publicly, I mean, come on.

2. Your friends, when discussing the clitoris, offer the follow-
    ing:
    a. "You should look at it every night. Be in touch with it.
       It makes you powerful."
    b. "We should draw diagrams and post them everywhere.
       You know, for men. So they can find it. It would be a
       public service."
    c. "That is not true of all men. Let me tell you about this one
       guy. He was like some kind of genius with it. A clitoris

savant. Let me tell what he did." This particular friend of yours is very graphic. Your other friends nod avidly. Some of them appear to be taking notes.

3. When researching the clitoris on the Internet, you look at the following sites:

    a. An article about an Australian urologist who has discovered that the clitoris is larger than previously thought, rivaling the penis in size. "If you lift the skin off the vagina on the side walls, you get the bulbs of the clitoris," says the doctor. All the anatomy textbooks, it appears, are wrong. Why the error, in this age of medical information? "It boils down to rivalry between the sexes: the idea that one sex is sexual and the other reproductive. The truth is that both are sexual and both are reproductive." Also quoted in the article is a representative of the sex toy industry. She says drily, "We have known this for years."

    b. Pictures of bonobos, primates whose females sport enormous clitorises. The bonobos are known for their promiscuity—the women have sex with women, men with men, groups, individuals, etc. Also, they are known for their peacefulness. The bonobos are a model society. Coincidence?

    c. Nothing else. You are doing this research at work.

4. Writers who broach the topic of the clitoris should adopt the style of:

    a. Early-seventies-era *Ms.* magazine. Open discussion is the road to liberation, sister.

    b. *Cosmo.* Something fun and breezy, not too hard to read or process, with numbers and lots of white space—like, say, a quiz.

c. Why are these always the choices, especially, it seems, when it comes to women's sexuality? There is something brittle even in the writing that purports to be playful, something artificial about the confidence of even the empowerment texts, none of it somehow capturing the goofy, transcendental complexity of the issue, its nuances and contradictions, the body's messy ecstasy and its *profound privacy,* even and sometimes most of all when shared with other people.

5.   The clitoris is:
a. A locus of mystery and danger, the seat of all that threatens the world about women, their hunger for pleasure, their independence.
b. Simply part of a healthy sex life. Everybody knows that. All this empowerment rhetoric is old news. This isn't a big deal anymore.
c. Part of the body that, according to Amnesty International, is mutilated on approximately two million women each year. This is a big deal. A very, very big deal.

If you answered mostly:

a. You are free and self-accepting and glorious. You are a woman.
b. You are curious and multifaceted. You are ever-unfolding. You are a woman.
c. You are sometimes afraid and sometimes not afraid at all. You are a woman.

COCK

T. J. PARSELL

DEFINITION: slang for "penis."

To dispel all myths, when cocks are flaccid, there is no easy way to determine what they will be like when they are hard. Conclusions cannot be drawn in the shower, from your basketball shoes, the distance between the tip of his thumb and baby finger, the hair on your chest, or the color and make of your car.

−THE BIG COCK SOCIETY HOME PAGE

Of all the colloquies in the English language used to describe the penis, *cock* is my favorite word. There's nothing flaccid about it. It's a word that stands up tall and proud—like a rooster crowing or a peacock strutting its feathers. The pronunciation alone invokes feelings of power and masculinity—the way the letter *c* combines with the letter *k* and gives it that extra kick off the back of the throat. Cock! Suck my cock! Take my cock! Play with my cock, you cocksucker! Worship my enormous, *monster* cock!

I'm glad I have one, and that I'm able to share it (occasionally). It's a boy's favorite toy. Sometimes known as a decision-maker for man.

The other words fail in relative comparison. *Dick*, which is probably a close second, has the same *c-k* letter sound on the back end of it, but the *d* doesn't quite cut to the bone in the same way as the sharp *c* sound. And if someone calls you a dick—it's considered an insult. Other names include *boner, ding-a-ling, ding-dong, dork, hard-on, Johnson, joystick, one-eyed monster, one-eyed pants snake, package, pecker, pee-wee, pork sausage, prick, pud, sausage, schlong, schwang, shaft, stiffy, swollen member, wang, wee-wee, wiener, willy,* and of course the good old *woody*.

Whether you have a cock or not (or even if you don't care for them), it's almost impossible to avoid its influence. It's a word that suggests confidence and control. *Cocksure and ready*: marked by certainty and without reservation—*he was virile in every way*. A cock swordsman, a chief, to act big and to strut with a swagger: are these not the hallmarks of a successful man? To lift and place high: leaning back in his chair and cocking his feet up on the desk.

According to Webster's dictionary, *cock* was once used to describe someone occupying a position of success and power. A victor: often one dominating some field or leading some circle through determined, aggressive effort. As a verb, *cock* is the spring-loading of a gun—pulling the hammer back and readying it for firing. To be cocky, one has pluck and spirit and often with a certain swagger and arrogance—all the young cocks dashing in their new uniforms. Instead of Mr. Prime Minister, or Mr. President, perhaps we should all just shout, "Hail to the Chief Cock." After all, isn't the world just one big cockfight, where opponents are left bloodied and dying?

If you want to insult a guy, you don't call him a pussy snatcher or a crack snacker. You call him a cocksucker. Then you sit back and watch as he suffers the repercussions. It's like the dirty bomb of nasty words—first, calling into question the integrity of his manhood and then soiling it by inference. The cocksucker probably deserved it anyway.

In Freudian psychology, penis envy is the young girl's reaction to the realization that she doesn't have a cock. It's considered a defining moment in the development of her gender and sexual identity. The parallel reaction in young boys, according to Freud, is not pussy envy, but castration anxiety. What is castration but the rendering of someone impotent—stripping them of all power.

For ladies who might be looking *to tie one on*—they turn not to a pinot noir, but to a cocktail. A stiff, alcoholic drink—on the rocks preferably—and then they pound them back, hoping to get schnokered. Cockeyed drunk, plowed perhaps, maybe even shit-faced. All this, they endure, as the cost for losing control.

With all this cock standing about, at full attention, what does it really get us? What does the word mean and why have we empowered it so? What is a man—if he's not his cock? Here to conquer the world and to reproduce, expressing his masculinity in terms of a swollen ego. Or is it all just poppycock—a cock-and-bull story—a fabricated tale passed off as true—especially in self-glorification? We live in a cock-centric world, with a special emphasis on size, where our e-mail in-boxes are filled with penis-enlargement ads and the number one selling drug is Viagra—outstripping sales of even the most common pain relievers.

Cock, *n.*, from the French word *coc* or *cocc*—the adult male of the domestic fowl. It's a loaded word that's fun to mouth.

COITUS INTERRUPTUS

DAN POPE

DEFINITION: coitus in which the penis is withdrawn prior to ejaculation to prevent the deposit of sperm into the vagina.

In June 2001, in Columbia, South Carolina, a young couple fell to their deaths from the roof of an office building. They were naked and it was assumed they having intercourse on the roof when they slid off.

—VARIOUS NEWS SOURCES

The undergraduate and his girlfriend are having sex in the basement. It is early morning; they have just woken. Upstairs the girlfriend's parents are sleeping. It is summer vacation; the undergraduate and the girlfriend have not seen each other for three weeks. The undergraduate has traveled north in his 1979 Firebird some four hundred miles, crossing the border into Ontario. *What is the purpose of your trip?* the border guard asked. The answer, if the undergraduate had spoken the unfiltered truth: *Sex.* Instead he said, also truthfully, *Pleasure.*

Three times the previous night the undergraduate and the girlfriend engaged in sexual acts: in his car; in the den after the parents left for an after-dinner stroll; and in the woods behind her house.

But it is a new day, the morning light streams into the basement through the casement windows, they are young, and new desires are at work. The undergraduate and the girlfriend fuck speechlessly, he standing behind, she on all fours atop the ottoman. *This is the ottoman,* the undergraduate thinks, *where her stupid father props his feet while watching television.* Now his daughter squats atop it, naked, making birdlike noises, which she tries to stifle.

A word about the father. He is a burly, mustachioed man who works for the railroad. He speaks with a strange inflection, which sounds like a heavy Scottish accent, although the man is not of Scottish descent. A speech impediment, then. His words come out fast and garbled, as if he were barking the entire syllables of, say, a twelve-syllable sentence all at once, an eruption of vowels and consonants nearly impossible for the undergraduate to decipher, although the girlfriend and the mother have no apparent difficulty understanding him. *Rarr rarr rarr.* That is what the words sound like to the undergraduate, with a few intelligible words interspersed. During dinner the night before the father uttered such sounds to the undergraduate, and the undergraduate turned helplessly to the girlfriend, who said, *He's asking about the American exchange rate. Oh,* said the undergraduate. *It's twenty percent on the dollar.*

This narrative can only end one way. But the undergraduate and his girlfriend are not reckless. They are vigilant, even while their congress accelerates, even while the undergraduate grabs the girlfriend's hair and pulls her head backward at a sharp angle. Even in this state, they listen for footsteps overhead. The undergraduate watches the door at the top of the stairs, the only entrance to the basement. If the door opens an inch, he will disengage; she will duck out of sight. They are safe, therefore, against detection.

Then: *Rarr rarr.*

The lovers freeze.

An instant later, the girlfriend springs off the ottoman, pulls the afghan from the couch, and covers herself with it, her eyes wide. The undergraduate, fully erect, looks desperately around the room. Where is he? The door at the top of the stairs is closed, it has not opened. Then he hears the father's voice, again. *Rarr rarr.* The undergraduate turns to his right and looks up at the casement window, and there he is, bending down and looking in, his face against the glass, eyeballs bulging, mustache aflare.

A moment later, the face is gone.

Now, panic. The undergraduate scrambles for his pants, hopping around the room. The girlfriend, her face exhibiting shock and disbelief, says, *I can't believe my father saw me like that.* She repeats this sentence, the first of many repetitions. *I can't believe my father saw me like that.* The undergraduate waits for the basement door to fly open, for the next thing to happen.

But the door does not fly open, the father does not appear in a rage. After a certain interval, the undergraduate and the girlfriend dress and venture upstairs. The father and the mother are in the kitchen, making breakfast. The undergraduate expects physical attack or banishment, but nothing happens, not during breakfast, not during the remainder of the weekend at the girlfriend's house. The father makes no mention of the incident, although, once, he peers at the undergraduate from across the room and, perversely, winks. Thereafter the undergraduate avoids all eye contact with the father.

The undergraduate asks, *What was he saying when he caught us?* The girlfriend doesn't want to talk about it. Nor does she want to engage in sexual congress for the rest of the weekend.

Later, driving those four hundred miles in his 1979 Firebird back to America, back to safety, the undergraduate hears the father's utterance again and again, and suddenly the words are decipherable:

Stop that.
Stop that.

Twenty-five years pass.

The girlfriend is a vague recollection. The undergraduate can barely summon her face; if not for a few photographs, he might lose her image entirely, even though she was his first girlfriend, even though they engaged in some four hundred acts of sexual congress. He can remember certain things about her. He remembers her name, of course. Words they said to each other in anger or passion or boredom. The rooms they lived in that last year of college. Otherwise memory has all but banished her and everything they shared, what was unique to them. Would he recognize her if she passed on the street? If so, would he then recall all of it—the winter night they stood atop Mt. Royal, for instance, overlooking the city while a soft snow fell around them and she said, *This is something I never told anyone . . .* ? Or would she be a stranger to him, inhabiting the time-worn body of someone he once loved?

It was so long ago.

And yet, the father's face, framed in the casement window, remains, to the undergraduate, indelible, as vivid as shame, as clear as the words on this page.

Stop that.

COMMITMENT

ELLEN SUSSMAN

DEFINITION: the state of being bound emotionally or intellectually to a course of action or to another person or persons.

Dr. Phil digs deeper to find out what has triggered John to believe that marriage is "a scam." John was engaged when he was 27—and got dumped.
"But I'm over it," insists John.
"Everybody who believes him, stand on your head," says Dr. Phil.

—REPORT ON *DR. PHIL* WEB SITE

COMMITMENT: A DIRTY WORD

Don't fall in love with my best friend, Max. I'm warning you.

But you do. You fall hard.

He is a man who loves women. No, that's not it. He is a man who loves love. No, he is a man who loves falling in love.

Real love is something else—hard, complicated, messy.

But falling in love is a six-week endorphin rush, a sex fest, a love feast. And my friend Max is so damn good at that part. He gives you all his attention. He sits across from you at the restaurant, leans toward you, his handsome face intently focused on you—on you! He wants to hear all your stories—he wants to *know* you. Even more surprisingly, he tells you his dark tales. He tells you about his father's death when he was a kid, and when he talks, his voice cracks and he tilts his head; this is hard but he's willing to share. He's not fooling you; he's not seducing you with his sensitivity. His emotions are raw, exposed. He knows that your heart is open to him because you've said, That must have been so awful—and you meant it!—and that makes him feel—what—love? Need? It makes him feel connected to you. The waiter serves wine and you both get quiet for a moment and you think, *He's different.* He's willing to expose himself. And so you tell that story, that one story that you only tell the men you fall for, about your anorexia or your sister's suicide or your mother's addiction to OxyContin or your breakdown when you were in college, and he listens for a long time, holding your hand across the table. You've heard rumors about him, about his many women, but you think, *I'm different. Tonight was—what—real? Maybe he'll love me.*

He sends flowers. No one sends flowers. It's a little silly. But it's sweet. And so are his phone calls, all day long and into the night. I was just thinking about you, he says.

He calls you hon. You love how it sounds, a pet name, a sweet sound, his whispered word for you. You don't know that he calls all his girlfriends hon. You don't know that he worries what he'll call out during orgasm when you finally go to bed. *Hon,* he moans. You don't know that his last girlfriend broke up with him because he called her fifteen-year-old daughter hon—can you pass the orange juice, hon? You don't know that the next girlfriend will love how he names her hon.

He does love you—he does! He calls me and tells me about you—you're wonderful, you're perfect, you're the one! He tells me your story—who you are, how old your kids are, what you do, where you live—and I read Salon.com on my computer while he's talking, his words like Muzak in the background. He knows my rule. I won't meet you until he's been dating you for six months. Because in six months he won't be dating you. He'll be telling me about someone else he's fallen in love with.

He has lists, well-considered lists of reasons for his love addiction.

1.   He was chubby in high school, then woke up one day in college and was thin and handsome, and even now, thirty

years later, still thin, still handsome, he doesn't quite believe it and needs to confirm this, over and over.

2.   His father died when he was sixteen, leaving a hole in his heart. Fill it with love! But he'll leave you before you leave him, before anyone ever leaves him and breaks him in that way again.

3.   His mother was overbearing, too strong, too too, and he loved her—but the minute you say something that reminds him of Mom—whom he loved—still loves—he's out the door, like a teenage boy who forgets to clean up his mess.

He wants to change. He tells you—because you've become so close—that he's ready for a long-term relationship. He's sincere; you can tell that he's trying so damn hard. You'll be the one to change him.

Don't fall in love with my best friend, Max. But it's too late. You're hooked. You've got it bad. You've started to talk about next year, your parents, your best friend's wedding in Bermuda, visiting day at your son's camp in August. He's still sitting across from you at the table, he's still holding your hand, he's still handsome, and tonight he'll sleep with you and murmur *hon* in your ear, but right now, while you're talking to him, he's looking past you, at a table behind you, where a beautiful woman sits by herself, sipping a glass of wine.

CUM

LISA SELIN DAVIS

DEFINITION: semen, a viscid, whitish fluid of the
male reproductive tract consisting of spermatozoa
suspended in secretions of accessory glands.
AKA: spunk, come, cream, pudding, juice, love juice, load, jism,
jis/jazz, sauce, cum-snot, oyster, slime, man milk, squirt,
spew, spooge, spunk, lovin' spoonfuls, seed.

*Red meats, greasy food, dairy products, chocolate, asparagus, broccoli, or
spinach will cause the ejaculate to taste sharp, whereas a vegetarian diet of
fruit, especially pineapple and apples, parsley, celery, spearmint, and pepper-
mint will give it a mild flavor.*

–ROBERT CROOKS AND KARLA BAUR, *OUR SEXUALITY*, 9TH ED.

(BELMONT, CA: THOMSON WADSWORTH, 2005)

I'd grown tired of Americans of European descent with their polite
ignorance of my origins (wealthy Iranian community in Northern
California—no headscarves, but still). Twenty-nine for the seventh
time, I gave myself two gifts: patent leather "fuck-me pump"
Jimmy Choos and a free one-month membership to Salaam Love—
"Connecting Muslims Worldwide." Amazing, in New York City,
how hard it was for an almond-eyed girl with nice tits to get laid.

Perhaps it had to do with my prudish side—I liked the penis
all right, but not what sprung from it: snot, phlegm, to be coughed
up and wiped clean. Also, the smell: late-blooming ginkgo trees.

What surprised me was the site's democratic nature, men
searching for men, women for women. Muslims who drank,
smoked, were six feet tall and "firmed and toned." Black faces and
Chinese faces, scraggly beards or clean-shaven, hailing from Greece
and Australia and Canada. Mostly Canada.

The non-burka-ed wore come-hither looks, ferocious stares.

63

"Adikted to love," the screen name of another single Muslim woman from Brooklyn. I chose "Reluctant" as my handle.

On my first scroll down, I found him: "Aladdin," posing shirtless before the brownish waters of Coney Island. Muscular in the photo, though he described his physique as "average." A bone necklace at his collarbone. Never married. Kids? No. Drinking? Never. Not just no, but never. A smoker. A lawyer. An income over six figures. Looking for? Love.

We met at the most generic restaurant I'd entered since moving to my dingy Bed-Stuy apartment six years ago to pursue theater/temping—near his building in Midtown east. Tall. Handsome. Smile slightly crooked, looked down at his plate when he laughed. Complimented my outfit, specifically my shoes. Not afraid to talk about politics. Our feet touched under the table, his shined wing tips—a lawyer, with a lawyer's wardrobe!—against my black pumps.

I accepted the invitation to his apartment—generic, too: a corporate, L-shaped studio on the sixteenth floor, tiny slice of East River hiding behind the Citigroup Center. Framed family photos on his bedside table: good-looking sister cradling two children; parents flanking him on graduation day, Gothic buildings of Yale behind them. I inferred from the blankness of his apartment that he awaited a woman's inspiration.

One glass of sparkling apple cider later and his mouth was at my neck. Not on my lips, soft and slow as I'd imagined, but teeth gnawing against the flesh, against my Egyptian musk perfume (two dollars a vial, bought from Jamaicans at the Fulton Mall). He had no stubble on his chin, pure, brown, smooth, the faint scent of something—curry? cinnamon?—on his skin.

Prostrate, then, somehow, bitten-nailed-fingers (he wasn't perfect) unbuttoning my one really good shirt with abalone buttons and a lido collar. Peeling back my padded bra with his teeth, heavy use of the teeth, I noted, leaving the scene for a moment to evaluate. Popcorn ceilings—the apartment was cheaply made after all. Focusing on the architecture while he made his way down my body, slipping off my skirt, underwear—I wished I'd had something rich and expensive with a high alcohol content to drink. I made myself heavy, submissive, like a Real Doll. Not responding when he talked. "You like that? Huh? Do you? Do you like it?" Rhetorical questions.

I was naked save for the shoes, and when I bent to remove them, he said, "No. Leave them."

Then he slowed down. Hovered above me, looking deeply, inquisitively. I lay there while he ripped open the condom package. I didn't look, evaluate the width and the length—I didn't want to risk disappointment.

He did the deed jackhammer style—"You like that? Huh?"—and now I was present again in the situation, waiting for it to be over. "I want to come."

Okay, I thought. That's fine. Go ahead.

"I want to come. I want to come on you."

Luckily the penis was all wrapped up. I turned my head to the side, saw what must be a cum stain on his navy pillowcase.

"I want to. I want to." Said faster now with the furious pacing of his bounce. "I want to come on your shoes."

Did I hear him right? A truck boomed down Third Avenue at the same moment.

"I want to come on your shoes."

He narrowed his eyes in a way I believe he believed was sexy. "I want to come on your feet." His penis made harder by his own words. I could only think of my beautiful shoes, but my lips forgot to form the word *no*. It was too late for no, and I hadn't actually seen the stuff for years.

He resumed the bounce until sweat dripped off his hairless frame—average, I agreed now—and pulled out suddenly, whipping off the condom, rubbing himself over my beautiful patent shoes: $176. He had what could be called a really nice cock—long, thick, whatever.

It wasn't much cum. Perhaps he'd screwed recently, last night, or earlier today. Maybe with other desperate Muslim girls, coming on their humble brown flats. Just a few pearly drops, perfectly spread in radiating rays like flower petals. It smelled, yes, like late-blooming ginkgo trees, as snotty as I'd remembered. I pondered the stuff: all our sex-education lives we'd been warned against it, the messenger of unwanted children and STDs. More important for Aladdin (real name Jimmy) to expel this than secure a second date with me.

He breathed heavily, sitting back on his naked heels, hand wiping sweat from his forehead, then mine, smiling as if we'd shared something beautiful. Then, smile retreating, clearing his throat at the blankness of my face. He reached for a tissue, the blue-green-swirly cardboard box next to the photograph of his mother's smiling face. He gently wiped off the evidence, meticulously making my shoes generic again, not the site of some stranger's fetish. The shoes were cum-proof, it turned out, immediately restored to their glossy grandeur.

CUNNILINGUS

TIM FARRINGTON

DEFINITION: a form of oral sex involving
mouth contact with the vagina.
AKA: velvet buzz saw, bikini burger, growling at the badger,
lickety-split, gnash the gash, blow some tunes, giving head, muff diving,
paying lip service, eat fur pie, face job, kneel at the altar, lapping
the pink canoe, box lunch, mouth music, swing low, fuzzburger,
clam dive, speaking in tongues, Egg McMuff, tip the velvet.

The Tongue Tube: Roll your tongue into a tube (if you cannot do this, forget about it because it is genetic and you can't learn it). This technique works best in an inverted or 69 position. Roll your tongue into a tube around her clitoris. Slide it back-and-forth; in effect, your tongue is doing something similar to a woman's vagina around a man's penis. This is likely to bring any woman over the edge to an explosive orgasm.

—WWW.SEXINFO101.COM

The tarot card ruling the man's approach to cunnilingus is, clearly, the Fool. "May the gods give thee sense, Philaenis, who imagines it a manly thing to lick a cunt," said the Roman poet Martial, speaking for the ancient, and much of the modern, world. The Latin word for the vulva, *cunna*, was such an obscenity that Cicero wouldn't use it even in his notoriously uninhibited letters. Horace goes there, but only to suggest that it was Helen's *cunna* that caused the Trojan War.

As for the clitoris, *landica* in Latin, there are no literary uses; not even Martial, who seldom hesitated to call a *mentula* a *verpa*, employs the term. Cicero hints at it, but only in a pun—"It would be a greater wrong were I to speak of *that thing*"—with *illam dicam* cleverly suggesting *landica*. If it weren't for Pompeian graffiti, we might, indeed, not even know what "that thing" *was*. (*Peto landicam Fulviae,* reads one bathhouse wall: "I'm after Fulvia's clit." But look what happened to the Pompeians.)

Squeamishness so obscured the situation that as late as the sixteenth century the two leading anatomists in Italy could squabble over which of them had discovered the clitoris. It was 1966 before Masters and Johnson described the clitoral structures surrounding the vagina, and their role in female orgasms, while the first anatomically accurate illustration of *that thing* did not see print until 1981.

Such was the situation when I came of sexual age in the mid-1970s: cunnilingus (a word listed in none of the dictionaries then) was, it seemed from the scanty etymological evidence, a nearly universally despised act involving a *lingua* in the vicinity of the barely mentionable *cunna*, seeking *illa*, that completely unmentionable thing.

God knew what I was supposed to do with *illa* if I found it. The Pompeian graffiti, still the state of the art then, was graphic but lacked specifics. Even the *Kama Sutra*, that supposed encyclopedia of sacred eroticism and yogic precision, failed me, disdainfully noting only that "the ancient and venerable sages are of the opinion that 'the mouth congress' (*Auparishtaka*) is the work of a dog and not a man." (Here, at least, squeamish Tantrists and classical Western prudes agreed: Hesychius defines *scylax* (dog) as a sexual posture employed mostly by "the Phoenicians," dogs and Carthaginians apparently both being disposed to licking private parts.)

In truth, the best advice available to me on the topic, for years to come, would be John Cleese's heartfelt admonition, in *Monty Python's The Meaning of Life*: "for God's sake, man, don't go stampeding the clitoris!"

Fool that I was, I rushed in at the first opportunity anyway, attempting a blind kamikaze version of cunnilingus with my high school girlfriend. Using the most sophisticated erotic schema available to me, the prototype of the baseball diamond, I boldly slid my *lingua* into third base and rummaged around for a while to no real effect. Faced with a scoreless tie that threatened to go into extra innings, my long-suffering girlfriend finally grabbed me by the hair and yanked me back up to second base, where we both were happier.

Not until many fiascos later, in the eighties, was a glimmer of light finally cast upon what the hell was really supposed to be going on between *cunna* and *lingua*. A pilgrim in New Age California, I ended up one summer at a rural community built around a series of geothermal springs in the mountains north of Napa. Here I met Rox, a sweet spirit with marvelous long legs, who practiced Watsu, ate organic, perceived auras and past lives, and turned out to be way more sophisticated than the *Kama Sutra*. In the loft of my shack among the tan oaks and madrones, Rox patiently set about imparting to me the art of cunnilingus, beginning with the literal ABCs (one of her techniques was writing the alphabet with your tongue). I even had homework and spent time practicing suck-and-diddle and the twizzler on my forearm. Rox believed that we had shared past lives—as Phoenicians, perhaps. All I knew was that I had stumbled at last upon the master I had been seeking, and I was profoundly grateful. At least I knew where that thing was now.

The next stop on my erotic odyssey was—seriously—a non-monogamous commune in the Haight-Ashbury, where Rox's techniques were a hit with my various partners during the rounds of what we called the sleeping schedule. One of those partners was Suzi Bite, a sexual theologian of true genius whose magnum opus, "The Nine P's of Great Cunnilingus," was a marvel of depth and lucidity in its time and is still a classic thanks to the Internet. Space does not allow for elaboration here, but for the record, the nine P's are Perseverance, Patience, Precision, Pressure, Position, Penetration, Pace, Persistence, and Playfulness. (The sacred ennead had been scribbled down on a matchbook cover during Suzi's initial brainstorm, and I carried that holy matchbook in my wallet for years, like highly condensed Cliff's Notes or a piece of the Shroud of Turin.) A bonus side effect of these abiding principles of pudendal palpitation is that if you practice them in a heartfelt manner, you will become a better person. Also, if you trace the alphabet with your tongue, and begin with P, you end with O.

The situation faced by an aspiring cunnilinguist has changed since I set out on my own fool's journey. It is possible now to go online and seek instruction from sources as diverse as the Web site for Cake and Cunnilingus Day (April 14, if you want to mark your calendar), Grandma Scrotum's Guide on How to

Find the Clitoris and Perform Cunnilingus (be sure to write *cli-toris* in the subject line of your queries, so she doesn't delete the e-mail as spam), and Uncle Melon's "How to Eat Pussy," featuring a photo of a fire hydrant that illustrates "how to give good head." ("Lick here." "Or here." "Or here.")

There are also numerous how-to books available, plus instructional videos, graphic photos, and recipes for cake to go with the cunnilingus on April 14. An embarrassment of riches, far from the pathetic tool kit I set out with.

Still, I wouldn't take nothin' for my journey now. As Blake suggests, the fool who persists, perseveres, and practices precision, playfulness, and patience in his folly will become wise. And in the end, no matter how you go about it, the fundamental things apply: a kiss is still a kiss, and a sigh is still a sigh, no matter how it is induced. The world will always welcome lovers, as time goes by.

CUNT (*see also* PUSSY)

JONATHAN WILSON

DEFINITION: 1. The female genital organs 2. *Offensive* Used as a disparaging term for a woman.

"Cu" and "koo," both pronounced "coo," were ancient monosyllabic sounds implying femininity. "Coo" and "cou" are modern slang terms for vagina, based on these ancient sounds. Other vaginal slang words, such as "cooch," "coot," "cooter," "cooz," "cooze," "coozie," "coozy," "cookie," "choochy," "chocha," "cootch," and "coochie snorcher" are extensions of them. "Coochie snorcher" appeared in The Little Coochie Snorcher That Could from The Vagina Monologues.

—AMERICAN HERITAGE DICTIONARY

Cunt is the most powerful word in the English language. In the

United Kingdom, however, it's pretty much defanged these days, and, in usage, if not in meaning, no longer gender specific. In the United States, for reasons that are not altogether clear—Puritan hangover, feminist triumphalism, cowboy fear and loathings—it is THE WORST WORD IN THE WORLD, and that is a decidedly sorry state of affairs.

Some years ago I wrote a story, "Mother With Child," that was published in the *New Yorker.* In it a female character, a young Englishwoman named Tina, floats around in the Dead Sea while her Jewish boyfriend is trying to shove his mother across the water in the direction of Jordan. Suddenly Tina yells out, "I've got salt up my cunt!" A bunch of German tourists from the nearby psoriasis center start paddling toward her as fast as they can. After the story appeared, numerous American women of my acquaintance regaled me with the same criticism. "No woman," they said, "would ever say that." Well, one certainly did, my friend P., a young Englishwoman from whom I took the line verbatim along with the location and the activity.

Why the big U.S. taboo? In the UK, women have been calling other women and men who don't meet their approval cunts for as long as I can remember. The word scores about the same as *fuck* on the insult charts. Perhaps it is heightened aesthetic sensitivity that has caused the problem on this side of the Atlantic. Or, more likely, there is awareness, both conscious and unconscious, of the way that *cunt* reports the deep unresolved misogyny of American life as it persists amid a general horror of female anatomy below the waist. America has always been big on boobs and, until recently, reticent about vaginas.

Does the taboo stem from etymological ignorance? The letters *CU* have, according to the great scholar of slang Eric Partridge, indicated "quintessential femininity" since ancient times. *C* and *U* are the same shape turned different directions, and both, with curve and opening, are anatomically pictorial.

The precise etymology of *cunt*, yet unresolved, continues to engender the most arcane and complex disputes, yet everybody has his or her favorite ur-explanation. I've always been drawn to the Welsh *cwm*, which means a hollow place or a valley (the Welsh *W* is pronounced as a *U* in English), and which spawned the English knockoff *quim*. In England, men who get a kick out of female tennis players serving in short skirts are sometimes known as lovers of "Quimbledon." The earliest citation of *cunt* spelled as we know it is listed in the *OED* as around 1230. In the early Middle Ages there were streets in the red-light districts of both London and Oxford known as Gropecuntelane. In Oxford it shifted over time to *Grope* and forward to the bucolic *Grove*. In London it morphed through several changes to wind up as Milton Street. Yet, somehow, "You stupid milton!" doesn't quite make it.

My first prolonged viewing of *cunt*, the word, came around my tenth birthday, when my brother visited Paris and smuggled back to London a copy of Henry Miller's banned novel *Tropic of Cancer*. I stole it from his shelves and read the first couple of chapters in the traditional manner, with a flashlight under the covers. It was a disappointment, literary almost to the point of incomprehensibility, but it was full of cunt, one in particular that belonged to a woman named Tania. At about this time a girl, let's call her Rosemary, who went to my elementary school, decided that *in exchange for telling her the time* she wanted to reveal herself in the toolshed at the bottom of her suburban garden (I'm not making this up) to myself and my friend Derek. Our "Tania" stood there and lifted her skirt, she had nothing on underneath, and then she twirled around. Rosemary was ahead of her time, in that no pubic hair was in evidence, but probably that was because it had not yet arrived on her body. This was my first cunt.

Philip Roth's *Portnoy's Complaint* arrived in my life some seven years later. The masturbatory excesses of its eponymous narrator, Alex Portnoy, have largely obscured that one of its most potent chapters is called "Cunt Crazy." Whenever I teach the novel, which is now firmly in middle age, that heading still carries a wallop for American students, although the desire of some female and Jewish readers to flay Roth to his bones has greatly diminished. Everyone's cool with masturbation (see the *American Pie* movies), but we're still a *cunt*-crazy nation getting shivers from that lethal combination of letters. I think it's time for a moratorium on American anxieties.

When I was eighteen, I had a summer job working for the construction company Bovis on a north London building site. We were renovating the interior of an office block in High Holborn. My first day on the job I got in the elevator and said, "Four please," to one of my fellow workers. Instead of pressing the button he gave me a murderous look. A seasoned veteran got on board. "Press two, you cunt," he said to my fellow passenger. "Fuck off," my guy replied, and pushed the button. "Cunt," the new guy said. "Cunt yourself" came the reply. Everyone was happy.

CYBERSEX

JOSHUA FURST

DEFINITION: online sex-oriented conversations and exchanges.
AKA: Internet sex, netsex.

A 34-year-old woman married 14 years to a minister . . . discovered he was compulsively seeking sexual satisfaction by visiting pornographic sites on the Internet. "How can I compete with hundreds of anonymous others who are now in our bed, in his head?" the woman wrote. "Our bed is crowded with countless faceless strangers, where once we were intimate."

–JANE BRODY, *NEW YORK TIMES*, MAY 16, 2000

Spam! The message bounces like a hailstone off your in-box, but you read it anyway before you delete all. *Dear Joe Blowstein, I just moved here from Ukraine. I am very pretty girl and also very fun. But today I am very lonely. I have no one to play with. Are you very lonely too? I would like to talk to you. Please e-mail me or if you want to chat right now, click* here! *I'm waiting! xoxo Daphne.* And spam! There's another one, this time to Jeremy Schlemiel, from a nice Polish girl named Tiffany. And another. And one more. They arrive by the boatload, these fun, pretty girls, each with a different name, but an identical message: *I'm alone here and it's that haunting time after dark, won't someone come save me from myself tonight?* You know they don't exist. You know they're just phantoms conjured from the keyboards of hairy entrepreneurs, but these lonely Eastern European girls get to you. Their availability, their promise of communion and possible release, it won't let you forget how futile you feel alone in your tiny room. You, too, have no one. So you click the link, knowing the risk, and hope your computer survives the encounter. A new window pops up. A garish collage of women in thongs, and not in thongs—breasts floating at impossible heights, not a blemish on their skin, no chips in their nail polish, ten or fifteen of these girls all together imploring you to Enter, to become a Member. In the corner of the screen you find a smaller screen on which a woman's head bobs over a penis that doesn't appear to be attached to a body. These women aren't real, or they don't seem to be real. Their personalities have been airbrushed away. But inside, the site promises, you'll find girls, real girls, live girls, at their computers this very second, horny girls, girls with needs, ready to chat with you, standing by their webcams waiting to show you how valuable you are, if not to the world, at least to them. Your computer doesn't seem to have crashed yet. So far the site's legit. No viruses. No worms. And for a mere two dollars and ninety-nine cents, you can get yourself a three-day trial membership. Five minutes later, you're staring at a black square on your computer screen. According to the text box under this empty space, one click of a button will rouse a nineteen-year-old coed named Sabrina. You'll be able to talk to her through instant messages, and if you're charming, if you're gentlemanly, she'll smile for the camera. She'll put on some music and dance for you, and strip off her baby T, her miniskirt, she'll show you her panties and flash her shaved pussy, she'll squeeze her breasts together and massage her nipples. She'll do anything you ask her to do. You just have to make contact. You have to click that button. Here you go. Here she comes. But, now, you're buffering. Or anyway, your computer is buffering, the Web site, something out there is buffering . . .

. . . buffering . . .

. . . buffering . . .

. . . your sense of self is slowly diminishing. You didn't realize it could shrink any further . . .

. . . buffering . . .

. . . buffering . . .

You suspect you'll be buffering forever.

D

DILDO

JENNY MCPHEE

DEFINITION: an object resembling a penis
used for sexual stimulation.

*Some questions to ask before buying a dildo. Are you looking for a dildo
that . . .*

Is for clitoral stimulation?

Will put you in touch with your G-spot?

Is so quiet your roommate won't hear it?

Gives your hand a little extra oomph?

Is so discreet that airport security won't know what it is?

*Can be worn while you're fucking, so your hands are free to seek other
pleasures?*

Is so wonderfully intense you'll get off in seconds?

Features more subtle vibrations for the sensitive clit?

Is great for sex or masturbation in the bath?

Is an international celebrity?

Is so stylish your girlfriends will covet it?

−FROM WWW.BABELAND.COM

It was what we called each other, I and my many siblings, ono-
matopoeically. "Shut up, you stupid dildo." "Oh, don't be such a
dildo." "Eat me, dildo-head." It was 1970 and I had become child
number five of ten in a novel family in which exploration and ex-
perimentation, linguistic and otherwise, were strongly encouraged.
Previously, I had been sister number three of four, and a devotee
of Sunday school, which took place in the basement of a big, yellow Presbyterian church on the main street in the town where I

lived. Adding *dildo* to my vocabulary at age eight was for me a God-given blessing, even if preordained. When I was ten, my best friend, Sara, enlightened me that a dildo was more than just a derogatory epithet by showing me the actual *objet* where it lay snug at the back of a drawer in her parents' bedroom. "It even vibrates," she said, switching it on and giving it to me. I held it in my hand. It was more consistent, but less interesting, than a captured firefly. "You're supposed to put it in your mouth," she said. I was suddenly reminded of another crucial moment in my linguistic development when I first learned the word for those easily duped. During my parents' divorce, my mother had taken me and my sisters to visit her college roommate in Charleston, South Carolina. She had a daughter my age named Ishbel. Ishbel was blond and pretty and sang her words like a character in a Disney movie. Alone together in her bedroom, she commanded me to put my nose up to her ass. Still used to obeying commandments, I did as I was told. She promptly let out a loud and odoriferous fart. She fell on the floor laughing and said, "Y'all are so gullible." So upon Sara's suggestion that I put the dildo into my mouth, I hesitated. "You do it," I countered. "I already have," she said, taking the dildo from me and replacing it in the drawer. "It's no big deal."

DIRTY SANCHEZ

BRIAN BOULDREY

DEFINITION: after having anal sex, the man pulls out his penis and wipes it across his partner's lip, forming an authentic-looking Mexican mustache.

A few more specially coined sexual feats:

- *The Stranger—Sit on your hand until it falls asleep and then masturbate, eliciting the feeling of a hand job from someone else.*

- *Western Grip—When jerking off, turn your hand around, so that your thumb is facing toward you. It is the same grip that rodeo folks use.*

- *The Woody Woodpecker—While your partner sucks on your balls, tap the head of your cock on his or her forehead.*

- *The Fish Eye—From behind, shove your finger in your partner's ass. Thereupon he or she turns around in a one-eyed winking motion to see what the hell you are doing.*

—FROM VARIOUS WEB SITES

A friend who spent his youth dancing in a ballet company turned, after the inevitable injury, to choreography. "I wanted to create a dance piece that would include ugly moves," he told me. Football tackles. A body, dragged by a parachute after an unfortunate jump. A waiter tripping with your meal. But it never worked out: once an ugly move was identified, repeated, and transformed on the stage, the ugliness turned to a terrible beauty.

Kelly, another friend, has a golden retriever named Emma. Emma is a canine manifestation of a ballet dancer, but she has one awful habit—when you take her to swim in Lake Michigan, she prefers to "do her business" in the lake. Kelly has to wade into the lake with a plastic bag and, in her own version of an ugly move, clumsily scoop doodies up, a soup of poop, lake water, and weed. Kelly and I philosophize about this—it can't feel "natural" to defecate into water; the slight pressure in the other direction would feel awkward, especially to such a princess-and-the-pea pup as Emma. But she prefers crapping in the lake; she saves it for the lake. "You can only hope for floaters," I told Kelly. I had a partner of many years who was Dutch, and the Dutch, being a clean people, are obsessed with fecal matter. As the Eskimos have many words for the different kinds of snow, my Dutch ex had eight known words for the different qualities of shit. *Keuteljes*, I am told, are ideal: "floaters." Kelly and I, in an attempt to accommodate the leopard

78

in the temple, have given a name to a dog's crapping in Chicago lake water: a Hot Michigan Dutchy.

The Dirty Sanchez—the adorning of a lover's upper lip with a Frito Bandito mustache using the fecal matter from less than clean anal sex—has the visceral shock of an ugly move. Tell a friend about it so you are not so alone with the shock, and then you will not be so shocked. You can only be shocked once when I tell you what a Strawberry Shortcake is (punching your partner's nose until it bleeds while coming on them), how to perform a Cincinnati Bow Tie (insert penis into tracheotomy hole; repeat as necessary) or the Alabama Hot Pocket (defecate into a woman's vagina), or that somebody might find pleasure in the Angry Penguin (fellating a man while he stands, pants around his ankles, and bringing him near orgasm, then walking away, leaving the fellated man no recourse but to waddle away, pants still down, furious). Even more elaborate sexual deeds have perhaps been performed at outdoor rock shows (the Abe Lincoln: shooting all over an unconscious person's face, trimming their pubic hair, and creating a beard with the pubes and jizz; the Houdini: while fornicating doggie style, the male pulls out and spits on his partner's back, fooling the partner into thinking that he has ejaculated; however, when the partner turns around, the man lets loose the true load in his partner's face).

That these acts have names seems dirtier than the acts themselves. I imagine that they are private jokes gone public. In the movie *Klute*, Jane Fonda agrees to perform a "half and half," but we're never quite sure what that is. The imagination runs wild, and the imagination probably has more fun than Jane's john.

I like private jokes. Kelly, after a hard day's work picking up Hot Michigan Dutchies, likes to relax with an Arnold Palmer with Vodka—a "Mrs. Palmer," she calls it. On the other hand, dirty talk during sex seems a bit spendthrift—what we shout at somebody does not always require, necessarily, the articulate breath. Just the gist. Lovemaking, castigating, whining, begging—none of these truly need text, do they? Think of the dingbats used to indicate swear words in comic strips: &@#$!

But David Byrne once said the only reason he wrote words for his songs was so we could remember the tune more easily. Those are not his exact words, but you get the gist. And you'll probably remember the gist.

Perhaps all these names for outrageous acts of sex are meant to startle memory, fond or otherwise, or to tame the wild. The *Audubon Bird Guide* gives words to birdsong for easy identification. The white-eyed vireo announces, "Quick, give-me-the-rain-check!" The white-throated sparrow laments over "Poor Sam Peabody, Peabody, Peabody" (though up north, he yearns for "Sweet, sweet Canada-Canada-Canada"). The cardinal nesting outside my window dares me to "Party! Party! Party!" Philomela, raped by her brother-in-law and unable to identify her assailant because he also ripped her tongue out, was transformed into a nightingale. No words are given to nightingale song, for it is too varied, too virtuoso, and Philomela's is a wordless grief that goes on and on. The difference between the cardinal's song and that of the nightingale is the difference between sex and love.

My partner Jeff, who died fifteen years ago from AIDS, drowned in his own fluids from the weeping of Kaposi's sarcoma sores. In his last days, our intimacy was reduced to my examining his body for the advance of these and other opportunistic infections; he trusted me when I ran my fingers over his tender sores and opened his mouth wide while I placed a long rearview mirror from an old van into his mouth, to note the purple lesions on the roof of his mouth, the thrush on his tongue. I will not give a name to this long, varied, virtuoso, loving scrutiny of his body, but believe me when I tell you it was an act of both sex and love.

DIRTY TALK

TOBIN LEVY

DEFINITION: the act of using sexually explicit language
in an attempt to arouse your partner.

*To avoid sounding redundant with vocabulary, attempt using metaphors. "I
want to feel my/your essence leaking out of me." "I love it when my/your pole
reaches the bottom of your/my throat." For a more aggressive touch, using
cursing can be quite thrilling. Compare "You are such a great lay" to "Holy
shit! You are such a great fucking lay!" Other examples are "Fucking bang
me harder, bitch/bastard," "Fucking smack my God-damned ass," and "Jesus, it just feels so bloody good that I want to fucking cum all over you." Here
you are able to speak louder because these phrases tend to be more aggressive.*
—FROM WWW.SEXINFO101.COM

The first time someone uttered anything other than the requisite
niceties (e.g., you're so pretty, you have great legs, I love making
love to you) during sex, I cringed. And cried. Then cried some
more.

This did not go unnoticed by Mike, the great offender. We'd
had sex before, only without the dirty talk and the inconsolable
waterworks. He lived on the West Coast. I lived on the East. So
we had sex intermittently, whenever he was in town. I was in my
early twenties and not all that experienced. He was in his early
thirties and had had more than his share of bedmates. I thought I
loved him and believed that, at the very least, he thought of me as
classy, smart, an attractive friend with girlfriend potential. Then
he talked dirty to me.

What Mike said that night was not all that offensive. If I remember correctly, he merely whispered salacious directives in my
ear, then gave an expletive-heavy description of all the things he
wanted to do with and to me. But at the time, what he said and

81

what I heard were two very different things. When he said, "Get on top of me," I heard, "You're a hooker." When he said, "I want to fuck you from behind," I heard, "You're an ugly, trashy, deplorable skank."

My reaction was immediate and visceral. I'd hoped, in the way that naive twenty-three-year-olds are wont to do, that if we kept having sex, Mike would fall in love with me. Because in my mind dirty talk and intimate relationships were mutually exclusive, his saying "I want to tie you up" was a preemptive measure. It meant he'd never consider me dating material. It meant he didn't find me sophisticated and intelligent. Suddenly, I'd become a booty call rather than a paramour. Semantics, I know. But at the time, it mattered. I was lost in translation. He was lost in my histrionics.

During the next few years, I went out with several men who had a penchant for dirty talk. The instigation was always startling, and the outcome often less than ideal. (Steve had too much stubble on his back and chest—presumably from shaving—for me to pay attention to what was coming out of his mouth. And Ivan's Irish brogue was too thick to elicit much more from me than a mood-killing "Huh?" "What did you say?" "Can you repeat that?") Still, my appreciation for filthy, late-night exchanges grew.

You can only hear "You're so pretty" or "You have great legs" so many times during sex before the words begin to sound pat, formulaic, and meaningless. The more I had sex, the more I wanted to hear something different, be it a bawdy command, a lascivious question, or an obscene declarative about something I was doing right.

Contrary to my preconceptions, a person's intelligence and propensity for dirty talk were not inversely proportional. The gift of prurient gab required a sharp tongue and an active imagination. More important, dirty talk and intimacy were not mutually exclusive. It turned out that nothing exhibited trust like "I bought you a tennis skirt. I want you to put it on and sit on my lap." Nothing, that is, except being able to acquiesce and enjoy the match—even if Lycra was involved. By talking dirty, the men I was seeing were opening a private window into their deviate selves. By liking it, even reciprocating from time to time, I was, too.

Three years after my first dirty-talk debacle, I suspected that Mike had actually been quite gifted in that particular art form. He was a writer, someone I'd trusted, and he was also unapologetically sexual. We'd remained friends over the years, so the next time we were both single again, I paid him a visit.

"I thought you hated it when I talked dirty to you," he said. I'd requested a little foulmouthed behavior in honor of my being in between boyfriends and having traveled to the West Coast.

"I don't want to talk about it," I said, red-faced at the memory of my bedroom hysteria. And he didn't, opting instead to indulge me with some of the most deliciously dirty pillow chat that I'd ever heard.

DON JUAN (*see also* LOTHARIO)

JOSH EMMONS

DEFINITION: 1. A libertine; a profligate. 2. A man
who is an obsessive seducer of women.
AKA: Casanova, Lothario, Prince Charming, Romeo, heartbreaker,
ladies' man, lady-killer, libertine, philanderer, playboy,
rake, roué, seducer, stud, wolf, women chaser.

The word is full of semi-adult persons who secretly nurse the notion that they are, or that by rights they ought to be, Don Juan, Napoleon, or the Messiah.

—WALTER LIPPMAN, *A PREFACE TO MORALS*
(MACMILLAN, 1929), CH. 9

Every man "was made to be the father of thousands." So says the narrator of John Cheever's "The Good Husband" while its hero contemplates having an affair, and although this isn't literally true (for which we should all be grateful), the impulse behind it is. Men want to have sex with everybody they find attractive, as well as with many people they don't, and it has always been this way and will continue to be so until our species is snuffed out by a nuclear blast or flooded world or solar supernova. Is this okay? No. Yes. Maybe. We don't know.

Consider Don Juan. How you view him probably depends on your answer to the above question. He is either a reckless seducer who plows his way through fields of innocent women, leaving behind wide, clear swaths of heartache, or he is a well-meaning sensualist who no more deserves our censure for his actions than does a bee for pollinating a garden. A third possibility—that he isn't good or bad, but instead absurd, aware that eternity is a ruse and the world meaningless, and therefore, because in response to the void that chills the center of existence one must act, an episodic seducer—is worth considering, though its depressing likelihood makes it unpopular.

Who *is* Don Juan, and why has he become a synonym for tireless womanizing? His legend first appeared in the Spanish dramatist Tirso de Molina's *The Trickster of Seville and the Stone Guest*, in the early seventeenth century, and it has been retold and altered and mashed up since by everyone from Mozart to Byron to Kierkegaard to Camus. According to most versions, our villain/hero begins his erotic career as a teenager with a married friend of his mother's, and over the next few decades he cajoles, flatters, romances, persuades, pressures, and forces hundreds of females—with an athlete's brio he reckons the number to be over a thousand—into bed. His methods are ingenious and varied, such as dressing up as his conquests' actual lovers, promising marriage, threatening suicide, and bragging about his physical and technical attributes. Swinging from woman to woman like some priapic Tarzan, he outrages husbands and fathers and occasionally has to defend himself in mortal duels, which makes him, again according to your sympathies, also either a murderer or man-slaughterer. One version of the story ends with Don Juan meeting and inviting to dinner the statue of a man he's killed, who then drags him down to hell, where the devil tells him that everyone there is assigned a role, and that Don Juan's is the Fool. In another version he enters a monastery in old age and discovers that asceti-cism and sensual pleasure are in fact—amazingly, ironically—flip sides of the same coin of destitution.

Yes, Don Juan is a player, and, yes, he lives entirely for sexual pleasure, unbothered by the thought that his promiscuity hurts people and intent until the end—even the end that finds him a monk—to believe that his earthly incarnation is all there is, and that acting on behalf of an imaginary eternity, not just in terms of one's cultural or political legacy, but also in terms of one's im-mortal soul, is a mistake. In this way he is exceptional, for few people can live with the certainty that they do not extend beyond their mortal self. In every other way, however, he is as common as the Y chromosome.

According to pop folklore, men chase women because they fear death. Having sex affirms that men are alive, potent, attrac-tive, dominant, and vital, and that they are unbowed by time, and that they, like God, can create life. At least temporarily, sex silences their fear of irrelevance and obsolescence. When you're doing it, you're not dead. The problem with this theory is that in their pur-suit of sex, men often risk the very thing they're supposedly safe-guarding, life. Think of the jealous husbands and irate fathers Don Juan has to subdue, one of whom winds up escorting him to his damnation. Think of Bill Clinton's impeachment. Think of every man you've ever known—don't exclude yourself, if you are one—who has lost or almost lost something crucial (a wife, a job, a sense of well-being, hours and days and weeks of mental focus) because of sex.

So how should we account for the deep-seated promiscuity at the heart of the Don Juan story? Biologists say it's simple. Like all animals, men evolved with an urgent desire to pass on their genetic material, which given the high rate of infant mortality—not to mention women dying in labor: even now, in the twenty-first century, somewhere in the world a woman dies every minute of every day in childbirth—required that they try hard and try constantly to impregnate someone. Therefore no story is as understandable or natural as Don Juan's. His insatiable appetite for sex is of the same kind as his appetite for food, hardwired and unchangeable and, from a physiological standpoint, innocent.

If that's the case, why do many people feel such repulsion toward the don? Why were adultery laws ever written? Why is polygamy considered horrible by most Westerners? Why, if the desire for different sex partners is of the same ilk as the desire for different foods, is cheating any worse than eating out every now and then? Biologists have an answer for this, too, which is that rearing a child is better done by two people than one person, and that fathers who run around often choose not to come back. It's just as likely—considering that infidelity is also viewed as unacceptable when practiced by childless men—that our society condemns Don Juanism because we've developed a morality of commitment over wanderlust. And because something can be natural without being acceptable (our penchant for war, for example), we try to stop behavior we don't approve of and reckon this to be the basis for our superiority over other animals.

But to return to our original question, putting aside for a moment society's shifting mores, is it okay for men to be—or aspire to be—Don Juan? Should we think of Casanova and Lothario and Warren Beatty and your walleyed friend and her cheating husband and the lust in Jimmy Carter's heart as abominations, as evils, as threats to our noblest instincts and highest callings? Perhaps this is the wrong approach to the fathomless mystery of human behavior, which ever lacks consistency and can be justified or vilified depending on where one stands and which unspoken experiences, real or imaginary, lurk in our minds and bodies. It's true, after all, that although Don Juan was remorseless and self-serving and guilty of a thousand indiscretions, without his spirit most of us wouldn't be here to answer one way or the other.

DURATION

PHILLIP LOPATE

DEFINITION: the length of time something continues or exists.

"Continuous erotic arousal" drops from an average of nearly an hour in the late teens and early twenties to seven minutes in men in their late sixties. It is pointed out that under prolonged stimulation "many a teen-age male will maintain a continuous erection for several hours."

–KINSEY REPORT

Fornicating is like parenting: no matter how you do it, you have the guilty sense that somewhere other people are doing it more correctly. Myself, I wonder if I am lasting long enough. With all due attention to foreplay, penetration, and the bliss that follows, it is still usually over in half an hour, so that if my wife and I start going at it by ten thirty, even with the reverential postcoital snuggle and "love you" exchange, one of us still has time to say, "You wanna watch the news?"

Of course, a marriage going on fifteen years, with a little one sleeping down the hall, may hardly be optimal conditions for sustaining the heights of lust. Still, I can't help wondering, if making love a half hour is pleasurable, wouldn't making love two hours be four times as pleasurable? And then there is the "all night long" boast that Casanova and so many rhythm-and-blues singers have claimed. I have never done it all night long, with the best intentions, even in my youth, when I was more inclined to show off by going at it more than once. Afterward I would feel woozily satiated, preferring to drift off or talk, rather than keep banging away.

When I watch pornography, I am amazed at the variety and duration of these partners as they rotate front to back, top to bottom, with one orgasm after another. I take my hat off to their appetites as much as their stamina. Even knowing that filmmaking is a fragmented process, with time off for camera repositioning, I can't help believing on some level that pornography constitutes the norm for a *Homo sapiens* of another, sturdier disposition. As for me, if I am stroking intently for fifteen minutes, there comes a point when I begin to think, okay, I've got the message, I've had my fun, it's time to bring this thing to a conclusion.

What is wrong with me?

Henry Miller wrote in one of his novels that he kept a bowl of ice by his bedside so that he could withdraw when he felt close to ejaculation and plunge his balls into ice, to prolong the act. That strikes me as so . . . *industrious!* O. J. Simpson was widely reported to have contracted a hugely expensive coke habit, mainly in order to fuck longer. Not that either of these worthy gentlemen is my role model in other respects, but I cannot help wondering if they were onto something—if their almost puritanically conscientious focus on sexual duration may have brought them closer to a spiritual truth than I, with my laissez-faire approach.

I recently asked a few women friends what they thought of the matter. One woman said, "I get bladder infections, so I really wouldn't want to be pounded for more than ten or fifteen minutes." Good, I can do that. Another woman offered, "Great sex tends to be quick or long. Most sex is medium length. Obviously, most sex is not great sex." Women characteristically say that what matters to them is the quality of connection, not longevity. In the sixties, the feminist Germaine Greer wrote that she preferred men to express genuine passion, however short-lived, to the calculated marathons that seemed to arise from performance anxiety, and that suggested the man was dulling his brain by remembering train schedules in order not to come. Indeed, though the *Kama Sutra* and other Eastern sex manuals often stress the importance of a man's learning to defer his ejaculation for the woman's sake, it often seems that a man's desire to go long has little to do with a woman's pleasure, and more with his own competition to better his personal best.

In my own experience, sometimes when I've tried to be my partner's selfless servant in foreplay, she might say impatiently, "I want you inside me," just as when I try to prolong the actual stroking so that she can reach orgasm first, she is apt to whisper in my ear, "I want you to come!" Some women's orgasms are only brought on by a man's ejaculation. In other cases, I don't doubt it's because the man is not touching or stroking her sensitively enough, and so she may feel, Let's get it over with.

It's fair to assume that emotions affect a man's capacity to sustain himself in sex. But rarely is love the determining factor. First-time excitement and romantic ardor with someone frequently shortens the act. Tenderness, from long familiarity or long-term commitment, tends toward medium-length coital embraces. A disengaged, blasé mood may enable you to feel you can continue indefinitely. Similarly, anger: there was one lover who made me frequently outraged, whom I used to screw for a long, long time. On the other hand, an unacknowledged hostility or alienation from the other person can sometimes make it difficult to keep an erection.

Clearly, Viagra and other potency-ensuring drugs have thrown a wrench into that age-old suspense about whether or how long you will be able to keep it up. For the very reason that they rob the sex act of one of its quintessential dimensions, anxiety, and pump up the performances of ordinary schlubs, who come to have a distorted idea of their amatory capacities, they should be avoided whenever it is possible to do so.

DYKE

CRIS BEAM

DEFINITION: a slang term for a lesbian. Originally it was a derogatory label for a masculine or butch woman, and this usage still exists. However, it has also been reappropriated as a positive term implying assertiveness and toughness, or simply as a neutral synonym for *lesbian*.

San Francisco lesbian bikers have won a major battle with the U.S. Patent and Trademark Office.For more than a year the San Francisco Women's Motorcycle Contingent has been trying to trademark the name "Dykes on Bikes." The non-profit group is a fixture at San Francisco gay pride celebrations. It says it decided to obtain a trademark for "Dykes on Bikes" to protect the non-commercial use of the name and its meaning to the LGBT community from private commercial use. The Trademark Office twice rejected the group's application on the ground that the word "dyke" is disparaging to lesbians. The group submitted more than two dozen expert declarations from scholars, linguists, psychologists, and activists demonstrating how the word "dyke" has evolved to become a positive term and that lesbians view "Dykes on Bikes" as empowering. This week the appeal board reversed the decision and notified the group that it can trademark the name.

—WWW.365.GAY.COM

The women who get called dykes are the ones who look like boys. They embody a tricky kind of maleness in the kick of a boot, a thrust of a chin, a slim hip, a steady gaze. They're the ones who got arrested in the forties, vilified in the eighties, and are erased in this strange new millennium of L-word femmes and girl-on-girl celebrity exhibitionism. The women who get called dykes are shy and subtle despite their hands that grip like men and can quickly slip inside another girl—a fist, an offering. Dykes are proud butches, heartbroken, headstrong—they've weathered cruelty against their skins alongside a silent loathing aimed at their souls (importunate, insidious, worse). And yet their imagined cocks still rise at a wink of thigh, a flirt, a quick tease in the eyes. I go weak for daddies.

"Call me Daddy," she said, and then, "Beg."

I did.

Her hands at my wrists, my waist, my throat. A knowing when to let up, to press harder. "You're mine," she said, and in that moment, I was.

What is this thing, surrender? Between two women, it is power upended, longing, finding, loss. Also, it's pure beginning; without language or continent, lesbian tops and bottoms are a big bang. In a word, everything.

The butch I love is small and French. Her shoulders are minor mountains, her mind, a complicated, bright forest. She fucks like she thinks—intense, direct, focused. And then, tender. She is muscular, defined as a wing or a cut, and I want her with every moving cell inside me. I want her masculinity, but I do not want a man. To the blurry-eyed voyeur, we could seem to merely reflect heterosexuality, but our twinned mirror is cracked through with a different knowing. There is violence in this sex, and rage, culled from years of sidewalk scorn, of never being wanted. To want—for a dyke—is to touch the hate of what one has never been given. That hate, of course, is hot. In all ways. (The fear of burning, I imagine, is why so many dykes end up sexless, with cats and tea, and U-Haul jokes.)

A butch's aggression, internalized from the world, externalized in bed, gives her a place to rest, and a femme a place to root.

Because we've both been excised; tie me down with cuffs. We both need comfort; see me as the skirted girl and I'll desire you as the boy with breasts. I'll want you as a man and know you as a woman; I won't be afraid when you call me your fag (you need to top every slurry bruise). A dyke is the barrier that keeps out the sea; you are so tired, my Heracles, of shouldering the world.

EXHIBITIONIST

ELISSA SCHAPPELL

DEFINITION: a perversion marked by a
tendency to indecent exposure.

Sexual display or exposure has not always been an oddity, a type of "perverted" or "deviant" sexuality. It used to be common and was even indulged in as a sign of respect to a visitor—as with the famous ladies of Ireland. The Queen of Ulster and all the ladies of the Court, to the number of 610, came to meet Cuchulainn, naked above the waist, and raising their skirts.

—FROM G. L. SIMONS, *THE ILLUSTRATED BOOK OF SEXUAL RECORDS,*
1974, 1982, 1997-2001

At three she stands between the glass door and the curtain naked but for a pair of red sneakers. She is waiting for the mailman. Her mother cannot police her all the time. The postman thinks it's funny. After all, it is the sixties.

In the midseventies the radio plays the song "The Streak" ten times a day. Streakers interrupt baseball and football games, even the Oscars.

Her mother tells her a terrible story about a man in a raincoat who's been flashing girls at bus stops. He is in his late twenties, white, and wears a wedding ring—yes, really, a wedding ring.

"People like that just want to shock and upset you," her mother instructs. "If a man ever exposes himself to you, turn and run."

Her best friend disagrees. "No. You're supposed to point and laugh: *It's so small!* Or, if he hasn't been snipped: *Look at the little anteater!*"

Her best friend, whose mom is a shrink, blames the flasher's mother. She says if his mother hadn't emasculated him, he wouldn't be sticking his dick in everybody's face.

Her best friend, whose mom is a shrink, tells her she has an Electra complex. Which means she loves her dad too much. This is ridiculous. Her father barely notices her.

At slumber parties she and her friends make prank calls, conduct séances, and play truth or dare while the sun comes up.

Truth, would you rather make out with Tony Rosetta, aka the Italian Octopus, or dare, streak to the mailbox? Truth is she will always take the dare over the truth.

Heart racing, she bolts like a deer up the driveway to the mailbox. The thought that someone might see her nude—her small breasts white and pink—terrifies and thrills her. Picking up speed, wind on her skin, she thinks, *I am just a streak.*

Across the street a man in a bathrobe is picking up his newspaper. Safe inside the house, the girls scream and laugh hysterically. He's going to have to spank his monkey before his wife wakes up.

She publishes a poem, "Loneliness," under the name Anonymous in the school magazine. In the halls people say how sad and deep it is. When she confesses she wrote it, no one believes her. This bothers her for years.

At sixteen she sunbathes in the front yard in a yellow bikini so small it can sit in her hand like a baby chick. When she hears the mailman idling at their mailbox, she stands up and starts to stretch—arching her back, touching her toes, her bikini bottom riding up her crack—she does a back bend. She couldn't pick the mailman out of a lineup, but it doesn't matter as long as he's not fat or bearded.

Once he accidentally gives the neighbors a lawn job. The tracks filled her with a sense of accomplishment. Pleasure.

Of course were he ever to speak to her, ever get out of the truck, it would all be over. Her father would kill him. Her father's disappointment in her would kill her. Then bring her back to life.

What is it with mailmen?

At the neighborhood pool she and two girlfriends swim out into the deep end and switch bathing suits underwater. They think this is the funniest thing in the world.

The lifeguard's eyes are the color of pool water, his white-blond hair tinted green from chlorine. He's a senior and they are only sophomores. Until now they have been invisible.

From his perch he watches them treading water—giggling as they bounce and brush against each other, swapping tops and bottoms—and spreads a towel across his lap.

She and her friends are pretty sure they've got the world by the tail, or at least the cock.

In college she sometimes undresses in front of her dorm window. It is innocent. One bra strap comes down—flash—like a camera bulb. Then, she's so coy—flash—the other breast. She doesn't know if anyone is really watching. What is she doing wrong? Nothing.

On the weekends she dances up on top of bars and tables. Cute guys stop talking to their girlfriends when she pulls another drunk girl up onto the bar and French-kisses her. The boys are so still and so close she could step on the their heads. Walk right over them and out the door.

She never sees the man who delivers mail to the college.

During pledge week the sight of boys mooning, or *pressing a ham*, against car windows disgusts her. Forcing anyone to *stare into the unblinking brown eye* is wrong. Now, if they were dropping their drawers for a good reason, say to protest apartheid or nuclear war, that'd be different.

Senior year her creative writing teacher encourages them to write what they know. "Write something you wouldn't want your parents to read."

When they get to her story, someone says, "I like the part where you cut yourself in front of your boyfriend." The teacher interrupts, "Don't confuse the writer with the character."

On her paper he writes, "You've got to get more naked. Push it. i.e.: Make her get into a strange man's car and see what happens. Do they have sex? Why is she doing this?"

He stares at her in class. He finds reasons to touch her. She flashes her scars. She shows off. The other students start to hate her. She doesn't care. She's the star.

In his office, after he's done praising her story about a tortured mailman, they fuck. She sighs, "I am most myself with you." She plays with his wedding ring. She knows he thinks she means during sex.

After graduate school her stories start appearing in magazines. She feigns shock that anyone could ever believe she'd ever do the things her characters do. Break up a happy marriage. Trade sex for drugs. "It's not true. It's fiction. Can't you read?"

And she isn't lying because some was truth and some was fiction. "The truth is I'm only truly alive when you're looking at me. Look at me," she wrote. *Feel the way I make your heart beat fast.*

F

FACIAL

LAWRENCE DOUGLAS

DEFINITION: the slang term for the sexual activity in which one person directs an ejaculation of semen onto the face of another person, often following oral sex, intercourse, or other stimulation.

The pull-out cum shot was originally developed as a way for porn stars to prove they had truly climaxed. The "money shot."

—WWW.RUSHKOFF.COM/ESSAY/FACIAL.HTML

History

The source of the term *facial* to designate the disemboguing of ejaculant on the face, or more generally, head, of a woman, and less commonly, a man, remains obscure. Richly detailed descriptions of oral, anal, and genital sex abound in classical antiquity, and yet one searches in vain the works of Sappho, Callimachus, or Horace for any mention of the facial. Neither the term nor any of its several cognates—*face shot, face-fungus, head frost, milk mask, scalp vinaigrette, bonnyclabber, koumiss splat*, et al.—find mention in Boccaccio, Rabelais, and Cervantes; the practice is likewise absent in the work of Flaubert, D. H. Lawrence, and A. A. Milne. The *Oxford English Dictionary* traces the term to a passage in *The Bells of San Gabriel* (1914), a historical romance by the Californian novelist Gertrude Atherton (1857–1948), "I've got fourteen heads to dress . . . and most of them want a facial, too" (p. 84), but many scholars challenge the authoritativeness of this usage, noting the alternative meaning of the term—viz, as a cosmetic treatment. The first reliable naming of the sexual practice appears, then, in the eponymous 1982 adult-film western *Facial*

Squaws (see Milton Cack, *A Basketful of Fuzzy Kittens: A Lay History of XXX* [Booty Press, 2004]).

Prevalence and Development

From its murky origins to its present ubiquity, the rise of the facial has been swift and even stunning. Through the end of the 1970s, extra-genital ejaculations were typically directed toward the buttocks or abdomen of the sex partner. The resurgence of mammary intercourse in the 1980s turned the female breast into a favored objective of seminal fluid. Perhaps it was inevitable that this gradual upward migration would soon reach and include the neck (see Fanny Nosher, "I Wore a Pearl Necklace," *Exquisite Hump: A Journal of Erotica* 4). But it was not until the late 1990s and the waning years of the Clinton administration that the facial gained its present popularity (Scham & Haar, *Executive Power and the Forms of Ejaculation* [Warsaw: Pundal Press, 2003]).

The rise of the facial has no doubt benefited from the increasing popularity of its more familiar cosmetic variant. The marketing of bestselling antioxidant moisturizers such as Dr. Orgo's Abyssinian Ultra Facial Fuel, prepared, in part, from the sperm of the chum, coho, and sockeye salmon, has led to a more generalized belief in the toning and exfoliating properties of human seminal fluid. Though no scientific studies have yet been published in support of this specific claim, many persons and groups continue to accept its truth (see, for example, "Help Your Wife Fight Those Wrinkles," *Bulletin of the Christian Family Association of America*).

Mechanics

Ejaculation can be understood as the union of emission and propulsion. The standard facial delivers a "throw load" of 4.2 ml of ejaculant over an average distance of 14 cm. A facial throw load of less than 1.5 ml may be a sign of hypospermia, or low semen volume, a condition not to be confused with azoospermia, or low sperm count. By contrast, weak propulsion may result in a facial that literally fails to "reach its mark." Discharge distance is, of course, a function of many factors, including prevailing wind speed, barometric pressure, air temperature, and altitude from sea level. Doctors agree, however, that greater propulsion can be achieved by conditioning the puboccoccygeus muscle, which controls ejaculation (see Axel Felch, M.D., "Treating the 'Dribbler': Some Suggested Therapies," *Journal of Genitalia 8*). In addition, there is the matter of "shooting straight." In a fully erect state, 82 percent of penises deviate from the bodily meridian by an average of 17°, and doctors have recorded deviations up to a full 90° (the deviation angle should not be confused with the angle of erection; see *Calibrating the Penis, with Special Attention to Ethnic and Regional Differences: A Statistical Survey,* Bureau of Weights and Measures, www.usgov.org). The failure to take the deviation angle into account may lead to an errant or otherwise misdirected facial ("Not in My Eye, Please!" *Semen Today*, July 2007). Simple corrective measures include "righting" the penis with the hand or with the aid of such widely available devices as the standard bar clamp. Finally, men who suffer from anejaculation (complete ejaculatory incompetence) can nevertheless administer a suitable facial facsimile by using a plant mister and ersatz ejaculant (a simple but effective recipe calls for 1 cup water; 2 tbs cornstarch; 1 raw egg; 1 tbs plain yogurt; pinch of salt—stirred, not whipped).

Sociology and Controversies
Despite its prevalence, the facial remains a controversial practice. For some, it is a symbol of contemporary male pride, a demonstration of virility in a postindustrial society that provides precious few opportunities for traditional displays of manliness ("The New 'Iron John'?" *Maxim*, August 2004). Others are less sanguine.

Without doubt, the source of greatest concern remains the Japanese variation known as *bukkake* (ブッカケ, literally "splash"), a group sex act in which multiple men take turns ejaculating on a woman, usually prone or seated and dressed in the Prussian-blue sailor *sērā-fuku* (セーラー服) uniform of a Japanese schoolgirl. In sharp contrast to the OMTF (open-mouth, tongue-flicking) facial favored in America and northern Europe, the *bukkake* "receptacle" (ぶっちぎり) commonly appears in an attitude of submission, awash in a veritable tsunami (120–150 ml) of semen. This has led many feminists to condemn this practice as a virulent form of gendered humiliation, a fetishistic display of female degradation and male aggrandizement tantamount to ritualized group rape (see Katumura Makinnukami, *Hello Kitty, Goodbye Dignity: The Woman in Today's Japan* [Tuttle, 2005]). Many Japanese businessmen, however, defend *bukkake* as a culturally specific art form, every bit as valid as Kabuki theater, indoor golf, and hara-kiri. These debates suggest that it is too early to say whether the facial will go the way of other erotic fads, such as Greco-Roman pedophilia, or will show the staying power of such time-tested practices as sexual reproduction.

FANTASY

NATALIE DANFORD

DEFINITION: the forming of mental images, especially wondrous or strange fancies; imaginative conceptualizing. Psychology: an imagined or conjured-up sequence fulfilling a psychological need; daydream.

Conservatives have just as many fantasies as liberals—despite the fact that, according to one study, nearly half of conservative Christians feel sexual fantasies are "morally flawed or unacceptable."

—PETER DOSKOCH, *PSYCHOLOGY TODAY*, SEPTEMBER/OCTOBER 1995

I am fantasy-free.

It's not that I don't have a fantasy life. In fact, as a writer of fiction, fantasies *are* my life. I spend my days dreaming up stories, putting imaginary characters through their paces, reaching metaphorical fingers deep into my brain to tease out any damp subconscious nuggets that might help me build a plot.

And writing fiction is a lot like sex. Crafting a story, you massage the pieces into place and work to heighten the drama, building toward a climax. No coincidence that my writer friends and I refer to those delicious moments when it all comes together—the story flows, the pieces click into place—as a "braingasm."

But fantasies about sex? I have none.

Some fantasies I have had: A great-aunt I didn't know dies and leaves me an enormous Manhattan apartment with high ceilings and its own washer and dryer. A Democrat wins the White House and the party holds on to the presidency for the next twenty years, implementing excellent universal health care quickly and painlessly. An elf breaks into my office during the night and finishes my new novel—brilliantly; all that's left for me to do is clean up the typos entered when his stubby little fingers hit the wrong keys.

Indeed, I suffer from the writer's great occupational hazard: I've got an overactive imagination. Riding the bus, I make up stories for the people around me. That woman just got fired, but she hated her job at the Gap anyway and dreams of being a circus acrobat; his heart hasn't mended properly since the head cheerleader rejected him in high school. The driver was abused horribly as a child, locked in a cage, but he's gotten over it and has a wife and four daughters (the oldest is currently missing her two front teeth) and a respectable two-family home in Queens. I even feel a twinge of happiness for him, overcoming the odds like that, before I remember it's all in my head.

Yet, just as the cobbler's children have no shoes, the writer's sex life has no fantasies. I'm too concerned with originality to be satisfied with the cliché classics (desert island, late night at the office, strangers on a train), and the effort to come up with something believable and new, with just the right amount of quirkiness, exhausts me.

So when my sweetheart and I are doing what we do, there's nothing on my mind except *it.* That. In those moments, my brain is blank of stories. I sacrifice narrative completely and give over to sensation. Really, it's a relief.

FELLATIO (*see also* BLOW JOB)

ANN HOOD

DEFINITION: oral stimulation of a man's penis.
The sexual partner performing fellatio is a fellator;
if female, a fellatrice or fellatrix.

Cleopatra of Egypt has been represented as the "most famous free-love fellatrice of the ancient world." Cleo is said to have performed fellatio on a thousand men. Perhaps this is why the Greeks chose to call her Merichane (Gaper)—"she who gapes wide for ten thousand men—the wide-mouthed one; the ten-thousand-mouthed woman."
–G. L. SIMONS, *THE ILLUSTRATED BOOK OF SEXUAL RECORDS*, PUTNAM, 1983

As a teenager, I loved to kiss boys. Boys in Mustang convertibles. Boys on sailboats. Boys at shopping malls and amusement parks and beaches. I kissed until my chin grew chafed and my lips got chapped. I liked the feel of their sixteen-year-old man-boy stubble on my cheek and their thick curls or shaggy hair in my fingers. I liked the way kisses could make them breathe harder, groan. I kissed and kissed and kissed. But that was it. No second base, even over my shirt. No hands sliding up my dress.

They begged for more, those boys. But I remained virginal, moral, merely kissable. They explained what *blue balls* and *cock teaser* meant. I didn't care. There was power in my kisses. One boy, tall and blond, wooed me with steak and Caesar salad, a moonlight walk on the beach. We kissed, small, soft kisses. But later, parked in his Fiat in front of my house, the kisses grew bigger and hotter. Dozens of them. His hand, the same one that he used to pitch his baseball team to championships, found my breast. I pushed it away. We arm-wrestled, still kissing. He moaned, "Come on!" "No!" I said, fumbling for the door. "Can I call you again?" he said, grabbing the hem of my dress to keep me there. Before I could answer, he said, "Then we can do some fellatio." I paused. He dropped my hem. "You don't know what that means, Miss A Student, do you?" "Yes, I do," I lied. "Good. Let's do fellatio next time." I ran inside, straight to the dictionary. I read the definition. What? Put the boy's penis in my mouth? This was what kissing led to? This was what boys longed for? I closed the dictionary, disappointed. And never kissed with such abandon again.

FISTING

FIONA MAAZEL

DEFINITION: the act of inserting one's fist
into either a vagina or rectum.

The sex act called fisting is a source of confusion and misconceptions for many Christians. This is unfortunate, because it means that many Christian men and women are depriving themselves of what could be the most spiritual sexual experience of their lives. Like anal sex and BDSM, fisting is often mistakenly associated with the gay community or is considered a sex act too extreme to be appropriate for Christian couples. Not only are these views incorrect, but fisting actually has a scriptural precedent, as we will show.

—WWW.SEXINCHRIST.COM

Fisting. n. A weak hybrid: fist+fucking=. Inspired use of the *ing* suffix to express perpetuity of action borne in vain against solitude. Number of Google pages: ~9,490,000. Pages for Nabokov: ~3,310,000. The foregoing thanks to a lonely researcher whose romp with tedium at her place of work avails data of no interest to anyone but the lonely researcher, who will now wrest from it a few ontological observations. For instance, when options to bilk the forlorn include reading and fisting, fisting wins. For instance, brachioproctic rapture is an experience of metaphor that bests what pleasure is to be derived from living another kind of metaphor, *literary metaphor*, e.g., Nabokov's pale fire, which is probably the moon at night or the glowworm at dawn. For instance, we are cavernous and unexplored; fisting is a means to discovery. The researcher likes this last observation best. For though she has never known the rending of flesh that is intercourse, she has known her heart's foray into speculation. Speculation that includes the dark arts—the arrant arts—that aspire to religious consequence. Let us return to the dell of metaphor and consider a blogger who insists the fist can channel the stuff of God as per Psalms 145:16: *You open your hand and satisfy the desire of every living thing.* Imagine, then, that fisting simulates in body the rapport between me and Him who loves me best. Okay, but *what*? Really? The researcher has given chase to an idea without prepping for the finish. She takes another route, which makes her expose affinity for a certain fey indie band that has in song referred to a *fistful of love*—of love that imprints on the body evidence of devotion, the fistee's and fister's both. And there you have it: the lyrics are a retelling of the spiritual ecstasy espoused by the Christ blogger. Good grief. The researcher doffs her headphones and thinks, *My day comprises one horror after the next; soon it will be mice shorn their organs and let's see how well they do.* Google pages for *prosthetic kidney:* 154. Pages for *virgin researcher:* 21. *Stays against loneliness:* 14. The researcher has need of a prophylactic and looks for one daily. That is what we've been saying from the start.

FOBBING

SAM BRUMBAUGH

DEFINITION: crying during sex.

RELATED TERMS: *cryber* : to cry while having cybersex; *cheching*: to cry while masturbating (aka cry whacker).

QUESTION: *Is it normal to want to cry during intercourse?*

ANSWER: *Sex can be an intensely emotional experience, and crying is a normal expression of being overwhelmed with emotion. If you are concerned about your feelings of wanting to cry and feel that they may signal a problem, I encourage you to discuss it further with a counselor at University Counseling and Psychological Services.*

−FROM THE WEB SITE OF
OREGON STATE UNIVERSITY STUDENT HEALTH SERVICES

CRYING DURING SEX

Some cry because they don't know who they are when they are having sex. Some cry because they cannot love you as much as you love yourself. Some cry because it will not go on, because it will end. Some cry because they are giving in and it suddenly feels like too much and they draw back and all that is left from the feeling of putting themselves out there unaware is fear.

Some cry as to why all women leave them. Some cry at a

condom breaking. Some cry at a whip on their bare skin. Some cry because they sense disease.

Some cry because of the way a man pushes it in. Some cry because of his size, or the pushy duration. Some cry because the act is so bad, because it's always so bad.

Some cry out of vain regret for a better relationship they are wasting. Some cry out of recent guilt, out of fucking around elsewhere. Some cry because you have been fucking around elsewhere.

Some cry because sex is no longer play. Some cry because it becomes crude, animalistic, and emptying. Some cry because the release of tears is like a slow and tender drawing up of the quilt over the act.

Some cry because they are sentimental about how loving sex can be and how this is a warm and natural reflection of their relationship. Some have a lot of love for you and it's just another way to show it.

Some cry out of joy, but this is rare and usually a hopeful mimicry of something seen on the screen.

Some cry because it is the only time they are able to, whereas they used to cry all the time.

Some cry because the tears are such a shock, because they render men speechless and in this way feel strangely deviant. Some cry because not even sex jolts them out of the relentless private dormancy of their life.

Some cry because the roller-coaster swing of sex mirrors their moods. Some cry because of hormonal imbalances. Some cry out of a fear of the loss of control, some to reassume control.

Some cry because of an overwhelming rush of loneliness, because you are right there with them but they suddenly have no idea who you are. Some cry because you become such a stranger in the act. Some cry because sex is as close as it gets, and it's not near enough.

Some cry because sex lurches into past trauma—a memory of rape or abuse or assault—and they cannot give in to another person, tears a fearful withdrawal from the currents of flesh and blood into some unshakable, dark preoccupation. Some cry because they can never open up to the freedom of the present, cannot simply let go. And sex becomes the opposite of joy, no longer a distillation of life, but rather a slow form of sexual suicide, resulting not in orgasm but an explosion of tears—the endorphins usually flooding you with good feeling instead triggering a sense of terror, grief, and sadness, a sense of a memory locked so deep inside, so bottled up in your blood, the only way to let it out is to cry using the convulsions of orgasm. Some cry because this is a beginning.

FOOT FETISH

MICHAEL HICKINS

DEFINITION: foot fetishism or podophilia is a pronounced sexual interest in feet. It is the most common form of sexual fetish. However, a foot fetish can also be nonsexual.
(American Psychological Association)

Neurologist Vilayanur S. Ramachandran proposed that foot fetishism is caused by the feet and the genitals occupying adjacent areas of the somatosensory cortex, possibly entailing some neural crosstalk between the two.
—MORTEN KRINGELBACH, *BODILY ILLUSIONS*, WWW.KRINGELBACH.DK/
PREPRINT_BEAGLE_BODILYILLUSIONS.HTML

Get in a cocktail party conversation about sexual turn-ons, and everything from hair to ass is fair game. Red, shiny, pulpy mouths are substitutes, preferable to some, for pussies. Legs are a V-shaped embrace leading to the promised land. But feet? You mean those filthy things down there, pounding the pavement, collecting every imaginable smell and disease. Are you some kind of submissive wussy-man? Do you like to eat shit, too? Do you want me to piss on you? How about a knuckle sandwich?

Misunderstandings about foot fetishism abound, particularly in modern occidental cultures, which promote explicitly primal sexual totems that are representative of procreation, only tacitly acknowledging the existence of more sophisticated forms of sexual titillation.

Of these, one of the most prevalent is foot fetishism. Also known as Retifism, for Rétif de la Bretonne, the eighteenth-century French novelist and chronicler whose acknowledged adoration of unclean female feet, especially the laving of particles from between the toes of the object of his affections, has contributed considerably to fostering one of the many misconceptions surrounding this largely unspoken sexual proclivity, foot fetishism can be defined as the conscious inclusion of the foot in sexual activity; heightened awareness of the erogeneity of ankles, toes, insteps, and soles; introduction of the foot as a member in good standing of the society of erogenous zones.

The fetishist (who, incidentally, resents the marginalization implicit in being so designated, if for no other reason than because, when necessary, he can actually achieve orgasm without the active participation of the foot in the sexual act) derives sexual arousal and/or satisfaction from seeing or touching or smelling or licking or kissing or engaging in genital-pedal contact, or any manifold, polyamorous combination thereof.

Some men derive pleasure from sucking on the big toe of their sexual partner during intercourse; others want to insert their penis into the cleavage between her big and second toe (a pedal version of titty-fucking); yet others want to shoot the gap between the arches that is produced when both feet are pressed together, the toes joined together like fingers interlocking in supplication (the Chinese practice of foot-binding was developed to create a more perfect mock-vagina, since even the most beautiful maiden may suffer from fallen arches); others wish to feel their rectums invaded by their partner's big toe, or to feel her feet against his face, her toes pinching it like tiny crabs, kneading and mashing his cheeks, eyelids, and lips while he masturbates; or to fuck the space between the sole of her foot (the French for shoe is *soulier*, which some etymologists argue contains the root of the word *soul*) and her slipper; or to feel her toes tugging at the underside of his testicles gently, forcefully, painfully, violently kicking him in the genitals; all or some of the above.

The adored, sucked, or fucked foot can be clean or dirty, shod or unshod, encased in silk, nylon, fishnet, or cotton stockings, adorned with orchid-red or mother-of-pearl or turquoise nail polish, toe rings, ankle bracelets, leather thongs, or, as the nursery rhyme would have it, bells.

Alas, the modern foot fetishist is assailed as never before in a paradox that Tantalus would understand.

On the subway, at the supermarket, in the streets of our nation's greatest cities, the modern foot lover is like a breast man at a nudist colony.

Never before has the female foot been so available for adoring observation; the world's leading structural physicists and cutting-edge engineers have brought their science to bear, using the most sophisticated technology available to man, to create pyramids of pedestals that expose, elevate, and twist the female foot to greatest effect; those striding women, their hair flouncing from side to side as they sashay on city sidewalks, high-step as if through tall-grassed savannas, their toenails glistening with sexually charged colors, their ankles delicately traced by narrow leather straps, thin tribal tattoos, golden chains, their bare toes twinkling with rings.

Their toe cleavage draws the eye, and when they cross their

legs on the bus and flex their aching feet against the straps cross-ing over their arches, the moon-sliver crack that appears between their insteps and the insole of their shoes is vaginal. Their painted, bejeweled toes wink like a slattern against a lamp pole, whistling *Hey, sailor!* and their pink heels and the smooth soles of their feet beckon the tongues of casual observers.

There is no way they can't know this, no possible way on earth they don't know the erections and longing they are creating.

But, oh, the denial! Industry figures show that American women spend an aggregate $83 kajillion on shoes each year, all be-cause those Manolo Blahniks are sooo cute!

Why the unspoken taboo? After all, feet have raised the flag-pole of sexual desire from the first time that Aphrodite played footsie with Mars on the foothills of Mount Olympus, from when Abigail toed David (2 Samuel 25:41).

This is due to manifold misunderstandings about feet: They're dirty and smelly. They're ugly (especially if the nails are allowed to grow long and filthy, or if bunions, hammertoes, and corns are allowed to accumulate, usually due to hard labor or un-comfortable shoes). They're a symbol of subjugation.

Foot fetishists are themselves riven by factionalism. Shod feet versus unshod. Painted versus "raw" toenails. Cleansers (lick-ing dirt or particles from between the toes), fooders (licking chocolate syrup or eating berries from between toes), shrimpers (toe suckers), and cum lickers (who enjoy licking their own ejacu-late from the object of their requited desire) regard each other with undisguised revulsion.

When, one might ask, will foot fetishism attain the social ac-ceptance of, say, mammarian fascination or vaginal obsession? Perhaps the answer lies in linguistics. The same alliterative quality reinforces the false idea that he who loves feet is per force a fetishist—i.e., someone with an unusual predilection. It stands to reason that foot lovers must resolve to no longer use the demeaning term *fetish* when describing their libidinal cravings and thus escape the ghettoization of their sexual preference.

Then let the word go out in every corner of every dungeon, in every office where a man dare not stare at the red-painted toes of his bodacious colleague, everywhere that a man's mouth runs dry and his penis expands at the sight of a woman flexing her foot in her high-heeled, open-toed sandal, that there is a new word in the world, and that word is *Retifist*.

Let any man who has ever been stirred by the sight of a woman extending her foot, her instep arched and her toes pointed, say to his neighbor, "Man, I could really go for some of that. I'm a foot Retifist."

FOREPLAY

MARCELLE CLEMENTS

DEFINITION: stimulation or love play
preceding sexual intercourse.

Why do so many women fake orgasm?
Because so many men fake foreplay.

Why don't women blink during foreplay?
They don't have time.

What is a man's idea of foreplay?
A half hour of begging.

—WWW.JOKES4ALL.NET

In theory, the purpose of foreplay is to generate a level of desire sufficient to produce vaginal lubrication facilitating intercourse. But even if it is assumed to precede intercourse, many would agree that foreplay is the dessert of sex—the sweetest part, and often the most nuanced exploration of sexuality. Requiring copious measures of both restraint and sensuality, it may be the most entertaining segment of a sexual encounter, with the possible exception of the orgasm. However, an orgasm lasts a few seconds, whereas foreplay can extend over hours, days, and years.

The notoriously ritualized conjugal choreography that leads inevitably (or so it is hoped) to classical intercourse is only one type of foreplay. Many variations do not necessarily end with penetration: for example, the sensual exchange of same-sex partners; the tenderness of elderly lovers; the early, hot and steamy, and occasionally all-elbows petting practiced by pubescent boys and girls; the six-year-olds playing doctor.

Foreplay can include, but is not limited to, kissing of every sort, holding, licking, necking, making out—sitting down, lying, or standing—and also teasing, showing, smelling, touching, caressing, stroking, fondling, fingering, masturbation and mutual masturbation, donning lingerie or removing it, the use of fur, vibrators, and vibrating rings, dildos, porn films, dirty books, dirty dancing, dirty talk, passionate or concupiscent or innocent murmuring, moaning, breathing together, chest-to-chest or pelvis-to-pelvis contact. One of the mainstays of foreplay is frottage (from the French word for rubbing)—the pressing or rubbing of the groin against the lover's pelvis, leg, flank, arm, hand, chest, or heaven knows what else. It may or may not include oral sex.

Foreplay is a kinetic improvisation that relies on combining sensation with intelligence, delicacy, and empathy, a jointly created narrative in which the partners are exquisitely attuned to one another. Everything is noticed—every sigh, the slight opening of the lips, a movement of the leg, a shift in weight. Because it is akin to a work of art, its form, content, and style vary according to intention—whether one of the parties is more willing than the other; whether one or both is willing to be naked, or partially naked; whether neither, one, or both want it to lead to intercourse . . . (It should be said, however, that ambivalence does not decrease pleasure. Quite the contrary.)

In human beings, for whom so much of sex happens in the brain, foreplay begins long before bodily contact, with teasing, wooing, flirting, the excitement of looking and being seen, and the vast, nuanced array of messages conveyed by the eyes—but also, on the contrary, with hiding (behind sunglasses, a veil, a fluttering fan, a mask of indifference, or in a cyberchat room).

Love is foreplay, and occasionally, hate is foreplay. Emotion is foreplay, and so is thinking. In the West, with its tradition of courtly, idealized love, delaying climax is an erotic stimulant that can take many forms. Poetry, dance, music, and any display of intelligence, strength, and accomplishment can be seen as foreplay (or as sublimation, if no consummation ensues). Frustration is an essential aspect of foreplay.

The British, according to recent surveys, claim to have more foreplay than anyone else—an average of 22.5 minutes per sex session in the United Kingdom—closely followed by Germany, Ireland, Spain, Netherlands, and Switzerland. (Really? Switzerland?!) The United States lags in nineteenth place with an average of 19.7 minutes. But, then, it was only at the beginning of the twentieth century that marital counselors began to urge the practice of foreplay upon American males—to little avail, until the 1960s and '70s. Around that time, sex researchers and therapists Masters and Johnson began requiring the couples they worked with to agree not to have intercourse during treatment. The idea was to restore "sensate focus," a by-product of foreplay, which they helped popularize with their book *Human Sexual Response*, in 1966.

In the *Three Contributions to the Sexual Theory*, which Freud wrote in 1910, when both psychoanalysis and sex were goal-oriented endeavors, he spoke only of *vorlust* or "forepleasure," by which he means any pleasure experienced prior to orgasm "the same as that furnished by the infantile sexual impulse, though on a reduced scale." Therein may lie the greatest power of foreplay, which can transport us to states of blissful regression—and yet somehow retains an aura of innocence.

But then foreplay can always be disclaimed—even while it's happening! It is not burdened with the irrevocability of penetration. Penetration is a point of no return in which lust and longing are, at least in theory, meant to be obliterated by climax and dissipate. Whereas foreplay is all about not quenching lust but heightening it, playing with boundaries, going further than you meant to, or not, creating increasingly irresistible intimacy, complicity, desire, and moistness.

FUCK

RAND RICHARDS COOPER

DEFINITION: usually obscene : copulate.

After Norman Mailer's publishers convinced him to bowdlerize fuck *as* fug *in his work* The Naked and the Dead *(1948), Tallulah Bankhead supposedly greeted him with the quip "So you're the young man who can't spell* fuck.*" The rock group the Fugs named themselves after the Mailer euphemism.*
—J. MICHAEL LENNON (ED.) "CONVERSATIONS WITH NORMAN MAILER," 1988

ON *FUCK*: *À LA RECHERCHE DU FOUTRE PERDU*
How can any essay convey the force, the ubiquity, the flexibility, the sheer exalted status, of the mother of all dirty words.

Fuck—the great in-your-face fighting word, and a superb show-off word as well, the one-syllable way to establish your disestablishmentarian bona fides. Why does my father-in-law, Princeton of the umpteenth generation, insist on using it, except to show he is an iconoclast, unconstrained by hidebound proprieties?

Why did every *New Yorker* writer feel obliged to slip it into his or her book review, profile, or *Talk of the Town* gossip piece, as soon as Tina Brown took the chains off the word? For a writer, there's nothing like tossing a few casual *fuck*s into your prose to demonstrate that you're not some library gnome, but a worldly son of a bitch, genus E. Hemingway, who, if he weren't writing, would be out there carousing and profaning and smacking poets upside the head on a street in Key West. *Fuck* expunges the last bit of writing-as-manners from your rough-and-ready street thing and reassures your reader that above all, nothing, nothing can shock you—since the refusal to be shocked is the sine qua non of our been-there-done-that era.

Like many powerful words, *fuck* commands multiple parts of speech, a shape-shifting creature that surfaces as verb, noun, interjection, adjective, or adverb, creating such syntactically overdetermined but richly satisfying sentences as "Don't fuck with me, you fucking fuck!" The original verboten word, it is now so prevalent in everyday usage that it has lost much of its subversive charge and become, well, pretty fucking normal. Even the federal government agrees. When Bono, receiving a Golden Globe Award in 2002, exclaimed in a live NBC broadcast that "This is really, really fucking brilliant!" the FCC ruled it a violation of obscenity laws, arguing that the word "invariably invokes a coarse sexual image"—but a federal appeals court disagreed, calling Bono's utterance "a prime example of a nonliteral use of the 'F-word' with no sexual connotation." In other words, Bono wasn't really talking about copulation. He was just being happy.

But I wonder, how happy do we really want to get in America? Do we want a society in which *fuck* becomes a routine utterance— popping up in supermarkets and doctor's offices, rolling lustily off your grandfather's tongue at the Easter dinner table? "Bless us, O Lord, and for these Thy gifts which we are about to receive, may the Lord make us truly fucking thankful. Amen."

Of course, the truth is that *fuck* has always been a routine utterance—in private. *Fuck* signals the language of intimacy, anger, sex; it is a word we use to strip off layers of rhetoric and get down to Things as They Really Are. Do we want public and official speech to merge with the demotic and the private? Would it be better if our politicians abjured formal language and spoke, as it were, from the gut? In fact, last year Dick Cheney F-bombed Vermont senator Patrick Leahy on the floor of the Senate, urging him to "go fuck yourself"—but that was presumably a private endearment, not meant for public ears. Imagine a State of the Union address in which the president said, "My fellow Americans, the war in Iraq is fucked, and I don't have a fucking clue what to do about it."

A great leap forward for presidential candor, anyway.

For me, the real question is this: what happens when you defuse a dirty word, unhooking it from taboo and turning it into just so many inert and harmless vocables? Any college freshman who has read Sartre understands that all language is finally just sound, and sheer repetition eventually detaches a word from its referent. If we all say *fuck* in public often enough, in the end it will be about as dangerous as saying *wallaby*.

And what will we do for our thrills then?

I doubt any society can ever squeeze all the illicitness out of language. But in the United States we may be getting close. Consider the very book you hold in your hands, a collection of essays about dirty words. Ostensibly intended to shock, what it really conveys is nostalgia for the forbidden. Behind such a book lies the paradoxical wish that the book itself would be banned. Because—let's face it—dirty words stop being really dirty once you can publish them without getting in trouble.

Fuck is not the dirtiest word, but for generations of schoolchildren it has been the ur-swear, the dirty word that made all other dirty words possible. In the schoolyard you spoke it with a whisper and a pleasing shiver of transgression. Significantly, it was a word you almost never saw in print—literature, in those pre-Internet days, was a *fuck*-free zone. D. H. Lawrence notoriously used the word in *Lady Chatterley's Lover*, causing himself no end of trouble with censors. In *Ulysses*, Joyce sidestepped it with some winking wordplay, doggerel verse that slyly spelled it out (along with another, even dirtier word):

> If you see Kay,
> Tell him he may.
> See you in tea,
> Tell him from me.

Here in America, it took the moral cataclysm of World War II to push *fuck* into the light of print—and even then, Norman Mailer agreed to bowdlerize it into *fug* in *The Naked and the Dead.* Just a few years later, Salinger got away with dropping a *fuck you* into *Catcher in the Rye* (Holden sees it scrawled on a wall at his sister Phoebe's school). The dam had burst; and soon we were off, floating down the river that has taken us to Bono's happy and unpunished exclamation.

And now today, *fuck*—as a dirty word—is basically fucked. But dig down through the layers of its overuse, and you may still recover your own childhood impression of the word and its power, the way *fuck* provoked the erotic imagination. If you asked me, what is the *fuck* I can never forget, I might answer, the one on the page, seeing the word there for the first time: the *f*, peering like a Peeping Tom over the inert *u* to where the action was, in the *c* and *k*. At age ten I could scan a page and know instantly whether those two letters were engaged in steamy congress anywhere on it. Their appearance stopped your eye for a breathless moment and lent even innocent words, such as *truck* or *duck*, a strange jolt of raciness. Amazing, how the orthographic became pornographic—those four simple letters, unlocking the realm of sex and the forbidden.

À la recherche du foutre perdu . . . Like Proust's famous madeleine, the recollection sparks a frisson of memory, taking me back in search of the lost *fuck*—back to a time when *fuck* was truly, breathtakingly obscene, provoking agonies of pure desire for something you hardly understood, except that it was contained in this secret, thrilling, nasty, unspeakable word.

Life hasn't been that innocent in a long, long time.

FUCK BUDDY

JONATHAN STRONG

DEFINITION: a casual relationship based on
sex with no strings attached.
AKA: FWB (friends with benefits), NSA (no strings attached).

Fuck-Buddy Becomes Fuck-Fiancé

MIAMI, FL—In spite of the explicitly casual nature of their relationship, fuck-buddies Nora Ingersoll and Keith Hetzel are engaged, friend Tom Stipps reported Tuesday. "Keith and Nora have been fooling around for years, but Keith said they were just friends," Stipps said. "I was shocked when Nora showed up wearing a ring." Later that day, the couple reportedly opened a fuck-joint-checking account.

—ONION, MARCH 31, 2004

Q: Maybe I'm naive, but how do you even start?
A: You have a time and a place. Spur of the moment or on a
   regular basis.

Q: Is it purely physical?

A: Depends. Straights like to call it "a friend with benefits," but given men and women, that's got to be different. *Friend* implies you know each other better than, say, you and I do.

Q: So gays generally get right down to business?

A: You work it out beforehand. You know what you're getting into. You don't have to think about it.

Q: Sort of like doing it solo?

A: Nothing like doing it solo.

Q: I'm just asking. Don't get defensive. But you're saying it's predictable?

A: Whatever you're both into. You negotiate.

Q: And two men handle it better than a man and a woman?

A: I can't speak for a man and a woman, or a woman and a woman. Sometimes a man and a man can't even handle it.

Q: But *you* can?

A: I've had some pretty satisfactory arrangements.

Q: Then it does have a natural life span?

A: Could last for years. You might take a break and get back into it later. At some point, it usually peaks.

Q: What if only one wants to quit?

A: The other bows out gracefully.

Q: No heavy processing?

A: That's the beauty of it.

Q: How often do you have to do it to qualify?

A: Once a week, once a month, could be once a year. It's got to be mutual.

Q: I'm not saying I'm opposed to the concept. Now, what if one starts seeing someone else seriously?

A: Depends if he gets exclusive. There's still ways of having it on the side if you both abide by the rules.

Q: There's rules?

A: Be discreet. Be honest. Don't hassle.

Q: Isn't that a little disingenuous?

A: It's totally straightforward.

Q: But how does it even get started? You discuss it, like this, in the abstract?

A: Look, I'm not trying to get you to . . .

Q: No, I realize that, but I'm still finding the concept vague. What if one of you wants something the other isn't into?

A: Don't be such a perfectionist. I told you, it doesn't always work out.

Q: Sorry. I think I understand. And I admit I could see getting it on a semiregular basis with someone I barely know. Oh, but what if one of you falls in love?

A: The whole point is you don't!

Q: Yet isn't it a kind of love, giving the other what he wants?

A: Within clear limits.

Q: Still, I'm wondering how good you really are at it. I don't mean in bed. I'm sure you're terrific. I mean with those rules of yours. Are you as coolheaded as all that?

A: When it comes to getting hassle-free sex I am.

Q: Because I'm definitely not into complications. And I like to call the shots. Would that work for you?

A: Wait a minute here!

Q: Because I can actually see us setting something up. That's where this is heading, isn't it?

A: I've only been answering your questions. You seem so—I don't know—innocent.

Q: Innocence can be an effective negotiating position. Do you think you can give me what I'm looking for?

A: I'm not sure what that is yet. We'd have to work it out beforehand.

Q: Can't I wait till I get inside your pants?

A: But we should talk about it some more first.

Q: I prefer the nonverbal method. My boyfriend's given me permission to let off some extra steam. Come on, won't you help me out?

A: I didn't know you had a boyfriend.

Q: There's plenty you don't know. And what do I know about you? We'll keep it that way. I get off work at five. Do you have a place?

GAYDAR

KATHARINE WEBER

DEFINITION: slang: the ability to recognize homosexuals through observation or intuition.

AKA: queen meter.

A study by Philadelphia's Monell Chemical Senses Center, published in the Journal of Psychological Science, *found that "gay men were found to be particularly good at detecting the scent of other gay men."*

—YOLANDA MARTINS, GEORGE PRETI, CHRISTINA R. CRABTREE, TAMAR RUNYAN, ALDONA A. VAINIUS, AND CHARLES J. WYSOCKI, "PREFERENCE FOR HUMAN BODY ODORS IS INFLUENCED BY GENDER AND SEXUAL ORIENTATION," *PSYCHOLOGICAL SCIENCE* 16 (2005): 694-701

Gaydar—noun, portmanteau formation: from *gay* + *radar*. The ability to perceive homosexuality in others. Commonly, expressing faith in gaydar is to have an implicit belief that one's gaydar is a powerful and unerring detector of the homosexual inclinations of others. Some people believe they can spot the gayness at a glance, even from a photograph, while others depend on personal interaction to activate their gaydar. Speculating about the homosexuality of celebrities is a popular pastime that depends on the pooled resources of group gaydar. Most people have some level of gaydar, but in certain individuals it is highly developed through practice, while in others the gaydar sensibility has atrophied through disuse.

Does effective gaydar depend on response to body language, perceptive observation of style of movement and gesture, scrutiny of physical othernesses manifest in behavior and clothing choices? Or, as some believe, can it all be determined by perceiving giveaway elements in the tone of voice? Or are there true biological differences that gaydar detects, even if we don't consciously recognize these signals? Recent studies show that hair-whorl patterns on the top of the back of the head tend to be clockwise for heterosexuals and counterclockwise for homosexuals, men and women alike. Finger proportion distinctions are also both gender- and sexual-orientation-associated: for straight men, the index finger is usually shorter than the ring finger, while for most straight women the index finger is the same length or longer than the ring finger. Gay men and women tend to have exactly reversed ratios. Does well-developed gaydar detect these subtle physical manifestations along with all the other signals?

See also *hyper-gaydar*—an exaggerated estimation of one's infallible gaydar abilities that can lead to the conclusion that if one's gaydar has signaled homosexuality in an individual, then that person must absolutely be either gay or closeted, perhaps even to himself. See also *hypo-gaydar*—a form of gaydar suppression common to the sanctimonious and politically correct. These individuals deny that anyone can ever perceive anything about other people. The chief symptom is a tendency when questioned about the possible homosexual inclinations of another person to respond by saying, "I have no idea, and it doesn't interest me. You never really know about other people's private lives, and anyway, it's none of our business to wonder about anyone's sexual orientation."

GIGOLO

JERRY STAHL

DEFINITION: a man living off the earnings or gifts of a woman, especially a younger man supported by an older woman in return for his sexual attentions and companionship.
AKA: boy toy, poodle-faker, escort, companion, dance partner, playboy, lady-killer.

Police in Juneau, Alaska, acting on a tip, searched a hotel room and found the occupant had $10,000 in cash. Police suspected the money was from the sale of drugs, but the man said no, he was given the money by a Juneau woman because he was such a good lover. When asked, he told officers he could not remember her name. With no direct evidence of a crime, they let him go. "He left in a real hurry, but didn't say why," a police spokesman said. "Maybe he's afraid once the word gets out about him, all the women will be chasing him."

—ASSOCIATED PRESS

The notion of gigolo—as in the guy who supplies women of a certain age with thrills for bills—has a bit of a schizo image. Drop the word into conversation and people tend to march out Richard Gere—impossibly suave in *American Gigolo*; Rob Schneider—lovably lame-ass in *Deuce Bigelow*; or some third, more Rasta-adjacent cliché—the studly Island Man whispering "Got the good wood" to White Ladies of a certain age down for erotic fun far from whatever button-down world they'll be returning to, relaxed

123

and possessed of enough ganja-breathed masturbatory fodder to hold them until their next vacation.

My own experience falls somewhere in between—or possibly a few flights down from the above scenarios. Strapped for cash, in the late seventies, I would occasionally loiter with a gaggle of other lads in the lobby of the erstwhile gigolicious haunt the St. Regis Hotel, in New York City. It would be tempting to assert that I serviced the blue-haired spouses of CEOs and Titans of Industry with such dreamboat-studly expertise that they screamed "Enough!" and yanked out their checkbooks with arthritic fingers still aquiver in orgasmic aftershock. In truth, I did perform yeomanlike service between the parchmentlike thighs of a dozen or so well-heeled senior-itas. (And this was pre-Viagra, ladies and gentlemen, thanks for asking.)

Just as often, however, my gigolo duties involved either listening to the lady's assorted familial frustrations—something, sadly, no one in her actual family would do—or accompanying her, fresh-faced and cruising on the all-purpose social lubricant of heroin (as opposed to the lube the physical deed required), to high-dollar charity functions.

As jobs go, I've done worse for less. I would like to say that my stint as gigolo taught me, in a bottom-feeding, postadolescent, Grade Z "John Cheever on china white" kind of way, that everyone—including ultraprivileged, postmenopausal wives and widows—deserves compassion. (Among other things.) But in the end, I believe, this ex–love boy learned a more valuable life lesson: even if you catch the clap from a seventy-three-year-old grandmother of nine with Parkinson's and gray pubic hair over a vagina she wants you to call Lollipop, it's still the clap. And that, my friends, they don't teach you in Bible college.

GOLDEN SHOWERS

ADAM WILSON

DEFINITION: a slang expression for urolagnia: sexual
excitement associated with urine or with urination.
AKA: water sports.

How to enjoy Golden Showers:
Experts recommend drinking plenty of fruit juice 45 minutes before
engaging in sex play. The juice will not only dilute your urine, but can even
give it a more pleasant odor.

–WWW.ROTTEN.COM/LIBRARY/SEX/WATERSPORTS/

By the dawn of the millennium, one could type *golden + shower*
into a search engine and be bombarded by Web sites featuring cas-
cades of urine—male, female, hermaphrodite, horse—splashing
across foreheads, splattering against horn-rimmed glasses, and
falling gracefully into waiting mouths. In June of 2000, HBO's
Sex and the City ran an episode in which sex columnist Carrie
Bradshaw ends her short-lived relationship with a local politician
because he requests that she urinate on him. Carrie titles her sub-
sequent column "To Pee or Not to Pee?" and millions of American
women stood by watercoolers debating that very question. But not
until 2002, when pop singer R. Kelly (allegedly) videotaped his
own glorious arc as it collided with a fourteen-year-old girl's face,
then trickled down her cheek like salty, glowing tears, did the term
golden shower infiltrate the lexicon of mainstream America.

By 2003, my junior year of college, we all knew about golden
showers. And though we did not anxiously await their occurrence in
our lives as we awaited, say, a new season of *The Sopranos*, we were
curious about this phenomenon and sometimes wondered if the
stale smell that wafted through the hallway was not coming from
the rarely cleaned bathroom, but through the crack in a mysterious

125

dormmate's door, where, inside, he lay beneath a leather-clad soph-
omore and bathed in the waterfall of her stream. The scenario was
unlikely—I went to a sexually repressed liberal arts school where
coeds wore chastity belts and took castration classes at the local Y—
but I held secret hope that, behind locked doors, our campus was
sexually liberated and erotically eccentric.

I rarely considered the possibility that I myself would be
involved in a golden shower—it was hard enough to find girls
willing to have normal sex—and was quite surprised when, one
windy winter night, with snowflakes swirling across campus like
stray arrows from Cupid's army, I was initiated into the world of
water sports. Though, as is often my fate, I was a spectator, not a
performer.

We were in my friend's room playing beirut and drinking
cheap beer from red plastic cups. It was late, and all the parties had
been broken up by cops. There might have been cocaine, certainly
marijuana, and maybe some Percocets. The male/female ratio was
7:2. We videotaped each other being electrocuted by a police Taser
someone had bought on eBay. It was a fairly typical night. The two
girls were freshmen and didn't seem to be putting out.

At some point, those who had beds passed out in them. The
rest of us half-slept on the floor or the futon. The snow had been
falling for hours, and no one wanted to trudge back to his own
dorm or apartment.

We were woken, in the soft purple predawn, by a sharp cry,
like a stepped-on kitten. Someone flipped a light switch. The ceiling halogen flickered, paused, then poured white light onto a
beautiful spectacle: there, in the center of the room, a friend (who
will go unnamed) released his perfect parabola of clear current
onto the barely awake chaste face of one of the freshman girls.
The girl did not move. She was paralyzed, as if the beam of urine
held her in its grip and caressed her tired body.

"He's peeing on me," she said flatly.

The rest of us were awed. Someone said, "Holy shit," Others laughed. None of this distracted the pee-er, who was in dreamland, perhaps standing above a giant, diamond-studded urinal. His expression was Buddha-like: peaceful, enlightened. When he finished, he pulled up his pants (with some difficulty) and went back to sleep. The girl took it like a champ; she laughed with the rest of us and spent forty-five minutes in the shower.

Our friend spent the rest of college in shame, as the target of jokes, but eventually he graduated and met girls who didn't know he'd once peed on a freshman. Maybe, these days, he tells the story at parties, amused and invigorated by the memory of his (unconsciously) reckless youth. Or maybe he's in therapy. Either way, he fared better than R. Kelly, who, after five years, will finally be tried in a court of law on fourteen child pornography charges.

HAND JOB

MICHAEL KIMBALL

DEFINITION: a slang term referring to the sexual stimulation of a penis using the hands and fingers.

A guy walks into a pub and sees a sign hanging over the bar that reads:

Cheese Sandwich: $3.50
Chicken Sandwich: $4.50
Hand Job: $10.00

After checking his wallet, he walks up to the bar and beckons to one of the three beautiful blondes serving drinks to a group of wide-eyed men.

"Yes?" she inquires with a knowing smile. "Can I help you?"

"I was wondering," whispers the man, "are you the one who gives the hand jobs?"

"Yes," she purrs, "I am."

The man replies, "Well, wash your fucking hands, I want a cheese sandwich."

Hand job (or *handjob*) is slang for the manual stimulation of a sexual partner's genitals. There does not seem to be a more technical term for the act, though it does go by many other names. *Handy, hj, hojo, Hank Jones, hand fuck,* and *tug job* are among the more common usages. You might remember hand jobs from your adolescence, when you may have given one or received one. Maybe, for instance, you have given or received a hojo in a HoJo (a Howard Johnson). It may have been thrilling or you may have felt ashamed (or both). You may have enjoyed it so much that you wanted to do it again right then and were disappointed to realize that you had to wait awhile before you could. It may have been the upper limit of your sexuality at that point in your life, which is why some consider it a gateway act. Sadly, the hand job is too often abandoned after adolescence.

There are many ways to give a hand job, but before we get into that, a clarification needs to be made. You cannot give yourself a hand job. Technically, that is masturbation. A hand job involves two people. That is, the sexual act can only be considered a hand job if you are doing it to somebody else or somebody else is doing it to you. This is an important distinction.

A hand job can just be foreplay or it can provide its own sexual ending. A *soft job* is when a hand job is used to create an erection. A hand job that takes place after a full-body massage is a *happy ending*, which is also known as *hand release*. A hand job that occurs during anal sex is a *reach around*, though my gay brother-in-law tells me that this is a rare and awkward sexual act. He believes that the phrase is mostly used during bantering between heterosexual males, a way to verbally act out their homosexual yearnings. The hand job enjoyed a renaissance during the mideighties as a form of outercourse (no penetration) in which there is no exchange of bodily fluids. The hand job embodied safe sex.

The more preferred hand job techniques are meant to simulate penetration. The basic form and action of a hand job usually involves gripping the shaft, and, depending on the size of the penis, moving the fingers, the hand, or both hands up and down. Most hand job aficionados insist on lots of lubrication (though a small minority prefer a *sandy handy*, i.e., with no lubrication; the same phrase is used to describe a hand job at the beach). The preferences run from baby oil to the K-Y variants to different types of lotion to spit (for its general availability).

Some hand job technicians recommend that the giver use two hands, which usually makes the receiver feel as if his cock is quite large, regardless of its actual size. If you use two hands and a basic technique, the hand job is a known as a *two-handed slammer*. But the hand job can involve a variety of techniques: the *slippy grippy* (extra lubrication), the *wild butterfly* (fast fingers), the *washing machine* (two hands twisting in opposite directions; also known as the *twist and shout*), *starting a fire* (self-explanatory), the *switch-hitter* (alternating grips between thumb up and thumb down), the *doorknob* (involving only the slippery head of the penis), and the *headless hand job* (the inverse of the doorknob).

Two of the most popular hand job techniques are the *endless tunnel* (also known as *perpetual penetration*) and *milking the bull* (also known as *squeezing the juice*). In the endless tunnel, one of the giver's hands continually starts at the head of the penis as the other hand reaches the base. In milking the bull, it is a similar continual hand action, but in the opposite direction. Many practitioners consider it to be a hand job of the highest order when these two popular techniques are alternated with increasing speed until the result is ejaculation.

Ejaculation—at some point during the hand job that is going to completion (i.e., not part of foreplay), there is usually a noticeable tightening of the testicles and the scrotum, which indicates the hand job recipient's approach to orgasm. When this occurs, the giver should increase his or her grip on the recipient, thereby increasing friction, and speed up their motion, indeterminate of what hand job technique is being used. This is a momentous threshold and the sensation should be propelled to its fullest extreme—as it is determined where the ejaculate should be directed. Some practitioners prefer simply to finish in and on the hand itself, while others feel that the hand job reaches its greatest heights only if it ends with ejaculate covering the face of the giver (the aptly named *facial*) or being sprayed around the base of the neck (the infamous *pearl necklace*).

The end of the hand job, like many endings, can be awkward. There may be sticky hands, for instance, as well as other messy body parts. Further, the two people who were just involved in the hand job may not want to touch each other anymore even though that is all that they had wanted to do for the time that led up to the ejaculation. Many hand job experts suggest that it is this awkwardness, and the rare pleasure that accompanies it, that makes the hand job a fascinating sexual act for those who engage in it.

HAPPY ENDING

ELLEN SUSSMAN

DEFINITION: when a masseuse feels inclined to finish
your session with oral sex or manual release.

*Q: My boyfriend goes for massages about once a month. Recently, he con-
fessed that sometimes he lets the masseuse "finish him off." I was mortified! To
me, that's almost like he's paying for sex and cheating, but he insists that it's
just an intensified massage. He told me that a lot of guys do this. Is that true?*
—WWW.COSMOPOLITAN.COM

I was living in Paris, happily married (or close enough, which I
was willing to settle for, Paris being Paris), with two young children, a job teaching writing, and a great community of international friends. So why did I feel an inexplicable yearning? I joined
a gym. Foolishly I thought my itch might get scratched on the
StairMaster. Wrong. Months later, my muscles were toned, but
my brain was still scrambled.

Maybe I needed to relax, I reasoned, and so I made an ap-
pointment for a massage. The fancy gym I had joined prided itself
on American standards of fitness expertise and offered a range of
treatments in pristine rooms with New Age music. I chose a sports
massage, met Pierre, who looked as if he had just stepped off the
Chippendales stage, and followed him into the room, mumbling
something in mangled French about my poor tired body. He
didn't say a word. I stripped down and let his hands soothe my
body. He kneaded the muscles in my back, my legs, my arms,
told me to turn over, oiled me anew. His hands were strong, my
muscles melted, my mind drifted.

And so I thought I was dreaming when his hands moved farther and farther up my thigh, and because I didn't want to interrupt the dream, I let him open my legs a bit wider. And when I felt

warm oil dripping between my legs and his fingers seemed to appear, disappear, coax, tease, I kept my eyes closed, my mind quiet, my breath slow. I was so transported in that private room that the rules of the world didn't apply. Besides, I was innocent. I didn't ask for it—and I wouldn't ask for it to stop. I gave myself up to his wondrous touch and had a remarkable orgasm. I never opened my eyes. He slipped out of the room, I got dressed and left.

I remember my walk home from the gym. I wanted to tell everyone; I wanted to tell no one. I felt powerful, sexy, and wildly free. I could do anything I wanted. Here's the rub (so to speak): I didn't change my life. At least not then. Five years later my marriage would fade like my old photos of the Eiffel Tower. Soon after, I would fall in love with another man and come to know a much deeper passion. But right then, I walked along the glorious streets of Paris, climbed the three floors to my apartment, roasted salmon, and sat with my family at the dinner table. While my kids talked about their day at school and my husband told a long story about his business trip to London, I sat there, a smile on my face, and listened to the sweet song whispering inside me.

HARD-ON

CORNELIA READ

DEFINITION: the state marked by firm turgid form and erect position of a previously flaccid bodily part containing cavernous tissue when that tissue becomes dilated with blood.
AKA: boner, erection, stiffy, tumescence, woody

A man went into a pharmacy and asked to talk to a male pharmacist. The woman he was talking to said that she was the pharmacist and that she and her sister owned the store, so no males were employed there. She then asked if she could help the gentleman. The man said, "This is embarrassing for me, but I have a permanent erection, which causes me a lot of problems and severe embarrassment. I was wondering what you could give me for it?" The pharmacist said, "Just a minute, I'll go talk to my sister." When she returned, she said, "The best we can do is one-third ownership in the store and three thousand dollars a month in living expenses."

To truncate the words of Flannery O'Connor, "A good man is hard."

If you want to get all clinical about it, Bartleby.com will give you the *American Heritage Dictionary* definition of *erection*: *the firm and enlarged condition of a body organ or part when the erectile tissue surrounding it becomes filled with blood, especially such a condition of the penis or clitoris.*

But that doesn't capture the blistering splendor of thing itself: thin skin slipping along engorged shaft, flared peach-cap of glans, long, delicious ridge of corpus spongiosum running from pelvis to frenulum like a happy flagpole's halyard . . .

Damn. It's all good.

Little wonder, then, that hard-on homage is a major part of spiritual traditions around the world. Statues of Priapus—the Greco-Roman deity famed for his permanently engorged jeroboam of a member—were placed in ancient gardens to enhance the fecundity of all nearby flora and fauna.

These figures were also considered an effective deterrent to would-be thieves, such that they were inscribed with a variety of cautionary slogans, to wit: *If a woman, man, or boy thieve from me, she shall pay me with coynte, that with his mouth, this with arse.* And: *If I do seize you, you shall be so stretched that you will think your anus never had any wrinkles.*

Hindu worship of the lingam—the stylized phallus representing Lord Shiva—also gives the woody tremendous cosmological due. Devotees chant *Om namah shivaya* (roughly: "I bow down to the holiest of holy being Shiva—who is the God") daily in temples around the world, but the mantra is considered most powerful when uttered during the winter festival of Maha Shivratri.

The main form of worship is a puja during which milk, yogurt, honey, ghee, sugar, and water are poured over the lingam in succession, followed by an application of sandalwood paste—this final step held to be a necessary "cooling down" of the deity's hot-blooded nature.

The hard-on has equal pride of place in literary tradition, its exquisite qualities having been extolled in every language and alphabet—proportions limned in the poetry of Catullus and the chapters of the *Kama Sutra*, exploits chronicled by the likes of Rabelais and Anaïs Nin, Erica Jong and Harold Robbins (though one must admit that its greatest laureate has long been "Anonymous").

The best-known cinematic reference to the male state of erection has to be Mae West's quip "Is that a gun in your pocket or are you just glad to see me?" though Madeline Kahn's enraptured cry of "It's twoo! It's twoo!" while the screen goes dark in *Blazing Saddles* certainly deserves an honorable mention.

As to the musical hard-on, forget *Bolero*. At the very least, Bessie Smith outdid Ravel with both hands tied behind her back with her 1927 recording of J. C. Johnson's "Empty Bed Blues," that low moan in memory of the man who "When he put in the bacon, it overflowed the pot."

But it was the late, great Lucille Bogan who, in 1935, penned and recorded the wickedest "Ode on a Stiff Dick" ever to singe vinyl with a little ditty called "Shave 'Em Dry." Bogan's most scandalous verse therein describes a lover's genitalia in terms of religious architecture: his scrotum a bell "sapper," anus a church's door open to welcome a congregation of crabs, while his "dick stands up like a steeple."

Let's face it: the hard-on is nature's applause meter. I don't mean those random math-class stiffies that a middle schooler's flesh is heir to. I'm talking about the heady stuff of the true Dick

Rampant—hot sugarplum visions of which you *know* were dancing through Mae West's head when Cary Grant asked, "Haven't you ever met a man who could make you happy?" and she replied, "Sure. *Lots* of times."

Amen to that.

HERMAPHRODITE

MARTHA MCPHEE

DEFINITION: an individual in which reproductive
organs of both sexes are present.

THE HERMAPHRODITE
BY STEPHEN DUNN

I showed him mine.
Then I showed him his.

THE SEXUALITY LIBRARY

Eight years old, my stepbrother seven, we snuck into his father's library, the place where he saw his patients, lined with books, a red velvet chaise on which his patients lay while he examined their heads. We understood the concept literally, that he sat behind them and with his fingers he probed their heads. One was fat and short and ugly and she smelled like pee, another was a pair of Parsi twins, identical. There was a nun and a priest. Later they would marry on our vast front lawn. In the beginning, my mother was his patient. We snuck into the library because it seemed a lot was going on there about the mysteries of the adult world, and we wanted to get to the bottom of it. We were scared and thrilled and eager and reticent all at the same time. The library was off-limits, forbidden entrance there. The bookcases were tall and filled from floor to ceiling with books; the spines named titles that included words like *love* and *sex* and *desire* and *lust* and *agape* and *eros* and *philia*. *Sex*, the word echoed through the room. My stepfather had been a Jesuit priest, had left the order after having an affair with a fellow novitiate. He pursued Gestalt psychology and philosophy instead, earned his degree from the Sorbonne, devoted his life to the writing of a philosophical treatise on the psychology of love—a book that was to answer once and for always the nature of romantic love, what it means to be the lover and the beloved. Like Casaubon's *Key to All Mythologies* the treatise remained unfinished at my stepfather's death. But back then, so long ago, in the study, the sexuality library, it was part of the earnest work being done in the room that my eight-year-old self was determined to understand. So while my stepfather was out, my stepbrother and I snuck in. We carefully pulled the dusty, heavy tomes from the shelf, flipped through them hoping to find pictures. The words were just as heavy and dense as the books themselves. My stepbrother lay on the red velvet chaise as I tried to decipher the words. Philosophical combinations of words, nothing was illuminated for us. Then it happened. *Hermaphrodite*. I can't recall the title, but *hermaphrodite* was in it, another heavy tome. But the key word was illustrated. I pulled it from the shelf and took it to the couch. I was a scrawny child who liked to wear fancy dresses. My stepbrother was even scrawnier with long, curly hair, so long he was often confused for a girl. He had the sweetest, biggest brown eyes. Between us we had eight older siblings, many of them in their midteens, all of them on their own precipice of the adult world, getting into trouble for sex and drugs and driving too fast in cars. My stepfather went after one of his daughters' boyfriends with a shotgun, the boyfriend streaking down the driveway in the buff. The book was fully illustrated, as promised, glossy black-and-white photographs of normal-looking people with close-ups of their genitalia. The book was stuffed thick with the images, words: *denotes ambiguous sexual development or intersex or unclear gender. The result of inconsistencies between gene chromosome gonad and genitalia. But in a strict sense the word applies to those capable of producing both sperm and egg.* Images that awed us, that propelled us back to the library for more peeks, that made us wide-eyed, filled us with complexity and a secret understanding of the world both disgusting and magnificent. It was Greek, it was potent, scintillating through us, a wonder. We wanted to keep it for ourselves and share it, too. "Look here. Get a look at this." Show all the older kids how much we knew. A woman could also be a man, a man also a woman. But we kept it our secret, pulsing between us, for it also seemed to be saying something to us, about us, for us alone. I'd known my stepbrother since I was four and he was three. I didn't recall much of life before him. He was mine, my little brother. I loved him wildly. I loved him in that room, on that chaise—his curiosity pouring into mine. The book was between us on the chaise showing possibilities that seemed to eliminate simplicity. He wasn't really my brother. We could see down the road, into that adult world. Possibility was endless, refracting like images in those double mirrors cast into infinity.

Not long after that, we began to kiss—warm and sloppy and wet, we spent a good bit of time perfecting the kiss. His lips soft on mine, coming to understand them, gently, surely, certainly. He'd hold my head in his big hands, and pressing our lips together on the red chaise, we'd vanish through the portal.

HORNY

NELL CASEY

DEFINITION: lustful, sexually excited.

Two old ladies were sitting on rocking chairs in their retirement home. One asked, "Do you still ever get horny?"

"Oh, yes!" was the reply.

"What do you do about it?" asked the first.

"I suck on a Life Saver."

The first lady sat there for a long while pondering the answer. Finally she couldn't stand it any longer and asked:

"Who drives you to the beach?"

Horny is, for me, a nostalgic word. It takes me back to a simpler time, to a big and teenaged and grabby lust, filled with the devouring want of someone who knows nothing of what she seeks. Horny is to sex as puberty is to adulthood. Its motion, the energy behind the word, is best illustrated by the scramble of Fred Flintstone's feet as he races along in his car. If Horny were a woman, she would have a round face but she would not be kind.

The word dates back to at least 1889, which means that Henry James may well have uttered the sentence "I feel horny." A statement made all the more possible by the suggestion that James may never actually have had sex in his lifetime. The word comes from the slang expression *to have the horn*, which, in the nineteenth century, was used by men and women to express sexual excitement—though I would like to see this phrase make a comeback among men only. It sounds a bit like *you're giving me wood*, another phrase that transports me like a time machine to my youth.

For travelers (especially the yearning ones), *horny* translates to *corne* in French, *rogowaty* in Polish, *hoornig* in Dutch, and 角質の in Japanese.

The best use of the word I have ever come across in literature is in Jonathan Lethem's novel *You Don't Love Me Yet*, in which he describes a slacker thirtysomething character at work: "As she roused herself from the cubicle, Lucinda felt a sweet nostalgic stirring of affection, almost like green shoots of horniness under the pavement of her hangover."

I admire the use of the word *horny* in adulthood, its stubborn refusal to give in to one of the word's more mature—and therefore burdened with the contradictory knowledge that life brings—colleagues. No need to resort to *sexy*, *desirous*, or *erotic* when you're describing that plain old burst of gobbling need that only *horny*, the youth elixir of lust, can describe.

HUM JOB

MARY-ANN TIRONE SMITH

DEFINITION: specialized form of fellatio where the fellator hums while holding the testicles (or penis) in the mouth causing pleasurable vibrations in the testicles.

Instructions on how to give a hum job from Cosmopolitan.com:

Simply make "mmmm" sounds for a few seconds at a time in a smooth, steady tone as you move your mouth up and down his shaft. Varying the pitch of your voice creates different sensations: Lower pitches create slower vibrations; higher pitches create faster ones. Also, the vibrations are most intense at the opening of your mouth, so if you really want to make him explode, focus on the supersensitive head of his penis with your lips.

I was getting into this really good rhythm—think baby with pacifier—when I heard him slurrr . . . "Could you stop for a minute and give me a hum job?"

I peered up past his hairy belly, hairy chest, hairy face, and into his sex-drugged eyes. I stopped. "Say what?"

"Don't stop."

Make up your mind. "Sorry."

"S'okay."

I got back to business and he started talking again. He explained what he wanted.

Egad. But I'm game. Rather than risk another upset of the apple cart, I let my hand take over so I could ask, "Any particular tune?"

He immediately lost half his leverage. Then he laughed. Couldn't stop laughing, actually, and soon all was lost. So I said, "Well, I mean, wouldn't Antonio Carlos Jobim be more effective than, say, 'Me and Julio Down by the Schoolyard?' "

He kept right on laughing but I was intrigued; I ignored him and performed my first hum job. And what a performance! I started in with one of my all-time favorites, "A Nightingale Sang in Berkeley Square."

By the end of the first four bars, his battery had recharged, and with his laughing short-circuited he said, "Could you just *hum?*"

But my mind was racing. I was already swinging into "On, Wisconsin!" seeing as how he went there. Boy, was that a hit! Then, knowing how much he loved Sheryl Crow, I segued into "All I Wanna Do."

Remember how, when you're a kid, you suddenly and inexplicably produce a sound from your kazoo? Well, at first, humming with a mouth full of prairie dogs isn't easy, but once you get the knack, *whoa, Mama!*

I'd settled into a repertoire of American standards when in the middle of the prelude to "Our Love Is Here to Stay," he grabbed both my shoulders, pulled me up to him, became George to my upper-deck Martha, and we both reached orchestral heights at nearly the exact same time. (I was two beats ahead.)

The next day, he brought me a gift. One of those revolving CD towers that I've been wanting forever. There were six new CDs in it: Sinatra at his most romantic; a medley of college fight songs; Sheryl Crow's greatest hits; and Diana Krall singing Cole Porter. There were two more: Antonio Carlos Jobim, and early Simon and Garfunkel—for future reference. Oh, and a vibrator that plays "Yankee Doodle."

What a guy!

I

INCEST

ADRIENNE BRODEUR

DEFINITION: sexual intercourse between persons so closely
related that they are forbidden by law to marry.

BROTHER AND SISTER FALL IN LOVE AND MARRY

The bizarre case of Patrick Stuebing and Susan Karolewski has captivated the world since the couple crashed into the headlines in 2001 with the birth of their first incestuous son (two of their four children are disabled). Not just because their self-proclaimed love seems to break one of the modern world's last taboos. But also because last week the couple's lawyer, Dr. Endrich Wilhelm, lodged a plea with the country's highest judicial body, the Constitutional Court, in a bid to attempt to overturn Germany's ban on incest.

—RUTH ELKINS, *INDEPENDENT*, HTTP://NEWS.INDEPENDENT.CO.UK/
EUROPE/ARTICLE2326110.ECE

141

A SHORT STORY

It's been over thirty years since that day, which when you think about it, started out as any other: Cheerios? Cinnamon toast, perhaps? Could you even say for sure?

"Please," you whispered, and the word—moist and warm from your mouth—lodged itself in my ear. "Please." "Please." "Please."

Moments earlier, we'd scrambled to get undressed, our bathing suits landing in a heap on the floor, inside out, a wet stain expanding darkly on the frayed Persian rug. Evidence should anyone be looking for clues. Not that anyone was. Not at that time, anyway. What with all that was going on—the steady stream of boozy cocktail parties, the affairs, the divorce, the new husband, the new wife—no one was paying much attention to us at all.

They are now, that's for sure. Now, everyone wants to know what happened, why it is that we're not speaking. We're not telling, of course. Why would we? Our story belongs lost in some neurological Bermuda triangle where it can't disturb things. I mean, you can wait for years or decades, your whole life even, for that one tiny piece of information that will shed light on why what happened happened, you know?

What do you think it was that piloted us into that tiny bed that day? Upstairs, in the room at the far end of the hall. Yellow walls, I think. Or possibly everything was just yellow with age. It was an unremarkable room, no? A large rectangle furnished with twin beds, a pine bureau, and a rolltop desk upon which sat several faded photos in tarnished frames, old photos of young men grinning, men long dead now, probably long dead even at the time.

Then, there was us.

Naked.

In bed.

"Naked as jaybirds," Dad would have said.

There we lay, not speaking, skin to skin, a million tiny nerve endings shooting impulses through our spinal cords, transmitting delight to our brains. In the past, we'd only ever kissed here and there—a little tongue, sometimes a feel. You know, just two kids sneaking our way into some grown-up fun. Though there was that naked roll in the snow after a sauna on a ski trip, remember? Still, this was different—a plane crash, a gun gone off, discovering a lump. This moment would lead to the next and to the next and to the next . . . What happens in early childhood is the key to everything else, right? At least that's what the experts say.

"Please."

"Please what?" I answered, my leg twitching under the weight of yours.

Voices from downstairs hovered just outside the door—our grandparents, an uncle. Dad, of course.

Just "Please," that was all you'd say.

You lifted a shard of skin peeling from my nose and popped it in your mouth. You would have devoured me whole if you could, that's how much you loved me.

A beam of sunlight streamed through the window and landed on your face, picking out the tiny downy hairs on your upper lip.

"Please."

I brought my hands down alongside your erection.

I would turn nine in two months, enter the fourth grade, learn about the orange dot beneath the herring gull's beak where her chicks would peck to get regurgitated minnows.

Beyond your shoulder, a water glass sweated on the bedside table. A tiny droplet of water hung from its lip and trembled from the tension of its own minuscule gravity.

Hours earlier we'd jumped off the slick jetty into the ocean and then out across the sand. You'd tackled me. I'd kneed you and escaped. You'd snagged my ankle. Down I went again.

The droplet hung there, quivering, holding tight.

Then I touched you, barely grazing your velvety skin, and with that it was over.

J

JAILBAIT (*see also* LOLITA)

JASON BROWN

DEFINITION: a person below the age of consent with whom
sexual intercourse can constitute statutory rape.
AKA: clanger, jailhouse pussy, forbidden
fruit, minor, schoolgirl, nymphet.

What happens to a woman when she finds the man of her dreams, only he is a child? And if the woman is his teacher? American parents cringed at the story of Mary Kay Letourneau, who first met Vili Fualaau when she was his teacher in second grade. He did not start flirting with her until he was in sixth. She started to have sex with him the next year, when he was 13. Already the mother of four from a marriage that was disintegrating, she would bear the teenager's daughter, but not before she ended up in prison on rape and molestation charges.

—HOWARD CHUA-EOAN, "TIME MAGAZINE'S TOP 25 CRIMES OF THE
CENTURY," 2007, WWW.TIME.COM/TIME/2007/CRIMES/22.HTML

I grew up in Maine, the state with the lobster on the license plate. I didn't realize until I moved away that people in Maine were supposed to live in white clapboard farmhouses, speak with an accent, and spend their weekends tying flies and digging for fishing worms. I lived in a lime green vinyl-sided house and spent most of my time smoking pot and jerking off to MTV videos. After my father left, my friend Tom moved in with us because his stepfather was a midcoast coke dealer who had tried to poison Tom's mother. Not long after Tom moved in, my mother discovered the Valium/marijuana/Gallo cocktail, which is when she started showing up in Tom's bedroom doorway naked and whispering, "Cary Grant?"

"Don't worry," he told me at our first house barbecue, when we accidentally set the vinyl siding on fire, "I would never fuck your mother."

That was a relief. It didn't stop him from fucking my girlfriend, Alice, though. I was in love with her, but Tom said, "One man is not enough for her. You can't take it personally."

I didn't, but I still felt awful and so I took a bunch of mushrooms one night and shaved my head. It almost cost me my job at Friendly's, where I worked as a Window Scooper. The manager said I looked unfriendly.

Then something happened that, as a teenager, I could never have predicted: I fell in love with someone else, our new biology teacher, Miss Paine. Our old biology teacher had quit because she needed a kidney transplant or she was going to die. We had no idea.

"She has the face of a chipmunk, but she's hot for a teacher," Tom said.

When we dissected a pig, she guided my hand as I sliced open the pink abdomen.

"She wants you," Tom said. "Go talk to her. Tell her she's hot."

I went up to her and told her my name.

"I know your name," she said.

I told her I was writing a one-act play, which I was. I just hadn't gotten very far into it. I told her the play was about an alien from the planet Benelia, where everyone was good. An evil planet was invading their planet, so they sent a representative down to Earth to learn the secret of self-defense. Ultimately, the Benelians decided they didn't want anything to do with humanity. They would rather go extinct.

"I did theater in college," Miss Paine said, and gave me a smile. She gathered her quizzes into her bag and stood up from her desk.

All the other students had left the room, so I made my move.

"Can we get together sometime after school and talk about my play?" I said. "I need help with it."

Her mouth hung open. Her face was blank. The person who had been there smiling and making small talk was gone. I had called up someone else.

We met at the old railroad station. It was just getting dark, late October. She owned an old, rusty Subaru. I got into the passenger seat. We sat in the dark for five minutes. Finally, I asked where she lived, and she said in the old mill building that had been converted to apartments. She drove us there and parked around back. In the apartment, she went into the kitchenette and poured water into a kettle. There was a futon couch in the main room and a bed in the next room. Stacks of books on the floor. Nothing on the walls.

We sat down on the futon together. There was nowhere else to sit.

"Tell me more about your play," she said.

"It's about an alien," I said, and I began to repeat the synopsis I had offered before. She didn't seem to listen. She leaned sideways on the futon, her head close to my shoulder, and she sobbed into her hands.

"I'm sorry," she mumbled.

I lay my hand on the side of her head and stroked her hair.

She didn't know that I was on familiar ground now. Alice always cried before, after, and sometimes during sex.

"Don't worry," I said. I was sure I sounded older than seventeen, and she nestled her face into my shoulder. I wrapped my arms around her, smoothing my hand down her back as her chest quaked.

She told me she had been raped two years before in Providence, Rhode Island, where she had been a college student. Beaten up, then raped by two men she had never met.

"Now I've moved to this place where I don't know anyone and I can't talk to people."

"You're talking to me," I said, and her face flushed.

Most of the women I knew had a similar story. Alice, my mother, another girl, my first, back when we were thirteen. The details varied, but the damage was the same. I leaned over and kissed her. Her lips didn't respond, but she didn't pull away. If I kissed her again, I sensed, she would stop crying and stop hurting. Her story had been a confession, an accusation, and a seduction. I kissed her again. She pulled off her clothes and then helped me off with mine.

She lowered herself on top of me. "Leave your hands at your side." I nodded. I was inside her but afraid to move my hips or my arms or my breath. She pushed herself down on me, wrapping her arms tightly around the back of my head, and she let out a long sigh, more of relief than pleasure.

She drove me to school in the morning, dropping me off a block from the building so I could walk to homeroom and after the first bell to her biology class. I spent half the week at my house and half the week at her apartment. My mother had a new boyfriend down in Portland and hardly noticed whether I was there or not. I earned a C-plus in biology. The plus, she said, was a concession to our relationship.

Together we were holding something back from a world we did not trust. We could never be seen together, so when I went to her apartment, I was careful not to let anyone see me going in or out. On the drive to school in the mornings, I ducked my head if we passed anyone. We spent our time in her apartment, kissing on her futon and talking in low voices. Two months had passed before I realized I had stopped drinking and taking drugs.

In the spring of the school year, I was no longer in Miss Paine's class, and for some reason I stopped going over to her apartment. Tom and I were drinking more, every morning, and taking whatever drugs we could get from his uncle. I missed her, almost desperately sometimes, but I wouldn't let myself go to see her for several months.

One night I left Tom and biked the two miles to Miss Paine's apartment. It was two in the morning. When she answered the door, I started crying and couldn't stop. It was the first time in a long time. She wrapped her arms around me and squeezed me. We lay side by side all night with our clothes on, and she repeated over and over that I would be all right. No one had ever said that to me. I didn't believe her, but I believed she meant what she said. In the morning we said good-bye, our last good-bye. A month later she quit her job and moved out of state.

KISSING

VICTORIA REDEL

DEFINITION: to touch or caress with the lips as an expression
of affection, greeting, respect, or amorousness.
AKA: sucking face, swapping spit, first base,
tonsil hockey, make out.

*A kiss is a lovely trick designed by nature to stop speech when words become
superfluous.*

—INGRID BERGMAN

The first surprise of your mouth and mine, the instant way we
begin to speak together a language we have never spoken together, a little tentative, small promises, a fluency, accented, di-
alected, each vowel and consonant exactly formed, sudden native
speakers, pun and slang, the slip of tongue, intentional.

On streets, on staircases, in bathrooms, in the back of cabs,
in a field, against that wall and that wall and that wall, down on
the floor, my hair caught in it, the tongue, lightest tongue, hard
and pressed and reaching tongue, darted, flicked, down-your-
throat tongue, come up barely for air, in hotel beds, in a bor-
rowed bed, and in the same bed night after night after year after
night, through an open window, under pines, underwater, on a
raft, in rain, salty with ocean, a peck at the door, a have a good
day, or again slow, slow, the melt, the play of lips, a lower lip
caught flicked with teeth, pulling back just a little to breathe
together.

Into under with for beneath above inside away toward, our mouths, prepositional.

Eyes open, eyes closed, your face in transport. Your face so close to mine.

The whole universe ignited. Combustible.

At the sink, doing dishes and suddenly your mouth on my neck and you are turning me around to face you, biting and licking, lifting me up, saying, "Give me your mouth," and I am giving you my mouth.

Coming up out of it, stunned, discombobulated, like moving out from a dream.

Like there is another room inside and then there is another room inside.

Strawberries, sourness of coffee, a slight fizzy sweetness or the clean grass taste as only you taste.

Mornings, just wakened, the tongue still slow and thick and dreaming, turning away from a kiss.

Kissing like something windy, like good weather. Kissing in winter, our mouths the warmest place in the city. Kissing in rain, in sudden drenching rain and we are gladly wet.

Kissing like nobody's business.

Or trying not to, trying to hold back, restraint, restraint and then surrender.

Tongue and tongue and lip and tongue and, suddenly I am all twitch and pull and ache inside.

Snuck, stolen, last, first, unbidden, forbidden, sloppy, delicious, French, farewell, slippery, criminal kisses.

Sacred kissing, a private syntax.

"Was that legal?" I ask when we come up out of it.

Could I have known when Charlie R. took me up the Harwood building stairwell for my first, fast, dry, twelve-year-old kiss that I'd become a woman who loves kissing, a woman who'd drive across state lines for the moment just before the kiss begins.

"What I really miss is the make out. That's what I'd go for if I could have a night on the lam," the married woman said, looking at a couple who have rolled right off their picnic blanket.

One of us might say, "Only kissing," and then it's the first night all over again and we are making out and making out and making out, we are the tumble and press and wrestle, all pressure and rub, everything concentrated in our lips and tongues, all of it, every mystical, dirty, delicious thing that two people can manage.

"Kiss me good-bye," you say, and on a street with strangers in floppy hats and winter coats, we slip into one another to say to one another with tongue and lips the last apologies and promises.

In the bank line or sitting at a dinner table with friends, I touch my mouth, chapped, puffy, maybe a little raw, a souvenir of our intimacy.

I am drifting or you are drifting and one pressed against the other whispers, "Good night," and there's the last kiss, the day's punctuation.

L

LOLITA

STEVE ALMOND

DEFINITION: a young seductive woman, derived from *Lolita* (1955), a novel by Vladimir Nabokov.

Amy Elizabeth Fisher (born August 21, 1974), dubbed the "Long Island Lolita" by the press, is an American woman who was convicted in 1992 of shooting the wife of her lover, with whom she began an affair as a sixteen-year-old student at Kennedy High School in Bellmore, New York.

One night early on in grad school a bunch of us wannabe writers gathered at a bar to blab about the books we loved, and of course *Lolita* came up, because *Lolita* always comes up in such conversations. The other guys and I took a cold, analytical approach to the book. We wanted to say how much we adored it, how much we secretly identified with Humbert Humbert and his illegal passion for prepubescent Lolita. But we were also hoping to get laid (of course), and we figured such a confession would put us in poor stead with our female classmates.

There was one in particular, a women I'll call Rita, who, as it happened, had more than a hint of the nymphet in her. She wasn't exactly "four foot ten in one sock." More like five-one in black stockings. But she was small and pale and occasionally dressed like a schoolgirl, and this made us all the more leery about directly endorsing *Lolita*. So we sat around parsing Nabokov's intricate wordplay and nursing our beers until, toward the end of the night, emboldened by a shot of George Dickel, Rita stood up and addressed us in an imploring tone, "But you guys, don't you get it—he *loves* her!"

And that, ladies and gentlemen of the jury, is the whole ball of wax when it comes to *Lolita*. He loves her. Without the blinding force of Humbert's passion, Nabokov's 1955 masterpiece would never have endured its initial ignominy, nor become the most influential novel of the last century.

I feel vaguely qualified to speak about the book's influence, because I spent so much of grad school writing dreadful imitations of *Lolita*, or reading them as the fiction editor of our literary magazine.

There is no need to labor the plot of *Lolita* (man meets girl, man seduces girl, man loses girl—that about does it). Nor the oft-cited symbolism (old, refined Europe seduced by young, vulgar America). What matters, in the end, is the heartsick love song of Monsieur Humbert. Here he is describing the boyhood tryst that presages his eventual coupling with Lolita:

> She sat a little higher than I, and whenever in her solitary ecstasy she was led to kiss me, her head would bend with a sleepy, soft, drooping movement that was almost woeful, and her bare knees caught and compressed my wrist, and slackened again; and her quivering mouth, distorted by the acridity of some mysterious potion, with a sibilant intake of breath came near to my face.

To be overrun by feeling, yet able to marshal words with such elegant precision—this was Nabokov's knack. That he did so on behalf of a quivering pervert makes the achievement that much more astonishing.

There should be no doubt about that: Humbert is a perv. "The bud-stage of breast development appears early (10.7 years) in the sequence of somatic changes accompanying pubescence," he informs us. "And the next maturational item available is the first appearance of pigmented pubic hair (11.2 years)."

Lolita was originally published by a French press. Its American debut came three years later, after being dubbed "the filthiest book I have ever read" by a British critic. Such is our lust for scandal.

And yet it is Humbert's pathology that makes his seduction so powerful. He knows he's doing wrong. We know he's doing wrong. He can't stop himself. And we can't stop ourselves from watching.

Nor, if we are honest, do we look upon Humbert with pure disgust. In our covert hearts we root for him because *he loves her*, and because, when you come right down to it, most of our own wishes are illicit or feel that way to us. Humbert's crimes, in other words, may be of a greater scale than the ones we commit, but they derive from a common cauldron of deviance.

Lolita has enjoyed periodic resurgences owing to two excellent film adaptations, by Stanley Kubrick (1962) and Adrian Lyne (1997). But the novel itself remains the vital artifact, because only it can capture—with unflinching fidelity—the fevered consciousness of Humbert himself.

"There my beauty lay down on her stomach, showing me, showing the thousand eyes wide open in my eyed blood, her slightly raised shoulder blades," he tells us. "Every movement she made in the dappled sun plucked at the most secret and sensitive chord of my abject body."

In moments such as these, Nabokov is nothing less than a poet of desire. He is not writing about sex, but about the tumultuous feelings that illuminate our clumsy acts of love. These are what sweep us along—the bleatings of our conscience be damned.

Big ideas, witty observations, and tricky plotlines are all fine and well. But the engine of any great book is desire. And by that standard, *Lolita* is a Mack truck.

"Her legs twitched a little as they lay across my live lap; I stroked them; there she lolled in the right-hand corner, almost asprawl, Lola the bobby-soxer, devouring her immemorial fruit, singing through its juice."

This is the true scandal of *Lolita*. Not that a man should love a child, but that he should prove so helpless to stanch his desires. Wild emotion is the book's central transgression and its saving grace.

Never has this been more obvious than in the current era, which has placed carnality in the service of capitalism by stripping from sex any vestige of authentic feeling. We see more and more these days—a universe of fawning Lolitas await us online—but feel less and less. Everywhere we look, glistening parts are pumping away in congress, yearning to excite our wildest consumer fantasies. Every day, it becomes harder and harder to make a clear distinction between pornography and advertising.

But *Lolita*?

It has nothing to sell but the truth of ourselves: our afflictions of want, our shame, our elusive and horrible and blessed ecstasy.

LOTHARIO (*see also* DON JUAN)

MELINDA DAVIS

DEFINITION: a man who obsessively seduces and deceives women.
Lotario is a character in Nicholas Rowe's 1703 play,
The Fair Penitent, who seduces and betrays the female lead.
AKA: Don Juan, Romeo, Casanova, ladies' man,
lady-killer, lecher, libertine, lover, philanderer,
rake, seducer, skirt chaser, stud, wolf.

We have always known him by his contradictions—the raging moderate, the compassionate realist, the hardheaded dreamer. But now Clinton emerges as something new: a feminist Lothario, a New Age Don Juan, Alan Alda with a zipper problem.

—ANDREW FERGUSON, *TIME*, SEPTEMBER 21, 1998

A WOMAN'S POINT OF VIEW

If sex is the jungle—the deep, the moist, the entangled, the strange, the muskiness that comes at the parting of root, the smell of ground, the exquisite focus, the anticipation of animal leap, danger, rapture, endless sweat, you know, the *jungle*—then Lothario is the lion stalking therein. Let us praise him. Choose your jungle. For wherever he does his roving, his rogueing, he is identified by the same bestial swagger. Primacy. Coolth. Cock.

Urban nights—for this is the jungle in which you are prey— you are alert to his approach through the stand of all others, watering. Nocturnal music. Frolic, perhaps. Mouths to ears. You see the blood of others on him—but you are not deterred, for this is the scent that draws you to him. (Kill *me*!) You show him your palms as you finger your hair. (Here find surrender!) You show him your neck. (Here! Strike here!) You lower your lids to prepare for surprise. Oh, how you lust to be chosen from the herd! You feel his gaze—a tug at the button of the womb. (Do you lust for life or for death?) You squeeze the invisible squeeze. (There!) You use only the sides of your eyes in his direction. (Him!) It is he! The One! All are aware! But, alas, he turns to smell another. Just as well, you think, for he is a scoundrel, a rake, a ruiner, a destroyer, a creep, a cad, a dirty word. But now he turns in your direction! (Look at me! At me! See the swelling of my breast! See how I suck the bottoms of my hair. See how I am hobbled by the leather at my feet. I will tumble! I will tumble! I open! I give!) He speaks, and his words are jazz licks, jazz licks. He knows the words. He touches the places. He chooses. He chooses you. (Is this happening? Yes! To me!) Now.

Following the breaching of your flesh (however many times it might occur), you imagine the creation of cave, that you will be the one to tame the beast, that he will be content with only you as sustenance. That he will remain forever in your thatch.

You see him lift his nose to the wind. He moves on to devour another.

Desolation. The only recourse is to stitch up the wound. At least for tonight.

LUCKY PIERRE

MICHELLE RICHMOND

DEFINITION: the middle man in a "sandwich"
of three sexually entwined men.
AKA: daisy chain, meat-of-the-sandwich,
chicken on the spit.

The Adventures of Lucky Pierre *is a 1961 nudie cutie sexploitation film created by exploitation filmmakers Herschell Gordon Lewis and David F. Friedman. The first of its kind to be filmed in color, the film starred comedian Billy Falbo. It was unique for its time and genre, adding successful comedy to the nudity and sensationalist material.*

—ADAM ROCKOFF, *GOING TO PIECES: THE RISE AND FALL OF THE SLASHER FILM, 1978-1986* (MCFARLAND & COMPANY, 2002)

I've often considered it a travesty of both my gender (female) and my general sexual orientation (prudish) that I've never, no never, gotten to play the role of Lucky Pierre. If the term *Lucky Pierre* makes you think of Aidan Moffat, front man of the Scottish band Arab Strap, then maybe you've been spending too much time managing your iPod and too little time stroking your id. And if you think it's the name of the porn-star protagonist in Robert Coover's

157

2002 metafictional romp *The Adventures of Lucky Pierre*—"the man of the moment, the lord of the leg-over, the star, the one and only: Lucky Pierre," whose penis advances into the frozen landscape of the novel "ramrod stiff in the morning wind, glistening with ice crystals . . . batting aggressively against the sullen crowds"—then you're correct, but that's only the tip of the iceberg.

Coover took his title and inspiration from the 1961 nudie film of the same name, directed by Herschell Gordon Lewis. The film follows the picaresque adventures of a beloved porn star who wanders about getting his rocks off with one willing lass after another. Lucky Pierre is also the name of a tour company in Alaska that leads halibut-fishing charters and black-bear safaris. Although the FAQ page for Lucky Pierre Charters includes such questions as "What is the length of your boat?" and oblique references to its "vessel," the charter company appears to be just that—a charter company—so don't be ringing them up with expectations of a naughty northern weekend.

But I digress. A term of such hedonistic Sturm und Drang surely deserves a more direct, front-door approach. Or back door. Or to be more precise, an adequate explanation requires entrance through the front and back doors simultaneously. (Be patient. I'm getting there. I did, after all, grow up Southern Baptist.)

Lucky Pierre is, quite literally, the middleman in a three-way romp involving at least two males. The fellow in the middle is deemed *lucky* because he's both giving and receiving. Something must be going in, while something else is going out. The word *Pierre* is purportedly a reference to the popularity of the position in France, but I've found no hard evidence to corroborate that our fair-tongued friends across the pond are more into it than the Americans.

Physics being what they are, and a dildo apparently being contraption non grata in this arrangement, two men are absolutely required. A mathematical approach yields the integers of x, y, and

z, where x and y must always be male, and z may be either male or female.

In the case that z is female, either x or y may be the Lucky Pierre. On a rudimentary number line, given that all integers are facing east, our happy threesome might appear in either of the following configurations:

$x+y+z$
$y+x+z$

In the case that z is male, then z may also be Lucky Pierre, in which case the possible combinations are tripled:

$x+y+z$
$x+z+y$
$y+x+z$
$y+z+x$
$z+x+y$
$z+y+x$

One can see how a social encounter with so many possible configurations could go on into the wee hours. In the infinite sexual database that is the Internet, the all-male equation seems to be favored, although the two-man/one-woman approach is frequently acknowledged.

In a 2005 interview with *Barcode* magazine, Aiden Moffat, the aforementioned front man of Arab Strap, defined Lucky Pierre as "the man in the middle of a three-man bum chain." Aside from the obvious inelegance of the wording, Moffat's definition strikes me as unnecessarily limiting. Why, I ask you, should the boys have all the fun? Oddly enough, Moffat claims that his goal with the album *Lucky Pierre* was to make "music to fall asleep to," but the Lucky Pierre position doesn't strike me as particularly restful.

LUG (LESBIAN UNTIL GRADUATION)

NICK ARVIN

DEFINITION: adolescent lesbianism, usually nonpolitical, motivated most often by either:

- testing/rebellion/experimentation (adolescent differentiation process); or

- seeking a safe way of investigating sexuality ("trying out her carnal wings in a familiar nest"); i.e., a reaction of avoiding the typically demanding male sexuality (i.e., until male peers mature into a more co-equal sexuality—described by *GQ* as "the time when boys finally learn not to ram their tongues into tomorrow").

—WWW.NUMBER-ONE-ADULT-SEXUAL-HEALTH-TERMS-
ADVISOR.COM/SEXSLANG.HTM

AKA: bi-curious, tourist, fence-sitter.

Can any three-letter acronym capture the complexity of human relations, the history and psychology and false starts and true starts and forlorn endings and so forth? Hardly! LUG captures the merest fraction of a partial percentage of the omnivorous capacity of human life, and so it makes no sense to speak of *a* LUG in a general sense, or, God forbid, *the* LUG. The LUG does not exist! Only individuals exist. Let us speak of individuals. Let us consider some real-life examples drawn from my own actual life experience:

Miranda now offers highly paid legal counsel to the manufacturers of pastel-hued sweetener packets and drives a car made of aluminum by skilled Germans, but when I knew her in college, she grew her own vegetables and rode a bamboo bicycle. She shaved her body hair, including the head, for compost, and she never showered. Instead she scraped the grease from her skin once a week and rendered it into tallow for candle making. She was a lover of womyn. But, when I met her again years later, she was wearing mascara and a navy blue pantsuit and an engagement ring with a rock the size of a baby's eyeball! When I asked her what had happened, she would only say, tersely (this was during a break in a deposition during which she sat across from me asking really unfair questions about the slug of artificial sweetener—pastel *blue* packet—that had nearly choked me to death), that making love to women had been too much like making love to herself, "like dry humping a warm mirror." Really, she said that!

Sweet Tessa was called Sweet because everyone loved her so much, and her case just goes to show how tricky these definitions can be. Sweet Tessa was always monogamous, but sometimes she fell in love with men, and sometimes she fell in love with women. So should we say that when in love with a woman she was a lesbian and when in love with a man she was straight? Or should we say she was a bisexual? Such arbitrary categories! And if she was a bisexual, should we say she was a BUG? That's mean! I think we should simply say Sweet Tessa was a woman with a lovely dimpled smile, a kind word for everyone, and eighteen pet gerbils. She also used to buy lobsters from the grocery store and liberate them into the sea. After college she was engaged to a dental student who went to school while she worked—this is true—in a salt mine. This was in Detroit, the Detroit Salt Company, you can look it up. She operated a loader. Anyway, when he abandoned her (I had tried to warn her, but she was in love) on the eve of the wedding and took the gerbils with him, she renounced human love. She's now a showgirl in Branson, Missouri.

Shirley was a lesbian during her college years in the rollicking 1960s, and she is my mom. She always told me that she gave up on homosexual love specifically so that she could have me, exactly as I am. Dear old Mom! Way to go!

Jenna was excruciatingly shy, and it was a rare day that she spoke a dozen syllables, much less went on a date or such. But one night a drunk girl stumbled into Jenna's dorm room and fell into bed with her, and Jenna had a dream of making love, only to wake and discover it was true! Having enjoyed the experience, she decided she was a lesbian. After graduation, however, she had nearly the same experience again, except this time the person who tumbled into bed with her was me—a guy! It happened that we were staying in the same house because it was our parents' house. Jenna is my sister. But she's adopted, so it's okay. Play on!

Angel is the only LUG I know who actually called herself a LUG, and she called herself a LUG while she was still in college. She basically announced she would give up lesbians and take up men when she graduated. She was totally in your face about it! And she did it! My friends and I all talked about it a lot, because clearly here was a woman who knew herself and what she wanted. After college she married Mike, a round, little, bucktoothed pea-gravel salesman, and then I lost track of Angel and Mike for some years until one day when she resurfaced in the news. She had cut Mike into five pieces and sent the pieces by Express Mail inside coolers filled with dry ice and pea gravel to the leaders of oppressive regimes on five separate continents. Maybe you heard about this? During the trial, which was all in the news, lots of curious particulars came out, including that Angel had left college when she was three credits short of graduating—she never graduated, and so she was never technically really a LUG! Wow, we laughed about that!

Toni is a woman that I knew in grad school, slight and pale; she wore her black hair short and straight and she was hot hot hot and it always killed me that she was a lesbian. Since graduation, however, Toni has escaped the confining expectations of the academic ivory citadel and discovered that for her the opportunities of masculine love are ultimately more satisfying, and now she often thinks wistfully of me—maybe? Who knows! Write me, Toni!

LUST

MERRILL FEITELL

DEFINITION: intense sexual desire or appetite.
AKA: crave, hunger, covet, yearn, hot and bothered,
all worked up, cream, hot, urge, ache, pine, thirst.

If it is the dirty element that gives pleasure to the act of lust, then the dirtier it is, the more pleasurable it is bound to be.

–THE MARQUIS DE SADE

He blew in like a hurricane—a hurricane that was really into oral sex. There were the lost afternoons, the lost weekends, the messy hair and the dumb, glazed flush. There was the wreckage of condom wrappers, like fallen foliage, clinging to our bare feet whenever we padded to the fridge for those urgent late-night/early-morning/midafternoon sips of juice. He raised the lust level in my apartment as if it were the water table—and then he moved on, leaving me to slosh around in all that lust alone. What was I supposed to do while waiting for the pool of it to recede?

Would I ever find another lover like Big Todd? I wondered. One who could cultivate desire—and then satisfy it, again and again and again?

"Of course you will," my friends were quick to say.

And only a few days later, when I'd fled to the higher ground of my desk, there, aglow, in the hot, still swamp of night, I fell in hard again, this time with Google.

Oh, Google, sweet Google, tireless lover. Google could satisfy my every need.

From blogspot, to Friendster, to Flickr, to YouTube, we tracked Big Todd's course, dating his way across Central Park SummerStage, dipping into Queens for a rainy set at the U.S. Open, and, finally, really hitting ground up in the Bronx. Should

I mention that I have never been one for peeping in actual windows and that fevered stalking was never the passion in mind? But in Google I'd found the perfect rebound buddy for riding the surge of displaced lust still swamping the scene—and what with the laptop, wonder of wonders, the frenzy could continue right there in bed.

The new girl was named Carla. She had mousy hair and bloated lips. Six of her MySpace pictures featured her cat, who was listed, along with "good food" and "nice people," as interests she held dear. The blogroll revealed that their first date had been s'mores at Xando; their first kiss, of course, on the Brooklyn Bridge.

In truth, it took a while for me and Google to really hit our rhythm, the clumsy peg-legged pursuit of her last name and e-mail took several dates. But then, late one Friday night, something happened—something just clicked—and, suddenly, Google and I broke through the floodgate. And if ever, ever, I thought Big Todd could deliver, now here was a little search engine he had to meet.

Chugga-chugga! The little engine that could: we had her name; we had her roommate; we figured out the inevitable clattering route he must have biked to her house. We knew that she liked to cook—he certainly liked to eat—we had the image of them feasting in her Riverdale kitchen, the windows steamed with sex and farmers' market greens.

And, oh, how Google could make me laugh! Showing me that the *Cat Kama Sutra* was atop her Amazon wish list; producing pictures of all the nice people she knew; pointing out that her old eHarmony profile name was—get this—MissMysteryNYC.

The voice mail filled. The sheets twisted. It was Saturday, it was Sunday—what did time matter at all? The nightstand cluttered with glasses, the sprinkle of gum wrappers, like rose petals, romancing the floor. Like the best of all lovers, Google teased and titillated, nudging me toward desires I'd never knew lurked inside: What ridiculous things had she bid for on eBay? And what kind of dinner plates were on her sister's wedding registry?

Of course, throughout all of this, my real desire was emerging, desire for something even Google couldn't probably provide. We had confirmation, of course, that they were having sex—but was Carla enjoying it as much as I had? That perfect storm of lust shared by Big Todd and me was—wasn't it?—a pretty rare thing.

If only she'd lived in a top-floor apartment with a skylight directly over the bed, then we could just have zoomed in tight on Google maps and seen right then and there for ourselves.

But no.

So I thought for sure we'd hit a wall, when, early one Monday morning, Friendster, bless its heart, stepped onto the scene. I received notification directly in my in-box: Big Todd has posted a new image. Just click here to have a look.

We clicked. We looked.

There was Carla now, in the early-morning light of Big Todd's bedroom, the wall calendar behind her still on the same month as I'd last seen it. There she was sort of damp and windblown, her neat limp hair was wrecked, all matted and mussed. There she was, wearing my dopey eyes, wearing my dumb, glazed flush. There she was wearing my lust.

I thought that might be the end of it for me and Google, that we'd taken each other as far we could go. But, as happens in all extraordinary affairs, we rode the lust for a few gratuitous weeks more. Am I tireless lover? Oh, yes. Indeed.

Give it to me, Google. Give it to me please.

M

MASTURBATION

KATHARINE NOEL

DEFINITION: sexual gratification through self-stimulation.
AKA: wank, whack off, jack off, choke the chicken, yank, spank
the monkey, kill a kitten, polish the dolphin, beat off.

One of the curious things about sexual behaviour is that it correlates—in frequency, variety, etc.—with social class. Kinsey found that masturbation was more common in educated classes than in those groups concerned with unskilled or manual labour. Of all classes the professional groups masturbate most.

−THE KINSEY REPORT

My first porn: *Peter Pan* and *The Five Chinese Brothers*. I was three, not old enough to read but old enough to know what turned me on.

Peter Pan makes sense—Wendy bound to the mast, Lost Boys forced to walk the plank, Peter Pan flying in with a knife between his teeth—but *The Five Chinese Brothers* is a weirder choice. The book, for those with a less indelible memory of its plot, concerns five brothers, seemingly identical, but each with a strange and dazzling mutation. After the first brother is unjustly sentenced to death, his brothers replace him in turn. He's sentenced to be burnt at the stake, but the brother who is immune to fire goes in his place. When the judge then changes the sentence to drowning, it's the brother who can't be drowned who shows up. And when the sentence is changed again, to suffocation in an oven filled with whipped cream, luckily there's a brother who can hold his breath.

Suffocation in an oven filled with whipped cream! Surely I'm misremembering this. But no—really. Suffocation in an oven filled with whipped cream. It was this page that I thought about alone in bed at night when I couldn't sleep, this page that sent me under the covers to rock against a pillow. It was this page that got me into trouble at preschool, at naptime, where we had to lie still for ninety minutes.

The thing I most remember of those two years of Montessori school—besides my intense crush on another little girl because we had the same first name—is *how fucking bored* I was, awake for an hour and a half every day on my blue vinyl cot. I wasn't allowed to sing to myself. I wasn't allowed to sit up to watch the other kids sleeping. I wasn't allowed to look at books, but I could think about them. An oven. Whipped cream. Who in the mob of villagers bent on vengeance had thought of that combination?

I pressed and wriggled until a teacher—sounding repulsed, almost panicky—hissed at me to stop. Which I did, until her attention was elsewhere again.

At that age, I had no reason to associate sexual excitement with *sex*. I did know about sex: my kind, earnest, pathologically honest mother had committed herself to be open about it in a way her own parents had not been. This commitment often resulted in explanations far more careful and advanced than I needed. (A couple of years later, when I first heard other children say *That sucks*, my mother, blushing, painstakingly explained to me that sometimes people licked and sucked each other's genitals. I was horrified. That was what my friends were talking about? Licking and sucking each other's genitals?)

So, by three I knew *exactly* where babies came from, but there was nothing exciting about what I knew. Pressing against a pillow was exciting. Someone forced to walk the plank, someone tied to the stake, the bizarre specificity of someone stuffed into a whipped-cream-filled oven: that was scary and fascinating, disturbing and unsettling, and therefore exciting.

At three, fidgeting on my low blue cot, I had no understanding of those crossed wires, and no words for what I was doing. As far as I knew, what I'd discovered was a mutation, strange and dazzling: a way to inhabit my body and be outside it at the same time. To burn without burning, drown without drowning.

MÉNAGE À TROIS

RACHEL SHERMAN

DEFINITION: a relationship in which three
people have sexual relations.
AKA: threesome, club sandwich, cluster fuck, three-way,
three in a bed, Peter, Paul, and Mary, three-layer cake.

When a man and woman have joined together in a loving and holy marriage union, they may sometimes find that their love for one another and for God spills over outside of their relationship. Or they may find that other people are drawn to the joy, bliss, and passion that they radiate. In such situations, the desire or opportunity may arise to involve a third individual in their relationship—to form a threesome. Is this a temptation into sin, or a calling to a higher spiritual love? The answer is not clear in all situations, so we must turn to the Scriptures for guidance.

—WWW.SEXINCHRIST.COM

MÉNAGE À TROIS: A DEFINITION IN
THREE ATTEMPTS

I.

It is my idea, but my friend is French and says it the right way.
It is my idea, but she agrees.

First, I figure, ménage à trois needs two. You need to gang up. This is the plan.

We buy a Twister at the drugstore and take it out of the box and toss the spinner. We bring the mat in a bookbag (we are in college) and knock on the boy's dorm-room door.

He answers and lets us in. Not long after, drunk, we lay the mat down on top of his futon.

"All hands on red," I say.

There are only so many red dots. Then, my forehead hits the green spot, my knee on a yellow. Her knee on my shoulder, his arm on my ass.

You can only hold some positions for so long, but I let go quicker than I have to. We all come crumbling down, and then on top, and then on bottom.

My friend, the French girl, who is beautiful and sweet and far away from home, freezes midway between each of his hands on our breasts and our stomachs.

She pushes us, begins to cry, and runs out of the room in her underwear into the coed hall. She is my friend first (we started it together), so I follow her and kiss her, and we don't try it again.

2.

It is like a sandwich but not a good one.

"You have nice breasts," the one below me says, surprised in a way that I wish he weren't. Why wouldn't I have nice breasts? They are new. I am still in college.

We had been at a party. Some kind of bonfire. I was into tequila then, drinking it from a beer cup, when one boy and one girl said we should go do it. We should get some others to do it and have an orgy, they said. I followed them down the hill to a dorm.

It is a boy's room with colored Christmas lights around the

window. It starts quickly, and soon I am looking up at the ceiling, a boy, wet and tired-seeming, working hard between my legs.

I look around the room. Everything glows from the lights. There is no "en masse"; each of us falls into twos and threes.

I push the boy off, get up, and lie on the bottom bunk bed next to two people fucking. I try to talk to them and tell them how funny it was, me talking to them while one of them was inside the other. Then I lie back down on the floor and get inside the sandwich.

I don't kiss above or below. I know it is not working from the moment I get in. The wet and tired boy follows me back to my dorm where I hide from him in the shower stall.

3.

There are two boys with gold crosses around their necks, younger and Italian. They are in a fraternity and I've got them both. They are perfect, unbelievable and finally mine: identical twins.

One of them has a bit of a different nose, maybe. There is something about them that makes me tell them apart, but I don't mind.

I am no longer in college and suddenly I see clearly: you *can* begin with only one.

My idea comes to me as I do it. Sure, I have a friend. But she is small, more of a foil. She tries to kiss me while each boy kneels between our legs, but I am not interested.

We are in the girl's apartment, but I tell the boys what to do and they listen. They are good boys, mama's boys. One is smarter than the other. They take turns, then we come together.

Finally, a sandwich with meat! A perfect platter. It's over faster than you'd think.

I lie on my back, done, and reach. One of my hands rests, matching, on each boy's chest. I am stuck between the boys, dividing them. I cannot move, and I do not want to.

MILE HIGH CLUB

LUCY FERRISS

DEFINITION: two people engaging in sexual intercourse
at an altitude of no less than 5,280 feet (a mile above
the earth) in an airplane.

On February 11, 2007, Lisa Robertson, a Qantas flight attendant, was dis-
missed after having sex with actor Ralph Fiennes in a business class toilet
during a flight from Darwin to Mumbai on January 24, 2007. Robertson at
first denied the allegation, but subsequently admitted the encounter in an
interview with the Daily Mail. *She also said she had stayed with him at his*
Mumbai hotel.

−"HOW I LED RALPH FIENNES ASTRAY AT 35,000 FEET,"
DAILY MAIL, FEBRUARY 15, 2007

The setting: Business class in a Boeing 747, JFK to Frankfurt. ANITA,
a petite, redheaded executive, sits next to MATT, a prematurely bald-
ing junior attorney. Others in the cabin are asleep. As the scene opens,
a tall, imposing female FLIGHT ATTENDANT is clearing away
one set of martinis and crackers and setting down another.

MATT: Thank you.
[*The Flight Attendant exits, Matt eyeing her rump.*]
ANITA: . . . and the best invention is this fully reclining seat. A
good night's sleep between JFK and Frankfurt's gonna
make all the difference to my deal-sealing.
MATT *(sipping)*: That's not the only difference it can make.
ANITA: Tell me about it. My liaison, Crystal? She said she
joined the Club on one of these. Tokyo to Dubai.
MATT: You're not a member yourself?
[*Anita brushes crumbs from her ample but well-corseted bosom. The*
question discomfits her.]

ANITA: I met my ex on a red-eye from the Coast. We got sort of
    intimate but—

MATT: Kept your clothes on?

ANITA: We were in coach!

MATT *(polishing off his drink)*: Not a member.

ANITA: Then the weekend we broke up, I flew to Stockholm.
    There was this Swede—

MATT: Don't tell me. Lars.

ANITA: Fredrika.

[Matt chokes on his drink; recovers.]

ANITA: So I don't know if that—

[Matt pushes the attendant button. The Flight Attendant enters.]

FLIGHT ATTENDANT: May I help?

MATT: My seat partner and I have a question about the Club.

FLIGHT ATTENDANT: You're a member?

MATT: Of course! I— *(glances nervously at Anita)*. Actually,
    neither of us is. But we wondered if girl on girl counted.

FLIGHT ATTENDANT: Homophobia has no place in the Club.
    Muff diving counts.

ANITA: Knob polishing?

FLIGHT ATTENDANT *(nodding)*: But bottoms off, and not just
    fingers. With blankets, reclining seats . . . it's too easy.
    Everybody'd be in.

MATT: No mess, no risk, no membership.

FLIGHT ATTENDANT: That's the code. Glad to be of service.
    Another martini?

MATT *(winking)*: Later.

*[The Flight attendant shuts off the call button and exits,
tiptoeing.]*

ANITA: I knew you weren't a member.

MATT: I have one though.

[Boldly he takes Anita's hand, places it on his crotch.]

MATT: And if you brought him home, I'd love it.

ANITA: But then we'd be in Frankfurt, and no closer to joining.

MATT: Don't you need to—ah—go to the restroom?

[*Anita removes her hand and shakes out her blanket.*]

ANITA: Is that smelly stall the only option?

MATT: If you want to join.

ANITA: How do you know? You're not even a member.

MATT: You on the sink. Me standing up. I'm standing up right now.

ANITA (*pressing his recliner button*): Could you lie down?

MATT: That's a *huge* risk.

ANITA (*fiddling with Matt's belt buckle*): And a huge reward.

MATT: I don't even think nonmembers can initiate each other.

[*Anita reaches for the call button. Matt catches her hand, replaces it.*]

MATT: N-n-never mind. I'm sure we can. Especially if we— (*gasping as Anita continues*)—if we make use of the latest conveniences. Especially if we—

[*Anita has shifted onto Matt's seat and pulled her blanket over both of them. Straddling, she gently covers his mouth.*]

ANITA (*whispering*): If we go for . . . Mile High . . . Premium.

Curtain.

MILF

ZOË ROSENFELD

DEFINITION: Mom I'd Like to Fuck.

(*While looking at a picture of Stifler's mom*)
Guy #2: Dude, that chick's a MILF!
Guy #1: What to hell is that?
Guy #2: M-I-L-F—mom I'd like to fuck!
Guy #1: Yeah, dude! Yeah!

—FROM THE FILM *AMERICAN PIE*

The acronym MILF, whose letters stand for "Mother I'd Like to Fuck," seems to have caught on after its usage in the 1999 movie *American Pie*, about the sexual travails of a group of high school boys, though by most accounts the word was kicking around for many years prior to that. These days, the term usually means simply "hot mom" (which is why a woman can put her baby in a T-shirt that reads MY MOM'S A MILF without actually implying that her kid wants to have sex with her). Women may jokingly refer to themselves or to other women as MILFs, but at its core the term implies a male gaze, a male subject—particularly a young male. And though MILF most often refers to a hot mother of any age, the word also has a life—a lively one in the porn world—as a term for a sexually attractive woman from her late twenties to her early fifties, regardless of whether she has children.

The very existence of the term MILF suggests that a hot mother is the exception to the rule—or, as a witty friend once put it, "that most M's are people you wouldn't L to F." But why? The more one tries to unpack this simple pop-culture phrase, the more there seems to be to say about it. There are familiar terms—*hot mama*, *mamacita*—that equate sexiness with motherhood, and yet the idea of a sexual, sexually exciting mother still has an illicit air. Why do we see motherhood and sexuality as incompatible? What is the backdrop of expectations about mothers and their nondesirability against which the desirable MILF stands out?

Certainly, for some men, a whiff of the maternal in a woman kills their sexual response to her, and by the same token, a whiff of the sexual in a mother makes men uneasy. Is this need to desexualize mothers and see them as essentially wholesome related to a massive repressed Oedipal complex or perhaps to the old Madonna/whore dichotomy? In either case, it seems strange to lose sight of the fact that motherhood begins with sex. And to the extent that MILF implies an older woman, it also expresses the speaker's surprise that age and sexiness can coexist at all (reviews of movies that feature hot older women always comment on this as though it's a minor miracle). We're so used to equating looking good with looking young that we seem unable to pry the two apart and allow for the possibility that someone could look good—and sexually attractive—without looking youthful.

Insofar as motherhood often occurs within a stable relationship, a mother may be presumed to be off the market, not looking for a mate, and this apparent unavailability may add to the taboo that's explored by the term MILF (not to mention that many women also move away from courting young-male sexual attention when they become mothers). But a mother's lack of sexual currency is clearly about more than just her being perceived as unavailable. It seems that something about giving birth and nurturing a child (and particularly, making the child's needs a priority), for some men, places a woman outside the sexual fray.

Perhaps it's worth noting that celebrities whose professional identities depend on being hot have increasingly turned to scheduled C-sections for giving birth, thereby preserving their sexual image and leaving anyone who cares to picture their vagina with an image that is untouched by the ravages of birth, almost still virginal. We prize these slim, taut mothers who don't remind us of any of the messy realities of motherhood (the bigger, softer, looser body; the leaky breasts; the chaos and the resulting struggle to maintain one's equilibrium)—seemingly, the only way to be a hot mother is not to look like a mother at all.

Because a man is presumably throwing a woman a bone when he uses the term, and because a mother is presumably someone who desperately needs a compliment about her sexual worth, a woman is supposed to be flattered to be called a MILF. And though we may at times be flattered by the word, and some may even claim to find it empowering, most mothers are probably unsettled to discover that when people look at them, they see the mother first and then the woman. Maybe the real problem is our cultural imperative to be sexy at every juncture of our lives. We could all probably do with a bit of relief from the need to be hot all the time—at least in the rather limited way our society dictates. After all, there must be more than MILFdom to aspire to for women who see no contradiction between their roles as mothers and as sexual beings—something with more life, juice, verve, variety, possibility, and power in it. Maybe in a post-MILF world, we'll be able to be sexy in our own idiosyncratic ways, and motherhood will just be one of the many aspects of a woman—by no means the one that defines her sexual self. Maybe whatever ends up supplanting MILF will be something that encourages us to have fun, to play, something that reminds us that especially when it comes to sexuality, the many sides of ourselves represent not contradictions to be reconciled but multiple facets of who we are.

MISTRESS

TONI BENTLEY

DEFINITION: a woman who has a continuing extramarital
sexual relationship with one man, especially a man
who, in return for an exclusive and continuing liaison,
provides her with financial support.
AKA: really good friend, part-time pussy,
side-job, jelly-roll, concubine.

Famous mistresses:

Angie Dickinson (John Kennedy)
Blaze Starr (Earl K. Long)
Blaze Starr (John Kennedy)
Jennie Jerome (Edward VII of England)
Lola Montez (Ludwig I of Bavaria)

Anne Boleyn (Henry VIII of England)
Judith Campbell Exner (John Kennedy)
Lucy Mercer (Franklin Roosevelt)
Madame de Maintenon (Louis XIV of France)
Madame du Barry (Louis XV of France)
Donna Rice (Senator Gary Hart, presidential candidate)
Harriette Wilson (Duke of Wellington)
Jayne Mansfield (John Kennedy)
Madame de Pompadour (Louis XV of France)
Marilyn Monroe (John Kennedy)
Mary Pinchot Meyer (John Kennedy)

–DAVID TALBOT, "THE MOTHER OF ALL COVER-UPS,"
SALON, SEPTEMBER 15, 2004

Mistress (monarchist): what I have always wanted to be. Really.

Would I rather be Madame de Pompadour, beloved mistress to Louis XV, getting my portrait painted by François Boucher in my Versailles boudoir in my new pink, silk, ribboned bodice for the admiration of posterity? Or Louis's wife, Maria Leszczynska, who bore him ten children and took refuge in religion while the king took refuge in Mme. de Pompadour? God's voice is often heard, loud and clear, by the woman disappointed in love. (Or, as Liane de Pougy, the most beautiful courtesan of fin de siècle Paris, demonstrated, the convent can also be a place to rest after a lifetime of sexual festivities, suicide lovers, and too much jewelry.)

Closer to home, well, actually at home, I looked at my mother in the kitchen—cooking, cleaning, and crying—thinking there had to be another way. That's when Madame de Pompadour came to my rescue. A mistress gets what every wife wanted when she got married. Two words, and it's too late. The line crossed, the voice silenced, the erotic dead.

Here's the bottom line: a wife wears underwear, a mistress carries a thong in her evening bag (in case she needs it later).

Mistresses of old always had a story, their own story; wives were only part of their husband's story—and that's if he happened to be interesting. Mistresses always seemed so much more glamorous and mysterious than that other thing, the wife, or that ill-defined, unromantic, modern wife-in-waiting called a girl-friend. Skip the domestic, very important. Do your own laundry and let him, his wife, his assistant, or his maid do his. And when you're his mistress, you can get your own maid to wash, by hand, all that lovely French silk lingerie that he gave you. Thus preserving your manicure.

Being a man's mistress means he really wants you—too much trouble and money otherwise. Being a wife means he has you and will soon wish he didn't. A mistress remains true to herself, giving up little and getting plenty, while a wife gives up everything and gets little. A mistress is the magnet for those men with wives who aren't getting the fun, and those without wives who just want the fun.

Now, anything that you do together—Paris for shopping (thongs), and sex clubs (sans thong), Bayreuth for the *Ring* (thong on pillow), Baden-Baden for the waters (Wolford thongs)—he arranges. His people do all of it, you just say a sweet little yes or no when asked about the details. You will be queried about every detail because he now knows that you want to know everything—without asking. For planning, the wardrobe, the lingerie, the shoes, the furs, the fans—both kinds. Mistresses always have good sunglasses. Very dark, no rhinestones, that's a dead giveaway of a wannabe. Solid, dark, Audrey Hepburn in *Breakfast at Tiffany's*. And for God's sake, *no* tattoos. It dates your body and your ability to evoke eternity for him. Think Venus—Botticelli, Titian, Velázquez, de Milo, even Rubens if necessary (better armless and fat than tattooed). No art is too great to be your model. Being "in" now means you're "out" in every other century—a severe limitation.

The money? He can just deposit directly into your account at appropriate intervals. A good mistress is very, very grateful. For everything. The bracelets, the orchids, and all those little gifts you don't really like. Here's the poetry of it all: unlike a wife, who feels entitled and thus endlessly dissatisfied, a well-treated mistress *is* grateful—she is loved *and* being left alone—thereby giving her man what every man wants more than anything else (and that he can never give his wife)—her happiness. Making you happy is his desire, his job, his pleasure; it makes him hard. It is all those dissatisfied wives that make men run to divorce court, or to their happy, charming, witty, well-dressed mistress.

Of clothes and wit, a few words. Sweatpants are private, only for private, and panty hose simply don't exist, never were invented. If you own a pair of culottes, give up now and marry the first man who'll have you. Sexy, classy clothes are the mainstays, and walking the edge between those two is what separates the real mistress from a tart. On the other hand, a mistress is a tart, always walking the edge of slutdom in her stilettos, but never tripping over the line. Where, you ask, is the line? If you don't know, you're in over your head already.

But it is neither her sexiness nor her sophistication that ultimately steers her boat—and rings his bell. The tiller for this vessel is her wit. Now wit cannot be learned, only practiced. So if you are bright enough to know you have none, marry. (If you think you have some, but don't, well . . . may the mirage be a marriage.) But, if wit races through your mind like blood through your veins, then you can do it. The wit of a mistress can save herself, her man, and even his friends from the shame inherent in the shameless game of sex.

This is a basic road map. Remember, keep the domestic out—and laser, don't wax. If you're happy with shaving, I see a white picket fence in your future. Oh, yes, one other thing. Being a mistress is not for the fainthearted. All the clothes, and massages, and rubies, and mind-bending sex (he never quite has you + you never quite have him = consistent combustion) cannot make up for the loss, the inevitable loss. A mistress is not protected from heartache and heartbreak. Hurt, humiliation, and devastation will be yours—as they are his wife's. But you retain, in your pain, what she gave away. Hope. Dignity. Freedom. Courage, you see, to have these three is perhaps the most noted quality of a true mistress.

MONOGAMY

KAUI HART HEMMINGS

DEFINITION: 1. The practice or condition of having a single sexual partner during a period of time. 2. The practice or condition of being married to only one person at a time.
AKA: fidelity, coupledom.

Any intelligent woman who reads the marriage contract, and then goes into it, deserves all the consequences.

—ISADORA DUNCAN

I hear it early in the morning: the sex slap—that wet and lurid suction sound that occurs when thighs bang together then pull apart, together, apart. Whom am I having sex with so early in the morning? A townie or someone in my poetry class? A skater or that guy from Greenwich? The pothead from the dorm or the cokehead from Sigma Chi?

Why do I sleep with so many guys? Why not just one? Why can't I just commit to Brian, say, who possesses all of the above traits—skater, poet, pothead, and cokehead? Wealthy, but sloppy. He's, like, the perfect man.

I prepare myself, I get into the role. I am wild. I'm adaptable—I can drink a forty, wake and bake, go to the country club, play golf, go snowboarding, read, whatever. Guys love that I don't have needs, requests. I don't want to cuddle (but I do), I don't need their phone numbers (but I do), I don't want breakfast (but I do, preferably in public so all my other hookups can see I've done well for myself. I can be a girlfriend, too).

The slapping sound quickens. I wake up slowly, then fully. Something's not right. I am not in college. I open my eyes to see my toddler standing beside my bed, a huge grin on her face. She has poured K-Y jelly all over her hands and is frantically clapping.

"Sticky!" she says. "Funny!" Slap, slap, slap, slap.

"Oh my God," I say.

I nudge my husband. We laugh, kind of, almost embarrassed that it's our toddler making those sounds and not us. Our sex slaps aren't so loud anymore, not so frenzied, frequent, and desperate. They were in the early years of dating when I couldn't be monogamous and we had to have the kind of sex that teetered on the hysterical—a little angry, a little afraid, full of passion and humidity. For most of my life *monogamy* has been a dirty word, something unattainable, something horrible, just one body away from being alone. Being promiscuous was being smart—I was always insured. I had backup. And, in a way, it got me my husband. We met in a dive bar in Breckenridge, Colorado. We were twenty-two. He was playing pool, and a girl kept trying to hug him. He swung her out of his way and she accidentally kicked me in the face.

"Are you okay?" he asked. I slept with him an hour later.

My husband carries our daughter to the sink and she claps the entire time. Slap, slap, slap, slap, slap. I'm almost disappointed that this is the mess I've woken up to. I kind of miss the excitement, surprise, awkwardness, and sexiness of a one-night stand. Sometimes I see all these girls getting painted, blown out, waxed, and buffed, preparing, essentially, to get fucked, and a part of me misses the buildup, the expectation, the intensity.

When you don't stick with one person, you get to feel all sorts of things.

But then I remember the penises, all those penises you have to encourage and laud. All the bad penises you have to pretend look okay and feel okay, but you're really thinking, *Is that a penis in my mouth or a baby carrot?* I remember being with a new guy and enduring conversations like this:

Boy: "Take off that skirt, girl. They call me the plumber 'cause I can fix it."

Me: "I'm not wearing a skirt."

Or this:

Boy: "Look at that. My mojo is rising."

Me: "Wow."

Or this:

Boy: "Have you ever done it wheelbarrow style?"

Me: "No."

Boy: "What about tractor?"

I try to envision this, but I can't. "No," I say. "But I've done it big-rig style." This silences him. I have no idea what I'm talking about.

Lastly:

Boy: "Do you want to sit in the cockpit?"

Me: "That's so lame." Bottle of wine later. "I'm ready for takeoff, Captain."

I could fill a book with romance.

Though it took me a while, I finally learned the big secret: *monogamy* is not a dirty word. Monogamy means one penis. *Un chauve à col roulé*—bald one with a turtleneck. *Uno uccello. Uno chilito* (also served at Taco Bell). *Der phallus* (*Achtung!* It's a little-known fact that the average German penis can't fill the average condom).

Now, I only have one penis to deal with, and it no longer expects that much from me. In fact it's okay with a movie and a bowl of my coconut curry. It's okay with my ugly pajamas. Our toddler will most likely be the only person getting lubed up today, and this penis is okay with that. I don't have to primp or wax; I don't even have to bathe. I am the only thing this penis has.

My daughter's hands are clean.

"Cereal time," she announces. "The whole family!" She says this every morning, and it never gets old. We walk the same route to the kitchen. I pour the cereal into three bowls. Andy gets the milk. Then we sit in our chairs and share our morning in utter exclusivity.

NECROPHILIA

KIM ADDONIZIO

DEFINITION: obsession with and usually erotic
interest in or stimulation by corpses.

Necrophilia is an erotic attraction to corpses, with the most common motive cited by psychologists as the attempt to gain possession of an unresisting or nonrejecting partner.

—KATHERINE RAMSLAND, *ALL ABOUT NECROPHILES*, CRIME LIBRARY

Necrophilia is a term that is commonly misunderstood. You probably think it means being so attracted to dead people that you skip the dating part and go straight to their place with a little wine. They won't come to your place since they're worse than couch potatoes; they're, like, gurney potatoes. You probably imagine walking into a cold, smelly basement that has awful feng shui, spritzing with a good air freshener, and getting busy.

I, myself, misunderstood this word until one day, a year or so after the breakup of a long-term relationship, I realized that it was meant as a metaphor. Just as in the Bible. When Jesus said to become as little children, he didn't mean to throw your burned Lean Cuisine on the kitchen floor of the apartment you rented after letting your ex keep the house. Jesus didn't mean you should stomp on your dinner, screaming and crying. As for the wine that is Christ's blood, if I can offer an explication—which is the same as an explanation only more complete—what it means is, go ahead and drink the whole fucking bottle of pinot if it makes you feel less lonely. Just so we're clear on that.

What necrophilia really is, is this: sexual obsession for men who are incapable of having a real relationship because they have no heart in their chest cavity. What they have is an empty socket that will electrocute you if you try to get close and touch it or maybe just point a flashlight that way to see what's wrong. These men can't have feelings for anything but girl-on-girl porn, American League baseball, and the thought of the fortune they are going to make when their ship, which is lost at sea and listing badly with several leaks in its rotting hull, magically cruises in.

Exempli gratia, which means "free example," as in the better markets where you can get cubes of cave-aged Gruyère and pieces of artichoke, sun-dried-tomato pesto sausage and make a slim but upscale meal of it; e.g., in my single, i.e., oppressively solitary, state I developed a crush on this dead guy, of course before I realized he was dead. That's how you get in trouble: they look so lifelike. He was charming and talented, and about a week after we met he e-mailed me *u r beautiful* and that's pretty much all it took. I'd been alone for a year at that point, and—how shall I phrase this correctly?—living alone is a hellish nightmare (i.e., *id est*, a dream arousing feelings of intense fear, horror, and distress, e.g., you feel as though you are trapped in a small, dark crawl space with someone who is repeatedly hitting you on the forehead with a hammer), and I am still trying to wake up (cf *nonketotic coma*, *vegetative state*).

Tell me *u r beautiful* and I'll probably fall for you, dead or alive.

After this guy and I saw each other three times and I gave him two prolonged courtesy sucks (I am not one to tire easily, but even I was reaching the limits of my politeness), followed by one bouncing of the brillo, or dancing of the buttocks jig, and at no time did I experience *la petite mort*; and after he didn't call for two weeks and when he did it was only to tell me about the baseball game he went to with his friend who sounded retarded, I mean that metaphorically and excuse me if it's the wrong word—well, then I finally realized I had encountered a bona fide dead guy. My own case was confirmed by *The American Heritage Stedman's Medical Dictionary*. I had an "abnormal fondness" for being in his presence; I had "sexual contact with" and "erotic desire for" his body. I was a necrophiliac, a necromaniac, textbook case. I had all the symptoms, and no cure was mentioned.

I consoled myself with the thought that I was definitely sick, but he was definitively dead—*id est*, asleep, belly-up, bloodless, blooey, checked out, cut off, gone, paralyzed, spiritless, stiff, torpid, unresponsive. So maybe he did carry me to bed once and was a really good, in fact excellent, kisser; to him I was only a chick (I'm using slang here that I hope you understand): a pair of tits and a nice ass in tight jeans, heavy combat boots, and a cute hoodie. The e-mails I agonized over, trying to hit just the right tone—provocative nonchalance—were living side by side with the pervy forwards his infantile, also deceased or at least comatose, friends were passing along. Smiling snowmen with carrots for dicks. Jokes about hillbillies: Why do they always have sex "doggie style"?—because their womenfolk don't like watching NASCAR upside down.

Hahaha.

When I realized how stupid, that is to say how brainless, dazed, foolish, naive, and obtuse I'd been, I wanted to put a stake through his heart.

Then I remembered he didn't have one.

A corpse is pretty much empty. The blood gets drained out, the organs are harvested, the brain is plopped into a jar for the benefit of science. A corpse is not even really a body, only the outside of one. A lot of them look pretty sexy when they're embalmed: beautiful, unreachable models of imperfection. To a certain kind of person, they may present a challenge, a hope, a profound messianic desire: to raise the dead, to lift them from their graves and rented rooms and broken couches, brush them off, and dress them in better clothes.

If you are a necrophiliac, you know what I mean.

They are irresistible. They shimmer with energy, though they are inert. In the chill air, they seem to form clouds of breath that take the shape of the possibility of true connection.

NUDITY

MICHAEL LOWENTHAL

DEFINITION: devoid of a natural or conventional covering;
especially : not covered by clothing or a drape.
AKA: naked, au naturel, bare-assed, exposed,
in the buff, in the raw, buck naked.

The English painter Henry Scott Tuke (1858–1929) is mainly known for various depictions of boys and young men who swim, dive and lounge, usually naked, on a boat or on the beach, sometimes in a traditional "alibi" context, but after 1890 often just naturalistic, usually sexually innocent scenes with local youths in the Cornish fishing port of Falmouth where he settled in 1885.

Norman Rockwell's painting No Swimming *adorned the cover of the* *June 4, 1921 edition of the* Saturday Evening Post *with boys in various* *states of undress escaping from the local authorities.*

—WWW.ETYMONLINE.COM/

As a teenager I went to a Quaker summer camp whose founder transformed *that of God in every person* into a startlingly literal creed: because we all contain the Divinity within us, our bodies must themselves be divine; why, then, should naked flesh shame us? Counselors taught us Franklin D. Roosevelt's Four Freedoms for which it's worth going into battle—freedom of speech, of worship, from want, from fear—and an equally worth-defending Fifth Freedom: from clothing. Everyone, from the youngest dog-paddler to the gray-haired (and I mean the hair *down there*) maintenance man, was encouraged to swim—and play Frisbee, and, hey, let's weed the garden!—in the buff.

I was hammerstruck at just this age by lust for other boys, and our camp's clothes-free policy gave me endless fantasy fodder. At camp, I first saw foreskins, hard-ons that weren't my own, fiddleheads of manly pubic hair; at camp, I first slapped a boy's bare ass. My groin throbs when I recall our fevered version of Greased Watermelon, the eponymous fruit replaced by a naked nine-year-old, his every inch of skin slicked with Crisco; tossed into the lake, he was tugged by other boys (also nude and, as the game went on, increasingly lubricated) trying to haul him to one of two team docks and thereby "score."

Nowadays, when I tell these tales, my gay pals *ooh* with envy. But summer camp, for me, was no sexual paradise. Quite the contrary, it was a purgatory: I was trapped between desire and dread. Precisely because the chances to look at flesh were so frequent, I was forced to hone my skills of avoidance—lest anyone catch me and brand me a queer.

Thus began my linking of heightened availability (or its

semblance) with heightened isolation. Bathhouses, nude beaches, strike a mournful chord within me: all that stripping down, it seems, just expedites the process of people's deciding whom to overlook. And if skinny-dipping was once daring enough to mark my camp as kooky, now, thanks largely to the Internet's abundance, no one seems to bat an eye when somebody bares all. Would my camp's founder be happy? Am I?

It's fun being able to Google, say, *swimwear fetish*—or *nudism*—and get a zillion hits. And for those who've long hidden less sanctioned predilections, the sense of validation and relief must be deep—just as I was soothed, in those Fifth Freedom summers, to find that my equipment wasn't the smallest or the largest, and to learn that the fact of having glimpsed me in the raw didn't seem to change how my friends *saw* me.

But does all our self-exposing truly bring our selves closer? I know guys whose dick pics are e-mailed far and wide, but who, if you met them in a coffee shop or church and asked them what they dream of, what makes them laugh and cry, would stammer (or stomp off in a snit). At any hour of day I could sign on to Manhunt and browse through a thousand nudie shots of willing men, each of whom is similarly browsing. Maybe this should thrill me or give comfort, but it doesn't. I picture a thousand men at a thousand sallow screens, sitting in their thousand lonely rooms.

So, as the barriers to desire seem to fall—stripped away like summer campers' swimsuits—I'm skeptical about our liberation. My camp, I have learned, in the years that I attended it, was veritably a nest of pedophiles, drawn there by the crowds of nude children. The Fifth Freedom was for some of my friends anything but freeing.

O

OBSESSION

SARAH BIRD

DEFINITION: the domination of one's thoughts or
feelings by a persistent idea, image, desire, etc.
AKA: craze, jones, mania.

*Forward and Buck believe that rejection is the trigger of obsessive love. They
state four conditions to help identify it, namely, a painful and all-
consuming preoccupation with a real or wished-for lover, an insatiable longing either to possess or be possessed by the target of their obsession, rejection
by or physical and/or emotional unavailability of their target, and being
driven to behave in self-defeating ways by this rejection or unavailability.*

–S. FORWARD AND C. BUCK,

OBSESSIVE LOVE: WHEN IT HURTS TOO MUCH TO LET GO (1991)

Crushes, there had been crushes before, the sedate, unspoken
crushes of a shy Catholic girl. Crushes made you trim your split
ends and position yourself fetchingly over the Bunsen burner in
chemistry lab.

Obsession, on the other hand, obsession made you rearrange
your DNA.

Obsession may be called "love at first sight." If you do not
know the individual you are obsessed with, and he or she is a
celebrity, and you stalk him or her, your obsession will be termed
erotomania and you will be put in jail.

But true obsession, my obsession, stops time so that once
again I am sixteen, a studious, devout girl wearing a pink paisley
voile blouse and Shalimar perfume. I hover again on the edge of
the floor at a dance hall in what once was a theme park named for

an Indian scout in the *Red Ryder* series: Little Beaver Town. Little Beaver Town is now the place where Albuquerque teenagers go to get high, get knifed, get laid, get wild. The band is Vic Gabriel and the Pallbearers. They are playing "Little Latin Lupe Lu" when I first see him. At the speed of light, as fast as the rods and cones can translate his image, I am obsessed.

Obsession will make a shy girl do anything if it will bring her one fraction of an inch closer to the deliriously handsome object of her desire. She will not eat, she will not sleep, she will stop making straight A's and wearing a brown wool scapular beneath her blouse. She, uncoordinated and always chilly, always nervous, will become a skier so as to snowplow repeatedly into his path.

She will spangle her cheeks with pink comets' tails of glittery blush. She will varnish her lips with the glossiest of glosses. She will burnish her eyelids with iridescent lilac shadow. She will make her face a reflective surface, a mirror, in which he can see whatever he wants to see. She will become whatever will draw him to her.

Beware the answered prayer. My obsession accepts the offering of my self, my unconditional adoration. We have a tumultuous affair based on the fiction that I am as wild and heedless as he. Maintaining this lie and holding his wavering attention requires ever greater doses of manic extroversion. I scuba dive off coral reefs in the China Sea. I hitchhike alone from Manzanilla, Mexico, to San Francisco. I work as a go-go dancer in Tokyo, au pair in Tignes, France, a botanical-garden guide in Cap Roig, Spain. He gives me crabs; I give him herpes.

For seven years, I am obsessed. And then I am not. Not with him. I have a new obsession. This one only lasts six years. I finally awake from these dark spells, blink, look around, and realize that my young womanhood is over. Mindful of my propensity to plunge too deeply, I never again venture into the bottomless waters of obsession. From that day to this, I have been careful not to get in over my head. I have splashed contentedly in safe waters, always within sight of shore.

Married long and happily, I believe that I am done forever with obsession. Obsession, however, is not done with me. Some mornings I still wake drenched in longing, and it takes me a few seconds to realize that I have, once again, dreamed about the deliriously handsome boy I first saw at Little Beaver Town almost forty years ago.

ONE-NIGHT STAND

BLISS BROYARD

DEFINITION: a sexual encounter limited to a single occasion.
AKA: shag, fling, hooking up, beer-goggles.
The morning after: walk of shame.

According to the Durex survey (2003) 54% of Americans say they have had a real one-night stand. The country with the lowest percentage is Taiwan: 20% and the highest is Vietnam with 75%.

–WWW.DUREX.COM

The term began in the theater to describe a single performance of a play or show in a particular location, which is fitting because, in its sexual sense, a one-night stand features a single performance of me. It's the role of an evening. A character that comes (one hopes) and then disappears. With no past on record or future in sight, you can be someone . . . not else exactly but more: more risky, greedy, or servile than you'd normally be. Because your partner also exists solely in that single time and space, a one-night stand holds all the potential ingredients for improvisational genius—a narrowing of focus to this specific moment, a heightened responsiveness to its textures and turns, and a freedom from dog-eared scripts and past disappointments. But like any improvised act, the one-night stand doesn't lend itself to encore performances.

About ten years ago, I went one night to a bar in the East Village with the specific intention of having a one-night stand. I'd never done that before, but I'd recently ended a brief relationship with someone whom I suspected of being a little too crazy in a bad way. Sure enough, he'd begun bombarding me with hostile phone calls and accusatory letters that might have been appropriate if he'd found me in bed with his best friend after a few decades of marriage. I stopped answering my phone and tore up his letters without opening them, but I still felt contaminated by our contact, as if his craziness might be incubating inside me. The antidote, I thought, was to put some flesh between us.

The handsome stranger in the bar was a friend of some friends of mine, which made him seem a little safer, along with his having just moved to New York from California where he'd been a pistachio farmer. After a little flirting in a photo booth, I turned to him and said, "So, you know, I came in here tonight planning on picking someone up." His eyes widened and then he quickly smiled to hide his surprise. "Gotcha," he said with a decisive nod, and we went back to flirting and drinking.

It didn't take long for him to press me into a dark corner and begin kissing my neck in between narrating all the ways that he could delight me. "That sounds nice," I whispered back, and before I knew what was happening, the handsome stranger had dragged me across the bar into the solitary bathroom where he lifted me up, deposited me on the sink, raised my skirt, sank to his knees, and got down to business. But the bright fluorescent light was shining in my eyes, I was pretty sure that he hadn't locked the door, and I'd left my purse hanging, unattended, on a barstool outside. Also, in the middle of our gymnastics, the stranger had banged his head on the edge of the paper-towel dispenser and blood was running down his forehead.

I called for a time-out, and he looked confused. *Hadn't I said that this was what I wanted?* "Not here," I told him. "Let's go back to my place." But as we were paying our tab, I began to have second thoughts. I turned to the stranger and asked him whether we were going to see each other again, if he was going to ask me out on a date or take me to dinner. Without so much as a thoughtful pause, he looked me in the eye and said, "At this moment, it's not dinner that I'm thinking of having with you." Fair enough. And with that, I let myself go—the part of me that felt judgmental toward women who hopped into bed with someone, that turned shy in front of a new lover, that believed in self-disclosure as foreplay.

The handsome stranger and I had sex in the back of the taxi cab, and then again in the hallway at my place, and then again standing on the bed in order to better see my reflection in the mirror across the room. The woman with her hair plastered to the side of her face with sweat, saliva, and God knows what else was me all right—a dreamlike version whose authenticity felt so persuasively real as to make my waking life seem like a dream. After we lay back down, I began to sob in the stranger's arms. "I'm sorry," I said, "but it's been so long since I've been touched." What I meant was that it had been so long—perhaps forever?—since this buried part of me had been touched. And I was both shaken and exhilarated by her appearance.

But when the stranger *did* want to see me again, I could no longer conjure that dream self. Over our ensuing two-year relationship, we had plenty of good sex, sometimes even with a similar level of abandon, but I could never completely divorce myself from everyday life and all the competing roles it required of me. Unable to live up to the woman I'd been during our one-night stand, I was reduced to a pale understudy of myself, bluffing my way through our sexual encounters. And this self-deceit, more than anything else, eventually came between us.

ORGY

DANIELLE WOOD

DEFINITION: a revel involving unrestrained
indulgence, especially sexual activity.

*At the request of the Catholic Church, a three-day sex orgy to be held near
Rio de Janeiro was canceled last Friday. So instead I spent the weekend
cleaning my apartment.*

−TINA FEY

Orgy is a word that fills your mouth like a wild oyster that's just a
little too big to (comfortably) swallow. It rests in your hands like
a pomegranate: a round, ripe gourd of a word, full of fruity pips
and sweet, dribbling juices capable of engendering a plethora of
meanings. For only relatively recently has *orgy* come to specifically
refer to a sexual free-for-all. Back when Bacchus was gobbling
grapes, *orgy* signified the whole kit and caboodle of hedonistic
excess: eating, drinking, fucking, *and* dancing.

Who knows which of these activities was foremost for the
"unsteady fairies" in J. M. Barrie's *Peter Pan*, who encounter Peter,
asleep upon their path, when they are said to be "on their way home
from an orgy"? Was this unsteadiness the result of knee-trembling
activities or simply a consequence of too much moshing and elder-
berry wine? We do not know the answer to this question, but we do
know that the story's chief fairy, Tinker Bell, wears her skeleton
leaf gown "cut low and square" to show off her figure. Further, we
know that this figure is "slightly inclined to *embonpoint*," which
might indicate an ass generous enough to be shared around.

In contemporary usage, *orgy* continues to refuse monogamy.
We might like to pin it down to a lithe tangle of naked limbs, a
symphony of sucking, a cornucopia of variously filled orifices,

but *orgy* is a swinger. Promiscuous. Omnivorous. Ready, willing, and able to be pressed into the service of myriad miscellaneous pleasures. One might be said to indulge in an orgy of shopping, an orgy of chocolate, an orgy of sunbathing, an orgy of gossip. But not, I think, an orgy of ironing, or accountancy, or root-canal dentistry. Which makes me think that the tidiest way to define *orgy* is as a word, used by killjoys, to denote any kind of pleasurable event to which they have not been invited.

PANTY FETISH

THOMAS O'MALLEY

DEFINITION: fetish—something, such as a material object
or a nonsexual part of the body, that arouses sexual desire
and may become necessary for sexual gratification.

- *In February, a fifty-four-year-old man in Japan was arrested for stealing and hoarding more than 4,000 pairs of women's panties.*

- *In March, a twenty-four-year-old man in Washington state was found with more than 1,500 pieces of women's undergarments, including panties and bras.*

- *In May, Colorado police invited women to identify, by viewing photos, 1,300 undergarments stolen from laundry rooms near Colorado State University by a forty-three-year-old man.*

–D. A. KOLODENKO, SAN DIGO CITYBEAT, 11.06.07,
WWW.SDCITYBEAT.COM

PANTY FETISH: A STORY

I sit on the floor of my bedsit arranging the eighteen Sainsbury food storage bags on the ground before me. Twenty years have passed since I pilfered my first pair of used panties, and in more recent years I've added a multitude of similarly styled white cotton thongs from different exes and their various laundry baskets. I don't know exactly how or when my obsession with panties began, merely that one day I stood in the alleyway behind St. John's lunch hall with the understanding that for 50p Lisa Johnson would show me her knickers.

Give me the money first, she said, and when Lisa asked, two years older than me and exhibiting all the detached and severe maturity of a woman, I barely hesitated. I handed over my 50p piece, slick from my sweating hand. With a bored look on her face she grasped the hem of her skirt, hoisted it above her waist, and thrust her pelvis at me. It was over in a moment, and then, with severe propriety, Lisa was straightening her skirt again. I wasn't exactly sure of what I'd seen: the briefest of white panty, a flash of soft inner thigh, the flowered edge of a waistband, Lisa's pale, goose-pimpled bottom, the prominence and slivered shadow of something more mysterious and disturbing. I was embarrassed and my head thrummed with blood.

Well? she said, only slightly glaring.

Can I see it again?

Not for that fifty p you can't, you little toss. It'll cost you.

Seeing my condition, Lisa Johnson took pity on me. She reached under her skirt, eased her panties over her narrow hips, down her legs, and handed them to me.

The heat of her remained in her panties. The hairs on my arms sparked as if with a static charge. Beneath my fingers, the soft, porous texture of the cotton. I stretched the waistband and peered into their interior. The cloven impression of her secret folds of flesh lay in the white crotch winking up at me. I inhaled her most intimate of secretions. I was smitten and enthralled; destroyed and obliterated.

Look, if you can get a fiver by Friday, we can do it again, Lisa said. And I promise I won't rush.

I can't explain why Lisa Johnson did what she did, and now it no longer seems important. All I know is that she ruined me. At the age of twelve I was ruined forever. In that moment and in the weeks that followed a strange and sick desperation fueled and possessed me as our perverse ritual continued. I would have clobbered a geriatric pensioner on her way home from the dole office and made off with her handbag for the five quid that would allow me to look up Lisa Johnson's skirt again.

Slowly, I make my way through my storage bags, drawing each panty to my face and holding it there, saying the name of their owners aloud: Teresa, Katherine, April . . . and inhaling their smell, the dry and chalky stains of their juice. But sadly the muskiness of a woman is mostly gone from them—now they are merely old, mildewy-dank things in need of washing. I can still see Lisa wiggling her waist, raising her legs, and stepping out of her panties, and watching me as I stared into them and then as I placed them into my pocket.

You're a right dirty little wanker, she'd said, smiling, a label that fixed me then and there and for the rest of my young adulthood. I was a right dirty little wanker, and Lisa Johnson not only detected this in me, but also the aberrant gene that allowed such dirtiness to transcend the normal dirty compulsions of most prepubescent boys. As a right dirty little wanker, I was in a class all my own.

And then as simply and as impulsively as it had begun, it ended. Lisa Johnson and her family moved from their navvy row house in the Charles Dickens ward—I was never sure of to where, perhaps Derby or Stoke—somewhere in the middle of the country—and I never saw Lisa again, that is, until she appeared like an apparition on the bus the other day. Over twenty years had passed since I'd last seen her, and now we were sharing the #24A double-decker from the Portsea docks to Southsea. I sat behind her and had absently looked her way as she stood for her stop. The bus was already slowing when I recognized the angled profile of her face, the same long auburn hair.

Lisa? I said, clutching the bar rest above the seat so that my knuckles shone white, and then she turned to me. An unprotected smile came to her face, and when she spoke my name, I was filled with an immense happiness. Perhaps I wasn't the pervert I'd believed I was; perhaps I could find a way through all this and on to a decent, well-adjusted, productive life where the Lisas of the past considered me a decent and worthy man. These thoughts came to me then but only fleetingly. Mostly I saw a vivid picture of us as twelve- and fourteen-year-olds and of Lisa lifting her skirt and squatting above me as I lay upon the ground.

And Lisa must have seen this also—was it in my expression or in my eyes? Had I leered lasciviously? And if so, was this an unconscious and involuntary tic of my perversion? It was as if she had just stepped into the theater of my mind and seen what has always been there—the horrid sickness of my nature—for, just as quickly, she reddened and a look of disgust came to her face.

For God's sake, she spat. Grow up, would you? We were bloody children!

As she made her way to the stairs, I couldn't help but stare at her bottom, at the visible panty line hugging such voluptuous cheeks—where had they been all those years ago!—and pulled by gravity into the generous and deep divide between, toward that rich, moist seam, that heavenly lubricious center.

I complete my inventory, and as an added touch before I place them in their Sainsbury bags and at the rear of a shelf in the hot-water closet, I fold each panty gently in pink tissue paper. I hesitate with Patricia Tanner's pastel blue G-string, spread it open in my hands, and bring it to my face. As I hold it there, inhaling deeply, I think of Lisa Johnson on the bus the other day and the sad pervert that I've become, still obsessed by the memory of her cotton-covered crotch twenty-odd years after she'd first lifted her school skirt and flashed me her divine knickers.

PHALLUS

PAGAN KENNEDY

DEFINITION: 1 : a symbol or representation of the penis. 2 : penis.

A sculpted and polished phallus found in a German cave is among the earliest representations of male sexuality ever uncovered, researchers say. The 20cm-long, 3cm-wide stone object, which is dated to be about 28,000 years old, was buried in the famous Hohle Fels Cave near Ulm in the Swabian Jura. Its life size suggests it may well have been used as a sex aid by its Ice Age makers, scientists report.

—JONATHAN AMOS, BBC NEWS SCIENCE REPORTER

I was dangling from a chin-up bar, trying to haul myself up one more time. My new boyfriend, Kevin, sprawled in an armchair below, reading his book and pretending not to watch my display.

"So," I said, after I'd jumped down. "How many chin-ups can *you* do?"

In every relationship, I want to wear the pants. I want what Jacques Lacan calls the phallus, that magic wand that confers power and privilege on whoever wields it. I look like the last person whom you'd expect to have a phallus. I'm a petite woman with an insipid freckled face, and therefore people tend to assume I must be perky and Kathie-Lee-Gifford-ish. But no. I'm more the type to challenge Kathie Lee Gifford to an arm-wrestling match.

Kevin and I had only been dating for a month. We were still in that period of courtship where the phallus was up for grabs—though not the real phallus, of course, because they're not detachable.

This morning, I'd showed up at his apartment with my power drill, ostensibly so that I could repair his kitchen cabinets. But mostly, I wanted to brandish the drill in front of Kevin—that big tool I had bought at Home Depot, twelve volts, twenty-one drill bits. While I worked in the kitchen, he went off to the bedroom, to escape the racket and read books on postcolonial theory. After I put down the drill, I noticed he seemed awfully quiet in there. Uh-oh. I knew that kind of silence from other boyfriends. I assumed he was lurking in the bedroom, nursing his wounded masculinity. After all, my power drill was so *very* big. But then he called out, "Hey, honey, while you're at it, could you fix the toilet?"

So it turned out he was okay with my power drill. We'd passed over that hurdle. But what would happen if I trash-talked him? That's exactly what I was doing now, as I jumped down from the chin-up bar that hung in his living-room doorway. "Are you scared?" I jeered. "Are you too lazy to even get up there and try to beat me?"

"Yes," he said, and he let his head loll on the back of the chair.

"What do you mean 'yes'?"

"Yes, I am too lazy." Indeed, he looked quite comfortable drooping across the chair, with a book tented on his stomach.

I hadn't expected this tactic. Any one of my past boyfriends would have been up on that chin-up bar by now. Kevin, however, went back to reading about the sovereignty of the modern nation-state; he even made a note in the book's margin, as if to prove to me just how he absorbed he was in that little printed world, a world in which no one was trying to make him do chin-ups.

I prodded his leg with the toe of my shoe. "Yeah? And what if I'm more of a man than you?" It was a mean thing to say. It was also a question of real concern to me. What if I was more of a man than he was? Could we possibly love each other, even so? Or would this relationship flame out the way the others had.

He laughed, shaking his head. "Look, if you want to be the man in this relationship, go ahead. Because I'm not interested in that role. It's too much work."

"Seriously?" I said, leaning down, hands on his shoulders, my eyes lasering into his.

"Yes," he said, then shrugged me off. "Okay, sweetie, I have to finish this." He stuck the book in front of his face.

For the first time ever, a man had simply handed over the phallus to me without a fight. I pictured it as a light saber, glowing orange, slung in the holster along the side of my leg. In my imagination, I was prancing around the room, drawing the light saber and waving it over my head, with a mujahideen flourish.

Then doubt set in. Had he really given me the phallus?

"So, if I'm the man, does that mean you're the woman?" I asked.

"No. I'm a man, too. But you're the alpha male."

"Really?" I strutted around in front of his chair, but then stopped midstrut. "Does this mean we're a gay couple?"

"I guess so. Whatever." He yanked off the cap of his pen and marked another passage in his book.

"But how come you don't want to be alpha?"

"Pagan, I like to watch my hockey games. I like to read. Occasionally, I like some KFC Crispy Chicken. That's really all I need to be happy. If you want to run around and conquer the world and—" Here he waved his hand in the air, in a series of figure eights, to indicate my grand ambitions. "Personally, it sounds like too much work. So go ahead. Be the alpha. Knock yourself out."

And that's how Kevin handed over the phallus for good. It was a stroke of genius on his part. Because once I owned it, I kind of forgot about the phallus—the metaphorical one, that is. It no longer seemed important.

Now, it's five years later. Kevin and I live together. He's working in the room next door; I can hear the clicks of his laptop keyboard. I'm here in my office, typing away on my laptop. And the phallus? I'm not sure where I put it last. Maybe I left in the back of the bedroom closet, underneath an old pair of sweatpants, where it collects dust and rusts away into nothing.

PHEROMONES

MAUD CASEY

DEFINITION: a chemical secreted by an animal that influences the behavior or development of others of the same species, often functioning as an attractant of the opposite sex.

San Francisco, March 20, 2002—Women's perfume laced with synthetic pheromones acts as a sexual magnet and increases the sexual attractiveness of women to men, San Francisco State University researchers concluded in a study appearing in the current issue of the quarterly journal Physiology and Behavior.

The study, the first of its kind in the world to independently test a sex attractant pheromone for women, showed that of the 36 women tested, 74 percent of those wearing their regular perfume with the pheromone saw an overall increase in three or more of the following sociosexual behaviors: frequency of kissing, heavy petting and affection, sexual intercourse, sleeping next to their partner, and formal dates with men.

—NORMA MCCOY, LISA PITINO, SFSU

PHEROMONES

1. On *Star Trek*, used by the female of the green-skinned Orion species to make men do their bidding and to give other women headaches.

2. Shot out of the helmet of Hank Pym, aka Giant-Man, in order to communicate with ants.

3. Were hanging heavy in the air that summer Myrna's best friend's older brother, Mike, and his best friend—called Red for no apparent reason—no longer spoke of the lady Orions and Giant-man. In Mike's basement bedroom, Farrah Fawcett tossing her hair from the wall, hard button nipples pressing eternally against that red bathing suit, Mike and Red talked instead about pussy fingers. Myrna and her best friend, who insisted these days on being called by her full name, Angelica, had learned a lot sitting on the plaid couch in the basement while pretending to watch TV. (A) Pussy finger referred to the middle finger, though, when pluralized, could also include index and ring fingers. (B) A girl who went to a different high school was letting both Mike and Red finger-fuck her providing one left the room while the other did the deed (Mike's word, from the AC/DC song).

Myrna and Angelica once saw this girl at Putt-Putt gazing out over the Putt-Putt lake, preparing for a difficult shot. She looked fierce and knowledgeable, as if she'd been through a war. They followed her around the course, and everywhere she'd just been smelled like Charlie perfume and cinnamon gum, with a hint of fresh dirt.

Sometimes while Myrna and Angelica watched *The Love Boat*, Myrna thought about Mike and Red and their pussy fingers and the fierce, knowledgeable girl and her sedimentary layers of smell. She thought of the poster on the wall opposite Farrah: a fake tennis-playing woman in a fake tennis-playing dress on a fake tennis court, an elaborate ruse (a word Myrna and Angelica used as often as possible) for her to scratch a perfect crescent of ass cheek, revealing her underwearlessness. The rest of her ass's nakedness lurked just out of view, like everything else that summer Myrna—all nipples (squishy, not hard-pressing buttons) and just on the verge of curves—first got her period. She and Angelica tried to synchronize their cycles by rubbing their armpit sweat under each other's nose because they'd read an article that said you could, but it didn't work, which was a problem because the article also said that women who didn't like each other wouldn't sync, but then they found out you have to live together in places such as prisons, bordellos, or convents. Still, it caused tension that summer Myrna's body was no longer a house of purity and wonder (Look, I'm double-jointed! Look, my tongue is upside-down!), but a house that magically generated new, secret rooms. As *The Love Boat* couples fell in love on the Aloha deck somewhere off of Acapulco because love was in the air, Myrna's body would abduct her like the aliens in the Sunday TV movie who abducted humans to perform navel probes for information to take back to their planet. It made her sneak away from Angelica and run down the middle of the street in the dark until her heart pounded in her mouth and she thought she might die and it might be fun.

"Where'd you go?" Angelica would ask when Myrna returned, panting. "You missed the beginning of *Fantasy Island* when they introduce everyone."

"Nowhere." The secret made Myrna miss her best friend already so she would sit close and steal sniffs of Angelica's hair, which smelled like the shampoo they both used and overripe banana, with the slightest trace of oregano.

One afternoon, after Mike and Red returned from the fierce, knowledgeable girl's house, they invited Myrna and Angelica into the damp basement bedroom.

"What do you want?" Angelica asked. She was tough. She had recently let a boy feel her boobs.

"We want to play you a song," Red said as if he were saying he wanted to finger-fuck them both simultaneously with all of his pussy fingers.

"Yeah, right." Still, Angelica took Myrna by the hand and pulled her into the dank, thrilling smell of chewing-tobacco spit and boy sweat.

Mike lifted the arm of the turntable delicately, placing the needle expertly into the groove of a record.

You need coolin'. If the smell of chewing-tobacco spit and boy sweat could talk, that's what it would say.

"Zeppelin's first U.S. single," Mike said, and for an innocent minute it seemed as though this were only a rock-and-roll lecture. "Nineteen sixty-nine. Their only U.S. Top Ten hit."

Way down inside. The chewing-tobacco spit and boy sweat played a mean guitar solo.

"They stole this shit from Willie Dixon," Red said.

"Fuck you."

"Fuck your mother harder."

"Hey, that's my mother, too," Angelica said. "Fuck your mother."

"Okay, that's it." Red gave Mike a now look. As fast as he was straddling Angelica, Mike was astride Myrna. "Smell." They shoved their pussy fingers in the girls' faces. Whole lotta love. It wasn't pure fish as they'd said. It was the smell of the music. It was the smell of electricity. It was a smell wave, alive and undulating: sour, sweet, cinnamon gum, Charlie perfume, fresh dirt, Slim Jims, chewing-tobacco spit, boy sweat. It was the smell of mystery and possibility and fate.

Was Farrah moaning?

Mike and Red rolled off Myrna and Angelica.

"That's Page playing a theremin, man," Mike said.

"A theremin, not a theremin man," Angelica said.
"Get the fuck out, Angie."

In the old-smelling book Myrna found in the library the next day was a picture of the first chamber orchestra comprised entirely of theremins, Carnegie Hall, 1932. Myrna read about the instrument's two oscillators: one operated in a frequency beyond the range of human hearing, the other required a hand to enter its magnetic field. When the two beat together, they made that quivering sci-fi wail. Myrna watched, trembling, as the men and women of the orchestra stroked the electrified air, their invisible, chemical yearning taking shape all around her.

PHONE SEX

HEATHER ROSE

DEFINITION: sex-oriented telephone conversations
with a lover or with a commercial service.

VIENNA LIBRARY RUNS PHONE SEX LINE
TO RAISE FUNDS FOR REPAIR

For the price of 39 euro cents (53 cents), a listener can place a call to hear recorded passages from erotic literature from the last three centuries. Many of these passages are being read by some of the more attractive and well-known film stars of the country.

—REUTERS, MAY 11, 2007

Some people like their sex standing up, some like it in rubber, and some like it remote. Phone sex is the safe sex of new love, it's the close sex of faraway love. It's fantasy sex for sale at three dollars per minute.

For those brave enough to play, it begins with a breath. With hello. With a request. *What are you wearing? Unbutton it. Tell me your fantasies. How do you like to be touched? Where are your hands right now?* Phone sex wears the cloak of distance with the gloves of intimacy and the cowboy boots of adventure. It avoids the exchange of fluids. It's the virtual bedroom electrified with a voice.

Some bodies might be made for love, but some voices are made for sex. In my late twenties I began a transatlantic relationship with a semifamous musician in America. He had a beautiful voice with a Bronx accent. It was the perfect inducement. He would tell me the food he had cooked that night—lemon and basil linguine, couscous stuffed zucchini flowers, fettuccine with clams, fresh rocket with Grand Padano, tomato and mint salad, tarragon and pancetta roast chicken—and somehow this always led to phone sex. Hot, slippery, down-on-all-fours, writhing-on-the-carpet kind of sex. It was so addictive that he had only to say hello and I'd be unzipping my jeans. Strangely, in the two years this relationship persisted the episodes where we were together were far less vivid and exciting than the sex we had at a distance. Phone sex is crème brûlée with wasabi.

Now my husband texts me to ask what underwear I'm wearing, what time I'm going to orgasm tonight, what position he's imaging me in. Our mobile messaging is foreplay, or afterglow. But our sex is the skin-to-skin kind. Our fantasies confined to the everyday limitations of what's in our dress-up box, or new from a shopping trip.

Phone sex lives and dies with fantasy. Accents are its fishnet stockings, innuendo its whips and feathers. In the singular seclusion of a telephone conversation, any outfit can be summoned up, any location imagined, any body part grown or changed, any moment in history recalled, any future dreamed. Phone sex is the ultimate liberation of two voices with the magic to entice orgasm from each other. But it presents the same challenges as chopsticks and a bowl of naked lychees. Timing and grip are everything.

PIERCINGS (GENITAL AND OTHERS)

THAISA FRANK

DEFINITION: piercing of a part of the human body for the purpose of wearing jewelry in the opening created.

THE TSA HATES YOUR VIBRATOR: HOW TO
SAFELY FLY WITH YOUR SEX TOYS

Traveling with piercings has proved so bothersome for some folks I inter-viewed that when traveling they just remove their piercings and pack 'em away with their socks and pasties. That's one option—but if you can't or don't want to remove your piercings, you have a couple of possibilities. Some piercings won't set off metal detectors, but large or multiple ones might. Stainless-steel, titanium and gold piercings are in the low-risk category. Be prepared for uninformed security personnel to single you out and possibly search you completely. Be calm and explain that you have genital or nipple piercings. Prepare yourself for your trip by carrying a drawing or photograph of your piercing to show security, but remember that on heightened alert the security personnel will likely need to see it for themselves—in which case they will assign a same-sex officer to take a look.

—VIOLET BLUE, SPECIAL TO *SFGATE.COM*, JUNE 14, 2007

He found me in my own closet at my own party. The closet, a walk-in closet in the bedroom, was piled with coats. I was buried beneath them, crying.

When I heard the door open, I froze. But soon I felt an arm squeezing my own arm through layers of wool.

Margaret? said a voice. Are you under there?

The voice belonged to Cory Whiting, a tall, blond graduate student whom I sometimes saw in the stacks. I'd invited him, along with other people I hardly knew, to the first party I'd given since my husband and I split up four months ago. We'd thrown a lot of parties in our run-down Victorian. They were famous for expensive grass, loud music, and cheap wine. We fought bitterly before every party—about whether to use plastic or paper glasses, spend money on good candles or cheap votives. But whenever the parties began, we felt an ineffable sense of excitement.

Cory squeezed my arm again. Margaret? How come you disappeared?

When I didn't answer, he began to unpeel the coats. I stayed still, hoping he wouldn't find me. But when he uncovered the last coat, I sat up and arranged my face in a smile.

Hey, you've been crying, Cory said.

I haven't. I just wanted to be alone.

Under all these coats?

I like coats.

I understand, said Cory, patting a windbreaker. Coats can be comforting.

The half-open door let in a shaft of light and I saw Cory clearly: he wore the mustard-yellow T-shirt he always wore, and the same dark green cardigan, unraveling at the sleeves. His glasses were slightly crooked. Suddenly he leaned over and stroked my hair.

I'm sorry you're sad, he said.

I'm not. And don't feel sorry for me.

I don't, said Cory. I just wanted to find you. He sat next to me and pointed to the small oblong window in the closet.

Have you noticed? he said. It's the first snowfall.

I looked outside and saw thick flakes falling by a streetlamp. They seemed preternaturally bright.

It isn't even November, I said.

Maybe it's in honor of your party.

Before I could contradict him, Cory closed the door and kissed me. His lips were gentle and his tongue was soft, making my mouth feel like tracery. He shoved the coats aside and held me in his arms.

People will see us, I said.

No one's about to leave.

You were.

I was just looking for you. Like I do in the stacks.

I never knew that.

Then I should have told you, said Cory, leaning closer and unbuttoning my blouse. Soon we were enveloped in a nest of coats and he took off his T-shirt and cardigan. I ran my hand along his back. I touched his thick blond hair.

It's been a long time since I've made love, said Cory.

Me, too, I answered.

I had, in fact, wondered why Cory spent so much time in the geology stacks—which happens to be my field. Since I'd known he was in linguistics, I'd wondered if it was because he liked maps; I asked him now.

In a way, he said. They tell bizarre stories because so many countries are changing. But I wasn't really looking at maps. I was looking at you.

He kissed me again—carefully, slowly—and I wanted to touch him all over, as touching him would tell me everything I wanted to know—why he'd looked for me, what he'd thought about. I hesitated, took one hand from his back, and put it on his stomach, then inside his jeans, moving cautiously. It was then that I felt two round metal knobs on either side of his penis. They seemed free—suspended of gravity—and I felt embarrassed, out of my depth. Maybe I'd discovered a secret he didn't want me to know. I took my hands away.

It's okay, said Cory. They're part of an ampallang.

A what?

A kind of piercing.

What a weird word.

Pallang means "crossbar" in Malaysian.

Did you get it there?

No! I got it at the Eye of the Needle Piercing Parlor in Brooklyn.

But I can't feel a crossbar.

You're not supposed to. It's where the knobs screw in through my—

He hesitated, not wanting to offend me.

Prick, I said.

Yes: prick.

How come you got one?

An old girlfriend wanted it.

The Goth in postmodernist French?

Well . . . yes.

Did it hurt?

A lot.

I touched the metal knobs again. Can you show it to me?

Not here. If I lose the knobs, we'll never find them. Want to see what it feels like when we make love?

In the closet?

Why not?

Cory pulled down my jeans and began to touch me so gently my whole body felt like lace. The knobs were cold: I tensed when he came inside. But when the metal seemed to melt and become part of me, I relaxed.

Does that feel okay? he said.

More than okay.

The knobs grew hot and the heat surged until it rippled through my legs and the two of us moved together, like swimmers cresting waves. I came again and again.

What do you think? said Cory.

I didn't have time to think, I answered.

Later, much later, Cory would unscrew the metal knobs and show me the ampallang. It would be exactly the way I imagined it—a small steel bone, strangely prehistoric, even totemic. I would tell him *ampallang* sounded like an exotic animal, and we would laugh. One of the knobs would roll on the bedroom floor and we would crawl around looking for it, still laughing. But now all I felt was a sense of warmth, a flickering between our skins.

We shook off the coats and Cory helped me get dressed.

Now come to your party with me, he said.

POLYGAMY

ALICE ELLIOTT DARK

DEFINITION: having several and specifically
more than two spouses at one time.
AKA: plural marriage.

A little boy was attending his first wedding. After the service, his cousin asked him, "How many women can a man marry?"

"Sixteen," the boy responded.

His cousin was amazed that he had an answer so quickly. "How do you know that?"

"Easy," the little boy said. "All you have to do is add it up, like the bishop said: four better, four worse, four richer, four poorer."

POLYGAMY: A CHRISTMAS LETTER

What a year this has been! So many men, so little time. But I did my best.

In January I married a sinewy runner named Tommy whose legs are sculpted like a statue. We went to Maui for our vacation and I really got off on watching him surf, and then going back to our hotel room when he was still pumped up. As we all know, however, that only lasts so long, and he did none too well in the afterplay department, i.e., going over every detail of how we met, what we thought of each other, et cetera. His vocab was pretty much limited to surfing lingo, so while I was indeed a rad Betty, I need more. So I was happy to get home to Evan, Klaus, and Mohan, who never tire of reviewing the romance with me. I bought them each a new BMW convertible—with Chauncey's money, of course.

Speaking of whom, in February Chauncey was made partner at his investment bank, and none too soon as we were running a bit short on funds. The state-of-the-art gym cost lots, as did my private spa, where Dolph and Andre are ensconced full-time now after internships at the Golden Door and Canyon Ranch. Dolph massages me every morning after my workout. His hands should hold up for a few more years.

Spring was about tiptoeing through the tulips—one of Jason's specialties (read two lips, ha ha!). I get revved up starting around April 10 and need some attention pretty much every day while the weather's hot. Sadly, I had to put Tommy out to pasture. (Remember, I have a big pasture on the back forty.) He pulled a muscle in his calf doing Bikram with me and gained twelve pounds. Luckily I met a new cutie named Stretch who wears cowboy boots and has a tongue like cactus. Andre stepped up, too. So nobody's getting too tired. I created a job wheel and rotate the guys nightly, which works well. When they aren't with me, they work out, watch movies, and clean. Anthony is in the kitchen all the time—I like my vegetables finely diced, it brings out the subtle flavors—but the others have to serve as sous-chefs for him if he asks. All for one and one for all—even if the bottom line is all for me.

Fall was devoted to remodeling. I redid my bedroom because it reminded me too much of Drake, God rest his soul. And I hired a trainer for all the guys, even the trainers. I don't want any midwinter slumps. Unfortunately I had to put Henry and Jim on probation. If they're not bringing in seven figures by this time next year, I'll have to have a trial separation. It's sad when that happens, but you snooze, you lose. I'm the one who decides when it's time to go to sleep.

Edmund is still doing well with hiding little prezzies around the house. Nothing like finding that egg blue Tiffany box when you're bent over the back of a sofa. He's smart—I like that in a man.

They say polygamy is a male game, but I'm managing okay with it. Sure it's a lot of responsibility and your management skills have to be top-notch, but the lifestyle has a lot to offer. I keep many men off the streets and satisfied—just ask them. And report back to me if they say anything other than yes!

So far so good with Stretch. I'm planning to marry him on Valentine's Day. On that note, I'll leave you all for another year.

God rest ye merry gentlemen. 'Cause they sure won't get any rest around here.

P.S. Photo of my guys continues on back of card.

PORN STAR

BRET ANTHONY JOHNSTON

DEFINITION: somebody who appears in pornographic films or photographs, live sex shows or peep shows.

What's your porn-star name? Take the name of your first pet and add the name of the street you currently live on. Mine is Christy Manuella. What's yours?

Porn star: an actor/artist/person of some distinction who performs in adult films/videos. Neither gender nor race is a criterion for consideration, but most actors/artists/persons fitting this bill are Caucasian females with radioactively blond hair. (Not coincidentally, according to an oft-cited Susan Faludi article, pornography is one of only three professions in which women consistently outearn men.) In 2007, the title/moniker distinction had also become a peculiar kind of merit badge/term of endearment. Attractive, seemingly well-adjusted, affluent, and intelligent young women could be overhead referring to one another as "porn stars" the way you might expect ranchers to refer to one another as "cowboys." The title/moniker distinction also occasionally appears on dainty T-shirts and bumper stickers attached to minivans driven by attractive, seemingly well-adjusted, affluent, and intelligent moms. The trend is either weirdly empowering or wholly disturbing.

Some actors/artists/persons achieve said title/moniker distinction through anatomical absurdities, such as extraordinary length or circumference: John Holmes and Kayla Kleevage; some make their name with specialized skills: Flower Tucci and Fallon, both known for reliable and epic female ejaculation; some achieve the status through such unadulterated beauty that watching them perform the requisite acts is more disorienting than erotic: Chasey Lain, Nikki Dial, Sean Michaels; and some (or, at least, one) achieve the title/moniker distinction against all odds and despite every law of attraction: Ron "the Hedgehog" Jeremy. And, irony of ironies, it's this short, rotund, back- and chest-hair-swaddled, balding, mustachioed, perpetually sweat-sheened, and generally spherical man who epitomizes porn, who is and will always be the industry's biggest and most paradoxical and (thus) most recognizable star.

I've met the Hedgehog. Long story, but I wound up in the back room of a strip club interviewing him for an article I had little incentive/intention to write. He's insightful and articulate, gentlemanly and funny in a disarmingly innocent, self-deprecatingly boyish way; he holds an M.A. in special education as well as the world record for most adult-film appearances. He was then trying to bridge the gap between adult and mainstream movies, and finding some success with it, but not enough. (He'd been an extra in *Ghostbusters* and a "special consultant" for *9½ Weeks*.) The current tack was stand-up comedy. He was touring strip clubs, cracking fairly hideous jokes between dancers, and selling signed glossies of himself for five bucks. The lines for his signature were consistently longer than those to tip the dancers; there were always dancers in his lines, paying for their autographs with singles.

And so we were in this back room, sitting across from each other, talking loudly into a tape recorder so as to be heard over the music pulsing through the wall, when this security guard interrupted us. "Mr. Jeremy," he said, "we've got a situation."

"How many?" the Hedgehog asked.

"Maybe ten, but one of them is getting antsy, *really* antsy. She's asked me—"

"Can you tell her I'm doing an interview? My next set is in—"

"She ain't hearing it," the security guard said. "Either you'll have to step out and say hello, or I'll have to ask her to leave."

The Hedgehog smiled his boyish smile at me, as if to say this happened all the time and he was sorry for the hassle. I smiled back, as if to say, *I know, brother, I know.*

To the security guard, he said, "Let her in."

Remember your mother's best friend, the one you either (a) first had a crush on before your crushes became more personalized, or (b) the one you kind of idolized, the one who always drank afternoon "toddies," the one you wanted to be when you grew up? That's the antsy woman. She looked like the kind of middle-aged woman/wife/mother who would work at Supercuts and talk to you about Bruce Willis movies while cutting your hair. Tight, silk, eggplant-colored blouse, not-quite-stiletto heels, a short, spiky hairstyle the same hue as her blouse.

The Hedgehog didn't get up to greet Your Mother's Best Friend; instead, he extended his right arm and hugged her sideways from his chair. He leaned his head against her hip, closed his eyes, and looked entirely sanguine. It was all so casual and wholesome-seeming that I figured they knew each other from college.

But then Your Mother's Best Friend started fanning herself and said, "I can't believe this is happening. I'm, like, your biggest fan. My husband and I watch your movies all the time. All. The. Time. He said I could . . . He said, that if you're clean, we might could . . ."

The Hedgehog had worked his sausage-y fingers under the hem of her blouse and was lightly grazing them over her belly. I was mesmerized/mystified/agog. Your Mother's Best Friend whimpered while the Hedgehog caressed her stomach. She said, "Oh, Lordy."

Through the wall, a smattering of applause as a song ended. After the next dancer's routine, the Hedgehog would take the stage again.

"Your husband knows you're here?" he asked.

The Hedgehog's hand had moved up to massage her right breast. Her head lolled back, exposing her neck. Your Mother's Best Friend whispered, "Yes."

I averted my eyes and started scratching notes into my notebook, not about Your Mother's Best Friend, but about things the Hedgehog and I had previously discussed so I wouldn't forget them. Such as, the Hedgehog, like most porn stars, had been arrested countless times, but the charges never stuck; the arrests happened when the cops needed to fill quotas or wanted to see "some tit," so they'd raid the porn sets in Chatsworth, California; when the Hedgehog was performing and needed to delay his "money shot," he would try to say the alphabet backward or think about his dead grandmother; sometimes, if he got into real trouble, he would say over and over, "Dead grandmothers, dead grandmothers, dead grandmothers"; he wanted to start a hot-sauce business; earlier in his career, he was capable of autofellatio.

When I looked up again, the Hedgehog had unbuttoned Your Mother's Best Friend's blouse just enough to slip out her left breast and take her nipple in his mouth. She stroked his hair. She moaned. He suckled. She looked straight at me and held my gaze, but her eyes were so glassy that I knew she never really saw me. I wondered if any of this was actually happening, if I was having one of those strange dreams wherein no one can see you but you can see all things, all at once. The bass-heavy music pumped and bumped through the walls. Later, without ever really finishing the interview, I would shake the Hedgehog's hand and we'd exchange contact information and I would tell him, and genuinely mean it, that he was one of the most interesting people I'd ever met. He'd leave a few friendly messages for me, and I'd do the same. He'd find still more crossover success on reality TV, someone would produce a documentary entitled *Porn Star: The Legend of Ron Jeremy*, he'd finally start his hot-sauce business. Later still, I would go to Supercuts and Your Mother's Best Friend would cut my hair and talk to me about Bruce Willis movies, and when she realized who I was—she *had* seen me!—she'd ask, with heartbreaking urgency, if I'd heard from the Hedgehog. I'd lie and say no and feign disappointment, all while feeling an odd mishmash of pride and sadness. But, in the strip club that night, I knew none of that. I just felt as if I'd wandered onto the set of a porn film, mostly because there was nothing sexy about it. I was nervous/bewildered/somewhat embarrassed, but totally enthralled. I wondered if I should remind the Hedgehog about our interview or, more pressingly, about his being imminently needed for his comedy routine. But then, as the music quieted through the wall and the deejay started his high-decibel introduction of "the hardest—get it? *Hardest*—working man in porn," the Hedgehog stood and collected himself—I can still see him primping his collar and patting down his hair—then he walked into the club to the sound of sparse, but enthusiastic, applause.

PORNOGRAPHY

TITA CHICO

DEFINITION: see essay.
AKA: porn, porno, hard-core, soft-core,
Tijuana Bible, filth, smut.

ADULT INTERNET PORNOGRAPHY STATISTICS

Men admitting to accessing pornography at work   20%
U.S. adults who regularly visit Internet pornography Web sites   40 million
Promise Keeper men who viewed pornography in last week   53%
Christians who said pornography is a major problem in the home   47%
Adults admitting to Internet sexual addiction   10%
Breakdown of male/female visitors to pornography sites   72% male, 28%
*   female*

—TOPTENREVIEWS, HTTP://INTERNET-FILTER-REVIEW.TOPTENREVIEWS.COM/
INTERNET-PORNOGRAPHY-STATISTICS.HTML

A HISTORY OF PORNOGRAPHY;
OR, A MIGHTY LEWD BOOK

Pornography has been around longer than the word; it was just called other things, oftentimes *lewd*. The word *pornography* comes from the Greek *pornographos*, for "writing about prostitutes," but did not emerge in the English language until well into the mid-nineteenth century. The *Oxford English Dictionary* tells us that pornography is "the explicit description or exhibition of sexual subjects or activity in literature, painting, films, etc., in a manner intended to stimulate erotic rather than aesthetic feelings."

The relative ease with which a lexicographer defines *pornography*, however, eludes members of the legal system. In 1964, Justice Potter Stewart tried to define pornography with what became informally known as the Casablanca Test: "I shall not today attempt

219

further to define the kinds of material I understand to be embraced . . . [b]ut I know it when I see it" (*Jacobellis v. Ohio*, 378 U.S. 184 [1964]). This famous characterization reveals a man of the law who may or may not consume pornography himself, but who will publicly recognize it in order to outlaw it.

One of the earliest accounts of someone reading pornography can be found in the private diary of the Englishman Samuel Pepys (pronounced "peeps"). From 1660 to 1669, Pepys documented his daily life as a civil servant in London, including his furtive taste for pornography, wine, and women. He wrote this diary in shorthand; it was transcribed and first published in 1825, but with the naughty bits expurgated. The full diary was finally published in 1970–83 in eleven volumes.

Pepys, whose name reminds one of voyeurism, adored having sex with actresses, prostitutes, and all manner of available women, whether at the playhouse, in a coach, or in his office at the Navy Board. But pornography was altogether different. For example, the entry for Sunday, February 9, 1668, begins and ends with his reading of one of the first modern pieces of pornography, *L'École des filles* (*The Girls' School*), first published in 1665. (The ample descriptions of intercourse, lesbianism, sodomy, and sadism in *L'École des filles* so enraged French royal authorities that, unable to determine the author, they burned the book.) Pepys describes the beginning of his day: "Up, and at my chamber all the morning and the office doing business, and also reading a little of *L'escholle des filles*, which is a mighty lewd book, but yet not amiss for a sober man once to read over to inform himself in the villainy of the world." And he concludes his day with pornography: "We sang until almost night, and drank a mighty good store of wine, and then they parted, and I to my chamber, where I did read through *L'escholle des filles*, a lewd book, but what do no wrong once to read for information sake. And after I had done it I burned it, that it might not be among my books to my shame, and so at night to supper and to bed." Eased with wine from dinner, Pepys gets off "for information sake" and then vows to destroy the offending matter (though we know he didn't). Even though he is alone and writes his private diary in code, Pepys suppresses his desire for pornography for the sake of decency. He tries to keep his enjoyment of pornography hidden from himself.

For Pepys, the pornographic is narrative—no glossy pictures, no DVDs or videos, no Internet JPEGs or video clips, no webcams. Old-time pornography was textual and made up of words. Pornography used to be just one form of silent reading, a practice that many feared meant using one hand to hold the book and the other to masturbate. And they were right. Pornography may stage sex between two or more people, or it may showcase one or more naked bodies, but its general purpose was to arouse the reader to masturbation or to other sex acts. It has the same general purpose today.

Whether in words or in images, pornography is representation. Pornography is not sex, but a collection of words or images that stand for sex. This is what makes it so alluring, for Pepys and for people today. Pornography is both a depiction of our sexual desires and the arousal of our desires. Pornography exposes the parts of the body that we clothe in everyday life, even if we cover them only to show off their shape or bulk. Whether it is straight porn, gay porn, fetish porn, hard porn, or soft porn, pornographic bodies seem to be almost *entirely* made up of genitals—close-ups can fill the computer screen, TV screen, or photograph. The plots of pornography may well be predictable, but the pleasure is in knowing that the ordinary activities of everyday life will soon transform into highly sexed bodies on display, and that the reader or viewer gets to see everything without being visible to anyone else.

PROSTITUTE

KAREN CONNELLY

DEFINITION: a woman who sells sexual favors and
the act of intercourse itself for money.
AKA: whore, sex worker, call girl, streetwalker, hooker, poontang,
hustler, hussy, harlot, strumpet, tail, tart, B-girl, bag, bawd, bimbo,
blower, broad, camp follower, cat, chicken, chippie, concubine,
courtesan, fallen woman, floozy, harlot, hostess, loose woman,
midnight cowboy, moll, nymphomaniac, painted woman,
party girl, pickup, pink pants, pro, scarlet woman, slut,
tomato, tramp, trollop, white slaveworking girl.

More than 90% of prostitutes suffered childhood sexual abuse, often incest
70% believed that being sexually abused as children influenced their deci-
sions to become prostitutes
Two-thirds began working in prostitution before they turned 16
Average length of career is 4 years
96% who began committing prostitution as juveniles were runaways
75% attempted suicide
15% of all suicide victims are prostitutes

—ILLINOIS COALITION AGAINST SEXUAL ASSAULT

I love the whore for her sauciness and unapologetic sexiness, for
her guts and sheer bravery. Prostitutes should be praised and em-
ulated, like fireman and doctors, for doing such heroic work.
How I have longed to be her, sometimes, wishing I could trade
my sexuality from a place of power, and for money, instead
of longing for love and companionship. I know that a "nice
woman" is not supposed to admit to such possibilities. Yet to be
a woman without a husband or a lot of money is to live that possibility, however remote. To be a woman is to live the history of

women, which is why, in a moment, I want to go back in time with my definition.

But first of all, today, at the top of the adman's bag of tricks is the promise of sex/power/freedom conveyed through blatant sexual images. With all the slutty women prancing in the media, movies, and music biz, you'd think we'd love our hookers for their honesty. But our culture hates the prostitute more than ever. What could be more threatening than a woman who owns her sexuality to such an extent that she can actually sell it?

Not that we often hear about sex workers who are self-determined, healthy contributors to society. Having sex with men who need to have sex (and are willing to pay for it) is a very important job. Some sex workers regard themselves as therapists, and sex therapy is also a very important job in a world that continues to be so fucked up about the pleasures of the body.

Sadly, the most common postmodern image of the sex worker is a desperate crack whore. It is true that sex workers who work on the streets in North America can be desperate, in part because they are doing such dangerous work. That danger is greatly increased by the legal system itself—from cop to lawyer to lawmaker to you and me, the voting public—which turns them into illegal, invisible women.

How else could Canadian Robert Pickton stand accused of murdering twenty-six prostitutes and be suspected of murdering more than fifty-five? These were *human beings*, with their own loves and fears and voices and laughter. Only those rendered invisible by their own society can disappear so easily, without any public outcry. Obviously this is no improvement from the abuse that prostitutes have suffered for centuries. In eighteenth-century England, even if she was a ten-year-old orphan, a prostitute was thought to be the pernicious seducer of innocent men. The early Christian Church asserted that she would go to hell and be raped by devils with burning spears. But how very far the fallen woman has fallen from her exalted origins in antiquity.

The word *prostitute* comes from the Latin *pro*—before—and *statuere*—to establish or to cause to stand. Hence *prostituere*, to expose publicly, to prostitute. But some historians believe that *pro statuere* originally referred to temple priestesses, those who had to stand in for the goddess in whose temple they served. The word *harlot* likewise has ancient origins. The Babylonian goddess Ishtar was also known as the great Har, mother of the Harine, who were her high priestesses. All the great goddesses of antiquity had their priestesses, who were the earthly link between man and the exalted goddess. To have sex with a harlot was to touch the power of those revered and universally worshipped goddesses. The men who had sex with priestesses were required to pay well for their experience of ecstatic renewal and power; the moneys contributed to the livelihood of the priestesses and to the upkeep of temples.

The *horae* priestesses of ancient Greece, like the Persian and Egyptian *houri*, kept the hours of night in certain temples, differentiating each hour with a new dance. *Horo* is still the word for dance in modern Greek, and *hora* is the name of one of the oldest Hebrew folk dances. *Har, horae, houri* . . . I wonder where the word *whore* comes from? The word *hor* in Hebrew means a hole, a cave, a pit, a pool of water: all common old symbols for the vagina and the womb as sacred wellsprings of fertility and power. Unsurprisingly, the root word of the common French and Spanish words for whore—*putain, puta*—are from the Latin *puteus*, meaning a well or a pit.

When the goddesses began to lose their power to male deities, the temple priestesses also lost theirs. When the big nasty God took over the ancient world, the holy women of the temples and sacred groves became despised as unclean, idolatrous fornicators, agents of Satan, and, of course, witches—an attitude that culminated in a frenzy of systemic, organized torture and murder during the five centuries of the Inquisition. Hundreds of thousands of people died during that long Roman Catholic slaughter, but we know from the historical records that a remarkable number were "witches"—wise women, healers, prostitutes.

Dear God/dess! To imagine a new definition for *prostitute* and to respect and love her for the work she does (which is, after all, the work of caring for the ever-longing, often lonely flesh), I once again turn to the past. The *hetaerae* were a class of prostitutes in ancient Greece considered to be the equals of men, debating publicly on the important philosophical themes of the day, transacting business, founding schools. They sometimes rose to positions of great power and wealth and married well in their later years.

Engaging in debate with philosophers, dancing, playing musical instruments, having sex with intelligent men. Being *celebrated*. It's a job description and a life of experience any woman could be proud of. When we repair our instincts for sensuality and pleasure, we will have more prostitutes like the *hetaerae*. I know that some already *are* like them, brave, rare, free women, in a class by themselves.

PUSSY (*see also* CUNT)

ROBERT BOSWELL

DEFINITION: the female genital organs.
AKA: snatch, tail, twat, pink Cadillac, flower, candy, the cockpit, cunt, gash, love tunnel, cooze, quim, quiff, her sex, the cellar door, kitty, nookie, poontang, oyster, the big slurpy, hole, bearded clam, button, beehive, cabbage patch, box, cave, bush, muff, cunny, fountain of love, fur, fur pie, hair pie, honey pot, jellyroll, keyhole, slit, beaver, poon, toolshed, coochie.

An old man was sitting on his rocking chair when Joe walked by carrying a roll of chicken wire. The old man asked, "Where are you going, Joe?" Joe replied, "To catch some chickens!" The old man told him you can't catch chickens with chicken wire, but a little while later Joe returned with some chickens.

The next day, the old man saw Joe walk by again, this time with some duct tape. The old man asked, "Where are you going, Joe?" Joe replied, "To catch some ducks!" The old man told him you can't catch ducks with duct tape, but a little while later Joe returned with some ducks.

The next day, the old man saw Joe walk by again, this time with some pussy willow.

"Hold on, Joe, I'm coming with you!"

PUSSY: A STORY

Three boys smoke and talk about sex.

Even her back, says Lee, *she had these shadows . . .*

He flicks his cigarette to the plank floor of the porch. They're in the mountains, alone in the wilderness, talking of girls.

She made me wear a rubber. Lee taps another cigarette from his soft-pack. *I felt like I'd put on a space suit.*

That's one big condom, says Greg, staring at the silver clouds above the pencil tips of pine that hide the moon.

The trip has consisted of one error after another—getting lost on the drive, the car stuck on a shoulder, the boys without a fish because they packed the wrong bait. They're on the porch without coats, having locked themselves out. They'll have to make a decision soon, but for the moment Lee says, *It felt so . . .* He strikes a match to complete the sentence. He lights his Camel, shaking his head, as if his lungs fill with wonder. Much of his tale has basis in lived events, involving a girl with braces on her teeth and a tenderness he knows instinctively to disown. Lee's father was caught performing an abortion and stripped of his medical license. His father's crime colors every aspect of Lee's sexual life.

She made this noise. I wish I had a tape of that noise.

226

Greg lights a cigar. Its aromatic smoke he associates with the men his father brought home. They'd gather in the kitchen, which would, come morning, smell of smoke, despite the pancakes his mother would have bubbling on the hot plate, standing in her underwear, red marks marching up her legs to her slanting panties, the cleft in her buttocks beneath the silky fabric visible to this boy even now every time he inhales smoke—a shimmering ravine ready to furrow into any girl passing before his imagination.

When it's his turn, Greg describes the forked body of a naked woman, the panorama of her body, the widening gate of her sex. It's actually a picture from a magazine, but it speaks to him more powerfully than experience. Through a keyhole as a child, he witnessed his mother passed among a throng of men. She took a man's cigar and dimpled her cheeks. His father's bright voice called, "First!" On hands and knees he made a ladder of kisses up her thighs, his tongue a serpent bent on pleasure, her panties at half-mast in its honor. His mother tugged the other men close, whose mouths touched her neck and breasts and parted the pink of her lips. And later, after the boy had returned to bed, applause came slapping down the hall.

Greg doesn't remember the night, but it lives inside him. Its weight settled his eyes upon the photo and now limns his description of the splayed woman with excited affection. *Even lying like that, the cheeks weren't flat, but kind of round, like those packets of sugar. You know that sugar?*

The third boy hesitates on the porch. This would be me, thirty-five years ago, posing with a cigarette, the distance between what I know of myself and who I actually am roughly the same as the distance between who I want to be and what I'll become. While I stall, the mountain air chills us, the stars flaunt their ancient light, creatures move in the wooden distance beyond our apprehension. In the bracing air comes the predatory fragrance of decay, and it's not impossible to believe the boys might smell it, might hear the gliding complaint of an owl, which directs their attention to the night sky, the million burning things hovering above their heads. They might stare at the world around them and see the actual world around them—the sky, moon, stars, trees, a brown patch of earth, three kids with uncombed hair and mud-spattered jeans: emblems of nothing yet freighted with a terrible beauty.

Instead, they see a universe nippled with light, the crescent moon (luminous curve of ass) riding seductively above the phallic pines. Their litany must continue, the push-me-pull-you stories of suck and satisfaction. Every word returns to the feminine body, how the friction of skin-on-skin lights the spiraling fuse they mistake for their souls.

Lee's father, by this time, again practices medicine. When the trouble came, Lee had been led to a bathroom in their house, where he settled on the rim of the tub, while his father sat on the toilet's lid. His father's hands shook as he explained himself. The woman, forty, mother of four, wept in his office. Can Lee forgive himself for what he said? He asked, *Was she naked?*

The betrayal rides in his shoulders, the dark space between the blades; in the narrow gap between bucket seats, the gulf that separates him from the girl with the braces; in the delicate silences among the words of every sentence, words that shimmy about a girl's torso more roughly than his hands. His actual touch had been gentle, laden with his father's shame, his fingers strumming her ribs, tracing the flared bones of her hips, his heart brimming with a rapacious delicacy. When he seeks words to describe the encounter, he can only say, *She was so . . . such great pussy.*

My turn to howl into the chasm: *At the party, after the Chandler game, she found ways to let me see her panties.* I tap the end of my Lucky; flakes of ash float on the frigid air. The white flash of panties stirred in me a desire that hibernates in the marrow. I didn't remember my favorite aunt but relived her jaunty walk across the porch of my childhood home, a walk I witnessed through gaping blinds, her man spinning her into his arms, his hands sliding beneath her skirt, revealing the white planes of her secret skin. What can a boy do with such information but store it in his body?

At the end of the party, that girl and I found an empty room. *I put my finger right there. I felt like my whole body was in that finger.*

They won't let me quit: *Did you fuck her?*

When I say *yeah*, it's only partly a lie. The power of that encounter speaks louder than simple facts. I describe my favorite landscape, the contours of a wheat field bordered by a canal, how wild the flowers grow along the bank, how bushy the patches of grass, how ready the field grows for the thrasher, and how, after the harvest, the stubble has to be burned. I substitute the body of woman for the body of earth, the geography of an upturned hip and slope of skin for the landscape of windblown wheat whose stalks genuflect and rise, a billowing movement that engages more than the eyes.

At least, that's what I think I did. We didn't know what we were saying, and yet we knew it more than what was said. Talking about the slender ribbon of dark hair on the taut surface of a girl's abdomen, I knew I was describing a thing whose real meaning was beyond my grasp, like a child who dreams of sex before he knows what it is, describing the mounds and valleys of his dream and the impossible wish to walk among them.

We were boys of no particular distinction, inventing our own history, perpetuating a species of desire as common as the cold weather that made our bodies tremble. Into the morning hours we continued our allegory of the body female, until we thought to try a window and tumbled in, and we crawled beneath our coarse blankets to talk again, elevating, as best we could, the fragile faith that our lives had meaning.

QUICKIES

RAVI SHANKAR

DEFINITION: sexual intercourse that is short in duration.
AKA: wham-bam-thank-you-ma'am, nooner.

A man goes into a restaurant and is seated. A voluptuous waitress wearing a short skirt comes to his table and asks, "What would you like, sir?"

He looks at the menu and then scans her beautiful frame top to bottom, then answers, "A quickie."

The waitress reaches over and slaps him across the face with a resounding SMACK! and storms away.

A man sitting at the next table leans over and whispers, "Um, pal, I think it's pronounced 'quiche.'"

ODE TO QUICKIES

Lunch hour. Time it takes
to meet in anonymity leaves
no more than forty minutes.
All preamble be damned:
hike up, hunker down, flush
the color of bruised peaches,
fall against casements in knots
of garment, tilt towards me,
so I'm exposed while you rove
a grove that grows in plum
with each sucked-in breath,
wordless communiqués
flashing between us, rapt to be

here, so roused beyond
the mere scope of skin,
only skin can suffice to hold
the charge of the rash
dance that fits the wan light
upon these chalky walls—
perfectly.

ROLE PLAY

ALLISON LYNN

DEFINITION: to experiment with or experience
(a situation or viewpoint) by playing a role.

Childhood games of cowboys and Indians take on a completely new dimension when played with your partner grown-up style. So pick up a hat, put on some warpaint and prepare for an afternoon of pleasure. The aim of the first part of the game is to take your partner by surprise and immobilize them. If you are playing the part of the sheriff, then you can use handcuffs; if a simple cowboy, then use your lasso or your whip. If you are taking the role of the Indian brave or squaw, then use a piece of thick trapper's rope. But no matter if you have little more than a dressing gown cord—it is the depth of your fantasy that counts.

–WWW.THELOVERSGUIDE.COM

Role plays are the intimate dramas of the bedroom, chamber theaters of the nude, one-acts of the aroused, curtain-raisers, community theater à deux—or à trois. First, there are the classics, the standard make-believe scenarios engendered to make it hot, scenarios popular since before your own grandparents were stripping with the lights out and performing their own play of "You be Mae West, I'll be Randolph Scott." You've seen them, you've heard them, you've played them: he's the doctor, you're the nurse; she's the landlord, you're the tenant; you're the bored housewife, he's a captain of industry; she's French, you're from Argentina; she's shy, you're an exhibitionist; he's the quarterback, you're the head cheerleader; you are the last two humans on earth, rabid hogs are clawing at the door, and the future of the species is in your hands. Then, there are the historical favorites: he's John Adams, you're Abigail (little played since the Marie/Pierre Curie story line took its place); she's Cleopatra, you're Mark Anthony (a favorite in the Mississippi River Delta); he's the asp and you're carrying a hatchet (rumored to be a standard between Anthony and Cleopatra, when they weren't playing themselves). And from there, the sky is the limit: he's the royal tailor, you're sitting in the throne; you're Little Jack Horner, she's the pie; you're the carpenter but he's got the wood; she's dying of dehydration, you've got a Snapple in your pants; he plays lead guitar, you're a breathless roadie; you're Pamela Anderson, he's Kid Rock (alternatively, you're Pamela Anderson, he's Carmen Electra; he's Carmen Electra, you're Tommy Lee; you're Kid Rock, he's Tommy Lee, and the yacht is on fire); she lost her E-ZPass, you control the tollbooth; she dances at the Moulin Rouge, you were born into the aristocracy; she's the rug and you're the floor; he lost his password, you're the naked techie in the IT department; he's the mouse and you've got the cheese; you're hard to get, she's emotionally impetuous; you're hard, she's willing; it's April 14, he's your accountant, and you forgot your receipts; he's got a touch of the poet in him, you're unerringly pragmatic; she's the lion tamer, you're the big-top medic; he's fast and you're loose; she's a damsel in distress, you're along for the ride; he's agoraphobic, you deliver his groceries; you're the rubber, he's the glue; he's him and you're you, only better.

SEX ED

ELINOR LIPMAN

DEFINITION: a broad term used to describe education about human sexual anatomy, sexual reproduction, sexual intercourse, and other aspects of human sexual behavior.

Eighty-six percent of the public school districts that have a policy to teach sex education require that abstinence be promoted. Some 35% require abstinence to be taught as the only option for unmarried people and either prohibit the discussion of contraception altogether or limit discussion to its ineffectiveness. The other 51% have a policy to teach abstinence as the preferred option for teens and permit discussion of contraception as an effective means of preventing pregnancy and STIs.

–D. J. LANDRY ET AL., "ABSTINENCE PROMOTION AND THE PROVISION OF INFORMATION ABOUT CONTRACEPTION IN PUBLIC SCHOOL DISTRICT SEXUALITY EDUCATION POLICIES," *FAMILY PLANNING PERSPECTIVES* 31, NO. 6 (1999): 280-86

When my son was nine years old, a family friend gave him *Why Do Our Bodies Stop Growing? Questions about human anatomy answered by the Natural History Museum.* Its anatomically correct illustrations were a big hit, as were its occasional half-goofy questions such as "Is it true that you can eat an apple standing on your head?" or "Is the skull one big bone?" On page 88, Ben found Question 132, the loaded one, which asked, "When do I stop being a child?" Beneath that were three paragraphs on puberty, including a sentence that got his attention: "Body changes in adolescence turn girls into young women who can have babies and boys into young men who can make women pregnant." That there was a connection between boys and babies had apparently never occurred to our third-grader. "How," he asked, incredulous, "do men make women pregnant?"

I, the evolved parent at childrearing's sacred crossroad, said, "Um. Let's go ask Daddy." And then, to prove it was science rather than cowardice, added, "He's a doctor."

Daddy was watching TV. I repeated Ben's question. My husband said in a voice I didn't hear often—therapeutic, pedagogical, Fred Rogers—"Well . . . sure. I can answer that. Do you want to sit down?"

And truly, Planned Parenthood could have videotaped his presentation and distributed it: the penis, the vagina, the sperm, the egg—logical, calm, no smirking. Ben listened and didn't interrupt. When Bob finished, Ben asked, not adorably or innocently, but suspiciously, "How does the seed get in there? Remote control?"

Bob said no. The man put his penis *into* the woman's vagina.

Ben asked, scowling, "Do you have to get naked to do this?"

Bob said, yes, you did.

"Did you and Mom get naked?"

Bob said, "I believe we did."

Our son stood up, exited the room, and yelled from the kitchen, "I'm never doing that."

We waited for his return and his follow-up questions. I said, "That was excellent. You couldn't have done better."

"We'll see," said Bob.

A few days later at the breakfast table, Ben asked me as casually as he could, "How do girls get pregnant?"

I said, "Ben! You remember! Daddy told you the whole story two nights ago."

His tone changed to one of weary tolerance, as if I were the one who needed the refresher. "Right, right, I know: the man takes a seed out of his tush and the woman eats it."

Well, why not? It had its own charm, and I was learning something valuable: one shouldn't push the facts of life at an age when they sound preposterous. I'd like to think I corrected his misapprehension on the spot, but I don't remember doing so. Nor do I remember his coming to us for more sex education.

Professionals handled the next step, a unit named Human Growth and Development, formerly known as Human Growth and Change, amended after someone (this was a lab school at Smith College) worried that the word *change* could alarm the children. The boys and girls were separated for the classes; the boys got Mr. Weiner, a seasoned and married sixth-grade teacher. Fifth grade proved to be good timing, developmentally, because Ben would study his vocabulary list without snickering. Again, Bob did the quizzing. "Vulva?" I heard him ask evenly from the next room, to which Ben would answer, equally clinically, "The external genital organs of the female."

"Vas deferens?"

"The main duct that carries semen."

When Bob said, "Clitoris?" I took a step closer.

"Female organ of pleasure," our ten-year-old answered as matter-of-factly as if the topic were farm apparatus and its inventors.

One of the last quips I recorded in his baby book—the date tells me he was fourteen—was Ben announcing on the ride to school, "We start Health today." A pause and a wry smile—I was his best audience and he knew it. "Fourth year in a row I get to learn about fallopian tubes."

He's a grown-up now with his own place, a fruitful social life, excellent hygiene, and good sense. I'd like to thank Bob and Mr. Weiner, the playground, his bunkmates at camp, the locker room, the Internet, and especially the Talking Transparent Woman at the Boston Museum of Science. It's an important job, and I couldn't have done it alone.

SEX TOYS

KATHERINE TANNEY

DEFINITION: any object or device that is primarily
used in facilitating human sexual pleasure.

We invented Fuckerware™ sex toy parties. Gather your favourite women and we bring the sex toys to you. Touch them, laugh at them, even turn them on (the sex toys, that is—adultery is not in our adult party plan). Then, a few days later when your Pleasure Box order arrives, the passion party truly begins!

—WWW.PLEASUREBOX.COM

TOY STORIES

Age 22

My boyfriend and I do it in the bright afternoon light of his bedroom. When I open my eyes, his face is impossible to read. I see only the sweep of his cheekbone, the glint of his smile. The rest is hidden behind mirror-black plastic. We are fucking in our sunglasses, like rock stars, like cops, like superheroes from planet Ray•Ban. For some reason, this really excites me.

Age 23

The man I go out with when my boyfriend breaks my heart works a banana slowly inside me. It's surprisingly large in this context—gasp-worthy. After I've come all over it, he peels back the skin and we take mouthfuls of the warm, sweet fruit. In the months ahead, we experiment with ice cubes, fudge sauce, rice pilaf.

Age 35

The divorce/birthday gift my sister sends me looks like an action figure propped behind cellophane. The box says, "It's Clitorrific!" Imagine the severed member of a Caucasian colossus, replete with bluish veins and goose-bumped ridges. In another year and a half, my hideous first vibrator refuses to start no matter how I bargain and plead with the battery terminals.

Age 37

I ask the Texan I'm dating to use his handcuffs on me. He assumes I want the sex rough, want him to ignore my pleasure and conduct himself like a rapist. He is easily insulted, so I pretend to enjoy myself.

Outside the bedroom, we argue about easily verifiable facts. When proven wrong, he says, "Do you want to be right or do you want to be happy?" I realize I want to be with somebody else.

Best sexual memory: he asks me to wear my one-piece bathing suit to bed. Then he gets in carrying my flashlight and hideous dildo (prebreakdown). For the next hour he makes me feel like a beautiful mountain range being scaled, explored, discovered, and mined.

Age 39

I fall in love with a beautiful, generously endowed older man who has made it to fifty without a good understanding of female genitalia. He knows where to insert his flawless cock and what to do with it once inside.

In an effort to educate him and expand our sex life, I ask if he likes sex toys. He dismisses the idea, saying confidently, "I've never needed them." To which I say, demonstrating my unfortunate urge to be right, "Nobody *needs* them. That's why they're called toys."

I then go online on a *Field of Dreams*–style shopping spree, reasoning that if I own them, he will come around. I also take him to see *The Vagina Monologues*. The toys don't interest him much, but the play makes him laugh and think and learn, baby, learn. I am still waiting for a thank-you note from the woman he now lives with.

Age 43

I'm once again seeing a man who loves sex, who views it as uninhibited play and is as curious about it as I am. On HBO, we learn about artisan glass dildos that can be heated or chilled, and "teledildonics" (machines that do a man's job without tiring). We visit a couple of stores that sell erotic clothing and an array of gadgets, books, videos, and supplies. I model various collars with rings in them. We consider a remote-controlled vibe that can be hidden in the underpants and operated discreetly in public. Mostly, we browse, quiz the staff, discuss, imagine. It's as if we're shopping for housewares at Target.

Back at his place, he slides a tiny vibrator on his tongue and prepares to thrill me. On the nightstand is the little purple buttplug, for him.

SILVER-BALLING

STACEY D'ERASMO

DEFINITION: read the essay to find out . . .

So, Beth and I are lying around in bed one morning, next to the computer. We get an e-mail from our friend Troy that reads, in part, "James will be at the party if he isn't too busy silver-balling his hot new boyfriend."

Beth and I look at each other. "What's silver-balling?" I say.

She says, "I don't know. Something with Christmas ornaments?"

We go out to dinner with Paul and George. Before the appetizers arrive, I say, "Hey. What's silver-balling?"

Paul looks abashed. "Silver-balling? Silver-balling?"

"I've never heard of that," says George.

Paul says, "I think it's when you're old and you have sex. Like having sex with silver foxes."

"What are silver foxes?" Beth asks.

"You don't know what silver foxes are?" says George.

Beth shakes her head.

"Hmmm," says George.

"It's being old," says Paul. "And having sex with men."

"You're lying," I say. "You don't know what silver-balling is."

"Do, too," says Paul.

I write our friends Katie and Liz and Jill with the subject heading "silver-balling." Katie writes back, "What the fuck is that? You dip them in silver? Who would do that?"

I ask my friend Adrian when she comes back from her date with the Frenchman. She says confidently, "Oh, it's Ben Wa balls. Definitely. You know, those balls you insert and then pull them out slowly? They're silver. That's silver-balling."

"Does it matter where you insert them?" I ask.

"Nope," she says.

I ask my friend Linda if she knows what silver-balling is. "I'm trying to figure out if I've done it," she writes back. "Have I? Have you?"

I'm not sure. I Google it. One definition appears to be "killing people"—i.e., shooting them. The term also turns up in a porn DVD description of something done in a "stall." A horse stall? A bathroom stall? The urban slang dictionary offers that it means: "when you skeet skeet skeet in your girlfriend's mouth and she spits it on your balls." Okay, possible, though not, perhaps, the last word. All other uses of the term have to do with jewelry. Perhaps it means hanging jewelry all over someone in a horse stall and then shooting that person? Or "shooting" on that person? I know James only slightly, but I can't quite see him doing that. Also, he doesn't have a horse, or a horse stall, as far as I know.

Beth and I are perplexed, and embarrassed, and we still don't know if either of us has done it, or not, and do we want to do it? This silver-balling? Whatever it is, I notice that I like to say it, that there is some sort of erotic charge in the sound of those *s*'s and *l*'s, that hard little *b* rolling around on the tongue, the slippery and receptive gerund, the invocation of silver shockingly close to the tenderness of balls—ouch!—the proximity of metal to flesh, the glamour of the juxtaposition of silver and skin. I don't know if I've done silver-balling, but after a few days I know that I have, at least, said and written *silver-balling*, and the more I say it, the hotter it gets. Beth and I say it quite a bit, and we ask nearly everyone we know about it, with the exception of Troy. We don't ask Troy because we don't want the silver-balling game to end yet. No one, it turns out, knows what it is, and we discover that there is pleasure in that, too: the erotic unknown. Surprising your friends, who like to think they are sexually sophisticated, with an act they've never heard of and that is possibly injurious. Like Catherine Deneuve opening the buzzing box in the Buñuel film *Belle de Jour*, that box of erotic mystery. What's in there? Why is it buzzing? Why does she look so happy when she opens it?

Silver-balling. Say it a few times. See what I mean? It's Seussian, also a bit Marie Antoinette. One can imagine they were silver-balling at Versailles. Lucky James, to be silver-balling said hot new boyfriend. It kind of turns me on that I can't quite see what they're doing in there, that the shadows don't make sense to me. In my mind, the silver is molten, but also cool, which isn't possible in reality. In my mind, silver-balling is special, dangerous, complex.

After a week or so, Beth and I finally give in and write Troy. *What is silver-balling? Oh*, he writes back, *I just made that up. I have no idea.*

Silver-balling. Silver-balling. Silver-balling. It rings in the mind, full of promise.

SLUT

ABIOLA ABRAMS

DEFINITION: a promiscuous woman.

Are we simply romantically challenged, or are we sluts?
—SARAH JESSICA PARKER AS CARRIE BRADSHAW
IN *SEX AND THE CITY*

Definition: The origin of the word *slut* does not stem from a sixth-grade bathroom stall encounter between Gina and Jaqui's boyfriend Jake as I originally suspected. The word *slut* derived from the Middle English word *slutte* for a slovenly woman and has come to mean a woman having multiple concurrent sexual relationships.

Politically correct synonyms: horizontally challenged, nonvirginal, footloose, lover of people, pussy-power advocate, indiscriminate, giving humanitarian, woman with the morals of a man.

Politically incorrect synonyms: skank, tramp, slag, sausage wallet, ho, hoochie, wench, trick, hussy, chickenhead, harlot, jezebel, tart, slore, whore, courtesan, jump off, sidechick, floozy, strumpet.

Related terms for nonmonogamous women: mistress, prostitute, nymphomaniac, polyamorous, sex-positive, fellacious, virtueless, loose, easy, promiscuous, lusty, dirty, low.

I was always jealous of the girls we called sluts. I was one of the finger-wagging, moral-policing high-roaders and former Girl Scouts that sat in the front row of every class and raised my hand practically before the questions were asked. When I grew up in the late eighties, *slut* was probably the worst thing a woman could be called. Nancy Reagan had taught us to just say no to all kinds of things, and AIDS seemed as if it might be lurking behind every toilet seat. Teen pregnancy threatened to ruin us. The so-called sluts seemed so much freer than the rest of us, flipping off society with their don't-give-a-damn attitudes. They seemed happy, as if by sleeping around—or appearing to—they were living slightly above the law.

I was one of a handful of kids of color at Brearley, an elite New York City all-girls prep school. I was reminded often by my parents and my peers that in addition to regular teenage concerns, I also bore the burden of representation. "You are not only representing yourself at Brearley. You are representing every African-American young woman in America," Mrs. Johnson, one of the two black teachers in the school told me when I racked up too many tardies.

Jeez, Louise. So if Abiola met a boy at Le Panto's, our after-school watering hole, and made out with him as Lizzie Paddock seemed to do daily, not only was Abiola a probable slut, but she was marking every young lady of African descent that might grace the halls of Brearley, Spence, Chapin, and Nightingale-Bamford (our neighboring all-girls schools) as sluts, too. My social life could single-handedly dismantle civil rights and set black people back forty years.

Madonna's *Sex* book, daring music videos, and cutting-edge lyrics made all of us girls at Brearley want to be exactly like her when we grew up. When our imitations of her wild style of dressing—cutoff shirts, rolled-up skirts, and public bra straps—compromised the integrity of our dull navy uniforms, our headmistress added a new rule to the manuals on proper apparel: no underwear is to be worn as outerwear. After all, we were not only representing ourselves, but also the Brearley School and its mission of providing an academically rigorous liberal arts education to girls, by truth and toil. Our playground motto was "Other girls marry doctors, Brearley girls become doctors." Evidently, our Madonna-wannabe wardrobes threatened to dismantle women's rights and set back the 110-year history of Brearley. My behavior as a young woman could again degrade my tribe.

So who was having all the fun while I was upholding the honor of my race and gender? The best known of the young women we called sluts in high school were Dana, who was caught having sex in the closet; Ariel, who claimed to have contracted a case of crabs by trying on jeans in the Gap; and Elle, who became a teen mother at sixteen. They are now respectively a real estate developer, investment baker, and day-care matron, so I guess that they were no worse for the wear.

Sluts are brazen outlaws. Male counterparts to sluts are called playboys, philanderers, players, ladies' men, man-whores, lady-killers, cads, womanizers, and rakes—all glamorous compared to the derogatory word *slut*. On the other hand, as a friend of mine says, a hoe is a garden tool, necessary for irrigation. The crops die without it.

STRIPTEASE

DANIELLE TRUSSONI

DEFINITION: the act, by a woman, of removing her
clothes one by one as a theatrical entertainment.

The People's Almanac *credited the origin of striptease as we know it to an act in 1890s Paris in which a woman slowly removed her clothes in a vain search for a flea crawling on her body.*

−RICHARD WORTLEY
A PICTORIAL HISTORY OF STRIPTEASE (1976), 29-53

Start balanced.
Show just enough skin to capture
Their attention, to inflame the eye,
To make them want more:
Give enough of the smooth, sweet stuff underneath.
But listen:
Not too much.
They need to think there's going to be a big pay-off.
This is about seduction.
This is about having a story
Only you can tell, the
One that explains the
Rough mechanics
Of desire.
(I'm always telling the same story,
The one about the night when I was
Twenty-three and drunk and dancing
At a bar in Chapel Hill called the Local 506.
Swivel-hipped, holding a gin & tonic in one hand, I stepped
Up onto the barstool and then
Oops-there-goes-my-drink-gimme-another?

Up onto the bar, where I danced a strip tease.
It was the summer, so hot nobody
Including me wanted to keep clothes on.
I wore a sweat-drenched white halter top and
Gold stretch 1970s spandex hip-huggers that read:
Van Gough on the back pocket.
I was too young and too drunk to know why
I was dancing on the bar.
An Indy-rock band from Athens, Georgia
Played on stage, oblivious to the heat.
Dancing was like telling them a story.)
One more thing:
Always tell them what they want to hear.
Say it like this:
Anything you want, anything at all,
It's worth the wait.
That's how I do it.
The heat was so overwhelming,
As it was on that summer night ten years ago
In a bar so hot that some of us began to
Go a little too far.
A white halter-top string loosened,
A shimmer of gold spandex,
Another gin and tonic hoisted up.
I began to like the idea of going too far.
The night was sultry and it didn't matter that a hundred
        people
Were standing around, smoking and nodding to the music.
I didn't care who was there,
So long as they were watching.

SWAPPING

HELENA ECHLIN

DEFINITION: Today what is called a swinger lifestyle
was previously known as wife swapping. This term is used
to describe a form of recreational social and sexual
intercourse between consenting adults.
AKA: the lifestyle, nonmonogamy,
swinging, play (as in *play party*).

RELATED TERM: the term *hot wife* refers to a married woman who
has sex with men other than her spouse, with the husband's consent.

As far as anyone knows, swinging (as this community exists today, in the
United States) had its roots amongst an elite group of U.S. Air Force fighter
pilots during World War II. These men were wealthy enough to move their
wives close to base, and the fact that their fatality rate was the highest of any
branch of service led to an unusual social milieu in which non-monogamy be-
tween these pilots' wives and other pilots became acceptable. These arrange-
ments persisted near Air Force bases throughout World War II and into the
Korean War. By the time the Korean War ended, these groups had spread from
the bases to the nearby suburbs.

—WWW.SEXUALITY.ORG

The directions to the international sex party take us to a damp
parking lot. The party itself is in a mansion somewhere on the
outskirts of San Rafael in Marin County, but in order to discour-
age gate-crashers, the organizers refused to disclose the address.
Instead, they have arranged for a van to pick up guests from here.
Earlier this evening, my husband and I had to attend his office
Christmas party, and by now, it's eleven thirty at night. I shiver in
my outfit, a skintight, silver evening gown that a friend picked
up in a Dallas stripper store (I wore another outfit to the office

party). I squint through the fog and see that the lot belongs to a Jehovah's Witness church. Can this be the right place? But after ten minutes or so, a van arrives, and we soon sweep up the driveway of a large ranch-style home. From the outside, it doesn't look like the venue for an orgy.

I am here because I'm researching a possible book about nonmonogamy. Jordan and I have already attended several partner-swapping parties, but this promises to be the most glamorous of them all. It's not advertised on the Internet or in swinger magazines. The only way to get in is through a personal invitation from the organizers: Smith, a man with blue eyes, a meticulous goatee, and a lupine charm, and his wife, Natalie, a pretty brunette in her early thirties. (All names have been changed.) I met the couple at Burning Man, the performing arts festival, where their camp was opposite mine. They gave permission for me to attend their party as an observer. "But you and your hubby can always jump in if you want to," Smith stressed.

Smith and Natalie are very picky about their guest list. Only couples and single females may attend, since single men can be aggressively competitive. You don't have to be a supermodel, but you do have to be attractive and, typically, under forty. Smith lets in a handful of "select early forties" (a loophole I suspect he introduced for himself).

Smith doesn't like the terms *swapping* or *swinging*. They summon up visions of suburban key parties of the seventies. He likes to refer to partner-swapping as "being modern," For instance, you might say, "They're a very modern couple." When Smith refers to the "modern world," he is not talking about global capitalism.

Tonight, when Jordan and I enter the party, there are beautiful modern couples everywhere. Smith boasted that couples fly in from London and Paris for this party, and now I see why. At most of the sex parties I've attended, when people have taken their clothes off, I would have preferred they kept them on. But, comparing these people with the clientele at the other parties is like comparing designer canapés with processed luncheon meat.

The party's theme is "Abracadabra, Ass, and Alchemy," and the women are dressed like magicians' assistants, in elbow-length gloves and evening gowns, or fishnets and corsets. The men are wearing top hats and tails, carrying magic wands and packs of cards. Everyone is drinking champagne or vodka. The mansion's owner, eager to protect his carpets, has forbidden red wine. I don't see why he's so worried about spilled drinks. He's going to have much worse stains to worry about later.

Jordan and I tour the mansion. The decor seems inspired by an English country manor, with polished wood panels, embroidered drapes, and four-poster beds. A veranda overlooks an aquamarine pool the size of a small lake, illuminated by burning flares. Steam rises from two hot tubs and evaporates among the palm trees. Mounted on the outside wall, a white stag's head surveys the scene with the disapproving expression of a chaperone at a school dance.

We should be thrilled to be spectators at this extravaganza, but the truth is, we're bored. We've been to too many of these parties and seen too many people having sex. We're suffering from orgy ennui. It doesn't help that we're starving. We skipped dinner to get to the office party on time, and all we've eaten tonight is a handful of peanuts. I promise Jordan we can leave after the Orgy Tipping Point. I've coined this phrase to describe the moment at a sex party when people actually start, well, partying. The OTP is a single point rather than a gradual process. It's as precise as the moment when the music stops in a game of musical chairs. This is because sex-party guests are goal-oriented. A period of small talk is necessary so that people can figure out who's going to have sex with whom. But then, as soon as the first couple or group gets down to it, everyone else follows suit.

Tonight, sure enough, guests mill about for an hour or two,

then—abracadabra!—suddenly everyone is naked and having sex, in the hot tubs, on the four-poster beds, and on the host's precious carpet.

It's easy to assume that a couple comes to these parties because something is missing in the relationship. Maybe sex has grown stale, or maybe they've fallen out of love. But everyone around us seems to be having fun. Maybe I've been to too many of these parties, but swinging no longer seems so exotic to me. I can see how for practitioners it is just a pleasant hobby. Some couples like to go antiquing. These couples like to have group sex.

"Great, now we can go," says Jordan. But to get back to the church parking lot, we'll have to find the van driver. We hunt high and low for him, peering at the tangled bodies in dimly lit rooms.

We end up in the kitchen, where three lovely women are having sex on the table next to a platter of cured meats and cheeses. Many men would pay to see this. But when Jordan sees the women going for it, all he says is "Great! Ham!"

I finally come upon the van driver outside, on the veranda, where guests are rutting under the chilly gaze of the white stag. I want to say good-bye to Smith before we go. But when I find him in one of the "play rooms," he is gymnastically entwined with two women and I don't want to interrupt. He is busy being modern—in fact, downright avant-garde.

T

TAINT

LES STANDIFORD

DEFINITION: Americanism for the perineum : that area of the anatomy between the anus and the male or female genitals.

The term was defined for me by Ray Sparks, my nominal supervisor on a street-cleaning crew employed by the city of Cambridge, Ohio, in the summer of 1963. One Friday after work, we were having a cocktail (Boone's Farm cut with 7UP) on the listing porch of a tavern in what was referred to as the city's Lower End.

"You a college boy, right?" Ray asked, apropos of nothing. "Next month," I told him. Ray nodded dolefully. "You know about the t'aint?" His tone suggested that it should have been a question on Ohio State's entrance exam. I shook my head.

Ray was not surprised. He'd already had to show me which end of a push broom to hold. He raised his slab of a hand, holding his thumb and forefinger about an inch apart. "It's that little place on a woman right in between," he said.

"In between what?" I asked.

Ray snorted. "T'ain't asshole, t'ain't pussy." His expression, as usual, suggested that his time was wasted on the likes of me. "There's women that like it when you fool around there."

I nodded sagely, but Ray was already lumbering off for another drink.

Some considerable time later, I found myself in a position to employ the advice with which my mentor had sent me into the wider world.

"What are you doing?" she asked.

"Uh . . . ," I began.

"Just make up your mind," she said impatiently. And we went on from there.

TANTRIC SEX

THORN KIEF HILLSBERY

DEFINITION: a slow, sustained form of sexual
intercourse founded on Hindu mysticism.

Tantric sex distinguishes between the experiences of orgasm and ejaculation. Although they often happen at the same time, men are capable of having orgasms without ejaculating. Ejaculatory control is what makes it possible for Tantric lovers to capture and extend the magical energy of orgasm. By holding back, men can experience a series of "mini-orgasms."

—AMY PAINTER, "TANTRIC SEX TECHNIQUES,"
DISCOVERYHEALTH.COM

When the Americans appeared at the outdoor café on the Campo San Stefano where Lorenzo Manin habitually drank his evening Prosecco, he beckoned the waiter. He nodded toward the new arrivals, a sunburned couple in their late twenties and a giant of a single man whose shoulders seemed as wide to the Venetian as the ornate matrimonial bed in which he slept alone in the Ca' del Duca on the Grand Canal. Manin said he was paying for whatever they might be having, not anonymously but with nothing in particular he wished to convey.

In short order they were joining him—after whispered assurances he could well imagine: *of the oldest of families, a man of refinement*—Sarah and Brendan from Chicago, who said they were

251

in town for the Biennale, and "Mikal with a *k*," origin unspecified, though Lorenzo Manin had noticed him before, striding across the Campo.

"I don't believe we've met," said Mikal. Stubble darkened his jawline, but his scalp shone pink and polished, as if freshly shaven. He wore a single gold earring, of masculine gauge.

"I thought I recognized you from the Giardini today," replied Manin.

Mikal settled in beside him, nodding. After the briefest of puzzled glances, Sarah and Brendan followed suit across the table

"The Public Gardens," explained Manin. "Napoléon's gift to Venice. Inadequate recompense for her liberty, perhaps, but a lovely setting for the Biennale, don't you agree?"

They agreed, volubly, over the first bottle of wine and well into the second, then gazed upon their host with evident wonder when he said wistfully that, yes, a lovely setting it would have made that year for his own work, too.

They no doubt supposed him a dilettante—

He raised a manicured hand to silence their objections.

"But I am sorry to say it is a matter of record, my invitation to exhibit at the Venetian pavilion. Followed by its retraction, at the eleventh hour."

What he had envisioned, he said, was a darkened room of glass within a larger gallery of wood, from which could be glimpsed at irregular illuminated intervals the initiation of sexual partners into the Tantric body postures, breath control, and meditation that led through volitional control of the male orgasm to ecstatic union, lasting hours.

Techniques first brought to La Serenissima in the fourteenth century by none other than Marco Polo, whose return to Venice with a Mongolian wife was well documented. What had remained secret for half a millennium was the couple's initiation of others into Tantric practice, commencing transmission of the mysteries leading to spiritual bliss through sexual pleasure that had contin-ued down the generations of Venetians, without interruption to the present day.

"To elaborate I will simply add that a heroic bronze may be seen in Campo Manin near the Rialto, depicting a man in com-pany of a ferocious winged lion, the most formidable in all Venice."

A man from whom he claimed direct descent.

A man whose private diaries revealed in coded entries that he sometimes engaged in intercourse for days without achieving release.

Several days.

Astounding as such a feat seemed to Westerners, it stood in the middling rank of proficiency to the cognoscenti of the East.

"In some radical Indian lineages, irreversible genital mutila-tion of the male has been practiced to ensure the complete im-possibility of ejaculation."

But that, he assured them, was quite the opposite of what had got him into trouble.

"In all artistic portrayals of Tantric practice, the *membrum virile* is shown to be of prodigious length and girth. I know of no exception. In soliciting volunteers to initiate I meant to maintain this tradition, and I said so when the curator asked why the men in my sketches were so uniformly well-endowed."

Only Mikal smiled, broadly.

"And that was the end of it. He told me that to recruit participants from those attending the exhibition, as I planned, opened the Biennale to prosecution for pandering as it was, and such a specification served only to strengthen the case."

He shrugged.

"Later I learned this gentleman is rumored to have, shall we say, personal sensitivities in this regard."

Only Mikal laughed, aloud.

Brendan said nothing.

Sarah insisted that size mattered not at all.

"At least to women," she added, shooting an accusatory glance at Mikal.

"But we are speaking not of procreation, or romantic love, but of sexual athleticism," replied Lorenzo Manin. He argued that many athletic endeavors required extraordinary physical attributes, and as he spoke discursively of coronal friction and esophageal G-spots, he thought Sarah's eyes betrayed a certain fascination.

Which betrayed in turn her husband's limitations, or so he suspected when Brendan put an end to the discussion. He rose abruptly, pleading their shared exhaustion.

As the couple made their good-byes, Mikal rose with them. He told Manin that after he walked them back to the Hotel Danieli he would make a point of swinging by Campo Manin.

"Check out the big lion," he said casually, his voice downplaying the intention even as his steady gaze emphasized, for Lorenzo Manin, the invitation.

He watched them depart, glanced at his wristwatch, and lit a Sobranie Black Russian. He was no artist; he had last attended the Biennale in 1993, for perhaps twenty minutes. And all he knew of Marco Polo's wife was that her presumed remains had been reported found a year or two after that, wrapped in Chinese brocade in an excavation on the site of her husband's family residence in the Castello district. But he was indeed a true Venetian, and no one had better identified the qualities that made him so than the incomparable Casanova, whose spirit he revered and whose example he relished. There was his pride, in the first place; his manners, in the second; and above all else, like the pendant pewter orb of waxing moon in the violet scrim of Adriatic sky, his absolute, impeccable discernment.

TOP/BOTTOM (*see also* BDSM)

WHITNEY JOINER

DEFINITION: a top is an assertive or dominant partner, or a person who prefers the assertive or dominant role, and a bottom is a receptive partner, a partner who is penetrated or submissive.

A female dominant is sometimes called a domme (IPA: dɒm), femdomme, domina, or dominatrix. In the English-speaking world, mistress *is by far the most common dominatrix title, while in most of continental Europe, the most common titles are, and some are etymologically related,* maîtresse, maid, maidress, matress, mother, mate, madre, *or* domina. *The most common dominatrix title in the Spanish language is* ama. *The equivalent Japanese term is* 女王様 (joôsama, *or* queen).

We bought the engagement rings before we knew what they meant. Before we knew each other at all, really. And even though I knew we had so much more to learn, I was still shocked when Sam told me—when the depths of what I didn't know about him became clear.

He'd been tinkering on my computer when I got home from class. Sam didn't live in New York, and during that visit—only a few days before—he'd asked me to marry him.

"What'd you do today?" I asked.

"Actually . . ." He hesitated. "I went to a club."

"A club?" I was confused. "In the middle of the day?"

"It was a . . . a sex club." He trailed off, guilt in his voice.

"What kind of sex club?" I asked, then suddenly flashed onto his meaning. "Like a dungeon?"

He nodded.

"While I was at school?"

Another nod. "I didn't do anything. I just . . . watched." He looked at the floor, as if awaiting punishment.

"So, you're . . . ?" I didn't know what to say. What was going on here? Watched what? And where? Some vaguely stygian chamber of depravity—sweaty walls, flickering candles, riding crops?

"I'm—" He started, then stopped. "I'm into that."

I just stared at him. What was "that," exactly? Leather? Whips? Chains? Nipple clamps? Hot wax? My tiny room started to feel even smaller. Sure, Sam got turned on when I was aggressive, but . . .

I'd never thought about S/M before. We were post–Madonna's *Sex*, but pre–*Sex Tips from a Dominatrix*. Before sex blogs. Before the mainstreaming of kink. I didn't get it: who'd want sex tinged with that kind of darkness? Throwing each other around, definitely. Tying each other up, sure. But . . . pain? Actual pain? And to be so mesmerized by the idea that you'd seek out a dungeon? Suddenly my adorable new boyfriend—fiancé!—seemed alien, threatening.

Sam didn't say anything; he was waiting for me. Okay, I thought. You love this boy. He loves you. Don't attack; don't jump.

I sat down on my bed. "Tell me about it," I said.

Sam didn't really talk about his interest in BDSM (bondage/disciple, dominance/submission, sadism/masochism), he said. His friends didn't know; his ex-girlfriends hadn't known. As a kid, he'd loved playing cowboys and Indians with the girls in his neighborhood: he loved the aching wonder of being completely under a girl's control, without knowing when he'd be let free. A few years before, during college, when his submissive fantasies became more intense, tentative online searches led him to alt.sex.bondage and the shocking relief of being one of many, instead of a lone freak, as he'd assumed. He'd joined local munches—informal groups who to talk about the lifestyle. He'd had a mistress, who topped him at an underground BDSM hotel. For those weekends, he was her slave, coming home on Sunday night bruised, spent, and in ecstasy.

Sam looked up at me hopefully. "I thought you might be into it, too."

I was into the pseudo-dominatrix dynamic with Sam. "I love that you're bossy," he'd told me after we first met. I didn't have to water myself down with him, act coy, passive. But codifying that—all the leather and "mistress" talk—was something entirely different.

I took a deep breath. "I can try."

And I did. After Sam left New York and I bought a handful of books on BDSM (a school acquaintance who was also a professional escort, well schooled in BDSM, gave me a reading list), his desires no longer seemed so heavy and dark. As soon as I had a wisp of understanding of the underlying psychology—the give-and-take of power, the enormous amount of trust and tenderness required for a BDSM scene, the incredible variety of sexual interests such an umbrella term encompasses—I relaxed.

Okay, so I didn't grow up with topping fantasies, I thought while I read. But Sam needs this, and maybe topping will come naturally to me. Maybe I'll channel the forceful side of my personality—Sam wasn't the first to call me bossy, just the first to think it was hot—into sex.

We watched porn together; I tied him up; we bought toys and strap-ons.

But the more I tried, the less natural it felt. The excitement of joining a subversive sexual club with its intimations of possible danger quickly fell away. I was left fumbling in the dark: masquerading as some dominatrix ideal gleaned from books, pop culture, and his vague descriptions of his fantasies. I started to feel as if he had a mental list of what he wanted from me—but he hadn't given me a copy. Instead of an organic, mutual experience, more and more it was as if I were performing, auditioning for a permanent part in his sexual bildungsroman.

Years later, long after Sam and I had broken up, I was on the phone one afternoon with Sam's mother. "Sam's with his strange girlfriend this weekend," she said disapprovingly. "She's much older. He hardly sees her. I don't know why they're together."

I didn't reply, thinking, I do.

TRANSGENDER

T COOPER

DEFINITION: an umbrella term describing people whose gender identity (sense of themselves as male or female) or gender expression differs from that usually associated with their birth sex.

It is better to be hated for what one is than loved for what one is not.

—ANDRÉ GIDE

1. I am the singular representative of all transgender (or *transgendered* if you like) people everywhere. Like if Oprah wanted to do a show about transgender people, and she had the budget to fly only one person into Chicago that day, it would be me.

2. Wait, I'm not even sure the word *transgender* should be included in this volume. It isn't a "dirty" word, and technically speaking, it isn't necessarily related to sexuality—except for the fact that many (well, probably most) transgender people, in addition to being transgendered, probably like to engage in sex, which, again, has very little to do with their gender expression—though it might have everything to do with their partner's or partners' gender expression(s). That is, transgender people could very well be sexually attracted to other transgender people, ones who present as traditionally masculine, feminine, or somewhere in the infinite spaces between. Or transgender

people might even be attracted to nontransgender (aka cisgender) people. Imagine that.

3. Seeing as the term is included in this book, and that I am the expert representative of all transgender people everywhere, I should start by saying that contrary to popular usage, *transgender* is not a noun. You know how in certain circles you're not supposed to say "The gays should be able to get married" or "The blacks sure have it hard in New Orleans" because of the slight tinge of implied homophobia or racism, even if you're trying to be nice? Well, in my opinion—which remember, represents all transgender people's opinions everywhere—you also can't say "Transgenders sure are snappy dressers," or even, if you're being honest, "Transgenders freak my shit out." Like on CNN recently, when they did a feature on "transgenders" during gay pride month, the hook for the segment was "What *are* transgenders anyway?" Don't say that. Say "transgendered people." Or simply "trans." And if you're bold and you know at least one personally, you might even use "tranny."

4. Some—but by no means all or necessarily most—transgender people feel as though they were "born in the wrong body."

5. Do you know that reality show about the dwarf family on the Learning Channel? I really like that show. (Stay with me here.) In some ways, little people are like trannies, in that they have bodies that don't easily fit into preconceived ideas about what human bodies should look like. So when average-sized people see a little person on the street, many feel it is well within their rights to comment, to ask, to prod, or just to stare. When I see members of the little-people family, the Roloffs, on the Learning Channel having dinner with other little people, or just hanging out and

literally being able to see eye to eye with buddies at the Little People of America Conference in Milwaukee, I totally feel them on a cellular level—how sometimes for transgender people, it's just so nice to have a drink or enjoy a meal with people who don't always fit neatly into the binary-obsessed world in which we live. Or maybe they do fit into the binary-obsessed world in which we live, and a stranger looking at our table would have no clue that anybody there was anything but a "real" man or "real" woman, but still, there's a shared journey and sensibility and experience, which I certainly saw mirrored at the LPA Conference on the TV show.

6. When you meet me at a wedding at which we are both guests, and you act nicer to me than any of the other guests, I feel a little like the only black person in the room at a Clinton fund-raiser. You're *so* cool with my visible difference that you've decided to *kill* me with kindness, just to show me and everybody else how *progressive* and *unfazed* you are by the fact that I am black or little or transgendered or disabled or poor or maybe even a Cambodian orphan. Being extra-nice helps you feel more in control—I totally get it, and I do it sometimes, too, only the difference is that I know what it feels like to be on the other end, so when I catch myself doing it, I stop.

7. As with most identity-based communities, unofficial rules and regulations emerge. "Pick a gender" is one example, because it apparently makes some of "us" feel more comfortable when everyone in our group adheres to an M or F completely, instead of floating somewhere in between. Those of "us" in the middle and comfortable with being there could ruin it for everybody else who just wants to pass as traditionally masculine or feminine, with the ultimate goal of being accepted by an admittedly transphobic larger culture. But that's sad, because the impulse that

tells nontrans people that it's okay to get up in my face and insist that I'm in the "wrong" bathroom (happens at least every other day) is the same impulse that some trans people indulge when insisting that other trans people are not "trans enough." It's called policing, and like its namesake, is based on a skewed power dynamic—and thus almost never fair.

8. Cutting your boobs off or not cutting your boobs off. Cutting your dick off or not cutting your dick off. Taking hormones or not taking hormones. Centurion, phalloplasty, tracheal shave, testicular implants, breast implants, hysterectomy, vaginoplasty, vaginectomy, labiaplasty. Any one or combination of these (and many others) are procedures that transgender people might—or might not—choose to undergo.

9. In fact, this entry for *transgender* is so incomprehensive precisely because (A) the term is alive and constantly evolving, impossible to define completely; even attempting to do so is fraught with anxiety that somebody's always going to feel misrepresented and subsequently pissed off; and (B) I am actually *not* the representative of all transgender people everywhere. I am merely one of them, who may or may not be in the midst of one or more—or none—of the procedures listed in #8 above.

V

VAGINAL EJACULATION

JONATHAN AMES

DEFINITION: the expulsion of noticeable amounts of clear
fluid by human females from the vagina during orgasm.
AKA: squirting, gushing.

Female ejaculation, or shiofuki, *as it's called in Japanese, takes the term also used to describe a whale spouting water.* Shiofuki *has become a household word in Japan largely through the efforts of one man—Taka Kato, the forty-four-year-old adult movie actor who has made a name for himself by making so many of his on-screen female companions ejaculate.*

—DR. KUNIO KITAMURA, HEAD OF THE JAPAN FAMILY PLANNING
ASSOCIATION, "SHIOFUKI AND THE ART OF FEMALE EJACULATION,"
AUGUST 2006

A GLORIOUS BAPTISM

Several years ago, I had a brief affair with a young, very attractive brunette. She had a full figure and was a fan of my writing. She contacted me via e-mail and we ended up talking on the phone. She said to me, during one conversation, before we met in person, "I figured that from your writing you were some kind of male slut and that it would be easy to sleep with you."

I wanted to protest this statement, but simply uttered, noncommittally, "Male slut?!?"

We fooled around, by my estimation, six times. The first two dates we simply made out. On the third date, we ended up in bed, but didn't have intercourse. I did go down on her, though, and noticed something curious: right when she seemed on the verge of climax, she would make me stop. This happened a few times and

I didn't question her about it. I figured that coming would make her feel vulnerable and she wasn't ready for that.

On our fourth and fifth dates, the same thing happened, though. Either by hand or mouth, I would bring her close, seemingly, to orgasm, but she would always halt the proceedings. Eventually, on the fifth date, I gently inquired, "Is everything okay? Why don't you want to come?" She mumbled something about not wanting to lose control, and this, I thought, confirmed my initial hypothesis, so I didn't press the issue.

The sixth time we were in bed, since she seemed to enjoy it for the most part, I went down on her, but, as usual, she wouldn't allow herself to have an orgasm. We made love, though, for the first time that night, and it was quite nice. She didn't come, but I didn't think she would.

After lying there, postcoitally, for about twenty minutes, I felt inspired and went back down on her. Something had changed—she wasn't stopping me every few minutes. The lovemaking seemed to have relaxed her, so I was happily licking away and an orgasm seemed to be approaching—she was pushing against my tongue with great urgency and she wasn't stopping!

Then, suddenly, she convulsed, and warm liquid gushed into my face and would not stop. I'm not joking when I say that I felt like I was drowning, but I kept on licking through this rainstorm as she thrashed about wildly. At first I thought she was urinating on me while orgasming, but then, though I was in a state of shock, it dawned on me that I was experiencing—as an observer and recipient—the first vaginal ejaculation of my life!

I had long heard rumors about such a phenomenon—it was kind of a sexual Loch Ness monster and I had always felt somewhat incredulous. But now there was no denying the empirical evidence of the geyser that was shooting into my face. Maybe because I was having a near-death experience, the girl's ejaculation seemed to last for a long time—seconds felt like minutes as I drowned and licked—and then her tremors subsided, and I could breathe and there was a hush in the air, a calming peace, like what follows a great storm.

Like the survivor of a shipwreck, I washed up between her thighs, my face resting in a substantial puddle on my sheets. I now knew why she had always kept herself from coming. If each orgasm was like putting a pin in a hot-water bottle and releasing a hurricane, I could fully understand not wanting to have such a thing happen until you felt comfortable with your partner.

I happily lay in that puddle, sort of reveling in the newness of it all, but not wanting to embarrass her. I eventually wiped my face on a dry bit of sheet and crawled up next to her. I held her from behind, and we lay there silently, not speaking about what had just happened, and then we both fell into a deep, pleasing slumber.

It's rather complicated to go into, but after that night I never saw her again. Subsequently, a few years later, I met a girl whose vagina seemed to hiccup when she came and a little bit of liquid would be released—my second female ejaculator—but I've never again had such a glorious baptism as I did that one night. I do wonder what became of that girl. I have to say that I'd love to see her again.

VIBRATOR (*see also* SEX TOYS)

PATRICIA MARX

DEFINITION: a sex toy that vibrates, often
used to stimulate the clitoris.

Around the turn of the century, entrepreneurs began to recognize the huge potential market for hand-held vibrators for home use. Vibrator innovation was in fact a driving force behind the creation of the small electric motor. Hamilton Beach of Racine, Wis., patented its first take-home vibrator in 1902, making the vibrator the fifth electrical appliance to be introduced into the home, after the sewing machine and long before the electric iron.

–TERESA RIORDAN, "HISTORY OF THE VIBRATOR SLIDE SHOW,"

–*SLATE*, JULY 5, 2005

Please don't tell my mother about this. When I mentioned to her the other day that I'd agreed to contribute an entry to an encyclopedia of sex, she said, "You can't. You don't know anything about that topic."

The thing is, as the following story proves, she makes an excellent point.

Where to begin? If you don't mind a story with a flashback, how about early one Sunday morning a few years ago? I step out of the shower and I hear a scary jackhammer-like noise. It seems to be coming from somewhere in the bathroom. But where? Inside the wall? I'd prefer not to risk being blown up while investigating.

For whatever reason—a sense of professional obligation perhaps or the wish not to be responsible for a lawsuit against the building—Drago, the handyman for my building, is persuaded to leave his trash-compacting duties, and together we tiptoe into the potential local television newsflash. I direct him into the still-intact bathroom. Maybe inside the radiator, I theorize; and Drago deftly takes apart the radiator. The blare continues. Maybe the faucet? And in a jiffy, Drago, who really is the handiest of handymen, disembowels that as well. The shower pipes are spared, at least for the time being, while Drago begins to ransack the drawers of the tall wooden bureau that sits along the far wall in the bathroom.

Ready for our flashback? Subtract a year. I am in Amsterdam for a reason irrelevant to this story. I have decided to check out a sex shop because, well, this *is* Amsterdam. And I am curious, having never set foot in a sex shop before. Mom, did you catch that? No Previous Experience. And so, I tentatively venture into Not Just Clogs, where I am so flabbergasted by the oddness and tackiness of the merchandise that I end up browsing for a length of time that I worry is perhaps unsuitable for a demure girl such as myself. In fact, I decide that after all this perusing, it would be rude not to purchase at least a souvenir.

Let's return home. Drago has, by this time, inspected all the drawers in the bureau except the bottom one. And now he is about to open that. I am struck by a hideous realization: I know what is inside that final drawer, what is juddering insanely against the resonant wooden walls. I bet you know what it is, too. In fact, given the title of this essay, you'd probably pieced everything together from the outset.

Let me make something clear, Mom: I never used the thing. I'd tossed it in the drawer when I got back from the Netherlands (the Netherlands!) and never even thought about it . . . until, well . . .

"Wait!" I say, lunging at the bureau, hoping to intercept Drago before he has the chance to show me that he, too, can do piecework. "You know, the noises have kind of grown on me now," I'd intended to say. But it is too late. Drago is holding up my souvenir as if it is a torch, except he is the one beaming.

NOOOOOOOOOO!!!!!!!!!!!!!!!!!

Drago looks at me with what I think is a look. What could I do? Drago is a blabbermouth, and the doormen he would no doubt blabber to would, I guess, not be all that tight-lipped, either.

Here is what I eventually come up with: "Oh my God! You found it, Drago! You found my mother's defibrillator!"

(What I meant to say, Mom, was . . . *my* immersion blender.)

VIRGINITY

LEWIS ROBINSON

DEFINITION: 1. The quality or condition of being a virgin.
2. The state of being pure, unsullied, or untouched.
AKA: v-card, honor, maidenhood, flower, chastity.

THE VIRGIN'S PLEDGE

Personal Declaration of Freedom: In order to claim my right to be free from pregnancy & STDs, a broken heart, and dishonest relationships; and, free to fulfill my life goals, find my one true love, and make a lifelong commitment; I, _____, have made the decision to abstain from sex until marriage. I will be accountable to (name of adult mentor) for this decision.

—SWEETGYRLNETWORK.BLOGSPOT.COM

Your friend Evan tells you he became a man on that bike trip in France, with a girl from Massachusetts, in a field behind a roadside toilet in Normandy. He gives you the details, including the expression on her face—concerned eyebrows, parted lips, panting—though you suspect he's borrowing the look from *Insatiable Swedes*, a movie he has also shown you. After dinner one night you and Evan climb the snowy roof of your school to look out at town, the Royal River a white shoelace in the dark woods. Up by Main Street, you see 7-Eleven's sodium lights, the police station, the quiet houses near the Route 1 overpass. Evan flicks his cigarette off the edge and says, "Someone out there, right now, is engaged in the penetration arts." The thought haunts you often. Somewhere in Egypt. Somewhere in Tasmania. Somewhere in Finland. Somewhere in Nepal. And the people of your country, too: Nancy Reagan, Ricky Schroder, Pee-Wee Herman, Dr. Ruth, Charles Barkley, Mary Lou Retton. The world ablaze, turbines whirring, lights flickering on and growing hotter, as if all that

267

fucking behind closed doors is generating electricity. Maine is dark and cold.

Then comes summer. Stacy LeClair brings you down to the icy ocean to teach you to swim. Freckles on her shoulders, straight flaxen hair, and a black one-piece, looming over you as you lie in the water, held up by her hands. Stacy is an older woman, nineteen, on summer break from college. Everything is frigid except her fingers and palms on your stomach. She watches as you stir your arms. When you cough seawater, she helps you up. The bulbous rocks underfoot feel like rolling pins. Your legs are numb. You want to lie back down in the cold waves just so she'll return her hands to your skin. For a few seconds you stand facing each other, shivering, both of you waist-deep, your reproductive organs cryogenically preserved beneath bathing suits. The sun is setting on what might be your last day on earth. She loses her balance on the round rocks, you try to steady her, only making her less steady, you tumble over together, nonswimmer and swimmer in a frantic slippery hug. The thought of drowning is less important than the feel of her arms around your back. But you're pulling her under, so she pushes you away, stands, then reaches out and pulls you to your feet. "Are you okay?" she asks. The swimming lesson is over. The shivering now feels religious. A cormorant stands on a nearby crag, drying its wings.

Her lips are blue. "I have a tub," you say. "I have a tub, a big tub, in my home." After you speak this astonishing collection of words, she nods and takes your hand and you are now walking together out of the water, you are now walking up the rocks to the road, you are now walking down the road to your home, to the tub in your home, to the long, claw-footed tub in your home. The sun is gone, but the asphalt is still warm. When you and Stacy arrive, your brother is in the yard doing push-ups, your sister is on the porch reading *Crime and Punishment* with the dog at her feet, and your mom waves from the kitchen window. In the icy water, you had imagined an empty house.

Stacy's smile is neighborly as she lets go of your hand and says, "See you around."

WET DREAMS

ANTHONY GIARDINA

DEFINITION: an erotic dream accompanied
by ejaculation of semen.
AKA: nocturnal emission.

The average teenager has four erections every night. And a wet dream, on average, every three weeks.

—WWW.BBC.CO.UK/ONELIFE/BODY_MIND/BOYS_BODIES/
WET_DREAMS/

THE MONSTER AT THE END OF THIS BOOK

To begin with, puberty was late, which was just fine with me. I already had pretty much everything a boy in the midsixties might need: long bicycle rides with my best friend, Barry Kennedy, Thursday nights with Elizabeth Montgomery in *Bewitched*, decent grades, a loving family. We're talking paradise. Who needed the thing that came after, the expulsion from the Garden, the confusing, agonizing thing that made my older schoolmates look so *troubled*? Let it take its sweet time.

That attitude, which seems, in the writing of it, so relaxed, doesn't fully explain even to me why, when puberty finally hit, I decided not just to accept it but to put up a fight. Maybe the answer lies somewhere in the fact that when puberty announced itself, in a way I couldn't just turn away from, it did so in the from of stiff sheets. Which I would wake up to, embarrassed, humiliated, and vaguely aware that the dreams that had led to the stiffening of the sheets—those dreams into which I didn't dare probe too hard (did they involve Elizabeth Montgomery? Barry Kennedy?)—were like nocturnal excursions into a cave, a dark, shadowy, haunting, rich, emulsion-causing cave. But I was a young teenage boy who liked the daylight world just fine: I didn't want to go into a cave. I wanted to pass the cave. I wanted to ignore and deny the existence of the cave. I wanted, even, to seal it up.

Which is why I conducted a summer-long assault on puberty, played out in my preparations for sleep, where puberty and its minions were most likely to catch one in an undefended state. I went out and bought a jockstrap and slept in it. I knew well enough—though I fought hard against knowing anything at all about the territory ahead—that what caused the monumental (to my mind, anyway) stiffening of the sheets was the stiffening of a part of my anatomy, and I decided, by a logic that now escapes me but which must have made sense to the boy I was then, that a jockstrap had the power to keep one from stiffening, even in sleep. And herewith this essay takes a brief detour into disgustingness (you may want to skip down a bit), because each morning I would peel off the jockstrap and feel it and sniff it, to see if I had indeed triumphed over the biological developments that insisted on despoiling my time of innocence, or whether, in spite of my best efforts, the God of Wet Dreams had found a way of foiling me.

And here's what's really heartbreaking as I look back on the boy who fooled himself that he really needed to investigate the morning condition of that overused jockstrap: you always know when you've had one. You're partly awake, after all. The feeling, especially for a boy on the cusp, is so unbearably sweet, so like being picked up by a perfect wave and carried, even against one's will, on the long ride to shore, that, upon waking, some part of it lingers. I could spend years investigating why I didn't want to give in to that sweetness, why I saw the cave as such a dangerous place to enter. (Does this perhaps have something to do with a childhood overexposure to that most potent of myths, "Hansel and Gretel," where unbearable sweetness is inextricable from ultimate burning? Has anyone studied the similarities of "Hansel and Gretel" to the orthodoxies of 1950s Roman Catholicism?)

It is not, however, "Hansel and Gretel" or even *The Baltimore Catechism* that I think of when I recall my valiant and ultimately doomed attempt to hold off the horde of puberty. It's another book, a *Sesame Street* book I used to read to my daughters when they were young, a book called *The Monster at the End of This Book*. On page 1, as I recall, that *Sesame Street* stalwart, lovable furry old Grover, announces to the reader that there is a monster at the end of this book. So don't turn the page! Which of course the reader does, and does again, to watch Grover build walls of wood and brick and mortar just to keep the foolish reader from turning another page. Until he gets to the end, where a surprised Grover realizes that the monster at the end of this book is him.

I didn't want puberty, so I tried not to turn the page. I built sea walls to keep my wet dreams from spilling over onto the beautifully manicured lawn of my childhood. The pages got turned anyway. Until at the end—well, who knew, all those years ago in my suburban Eden, that the monster at the end of this book would turn out to be so user-friendly?

ACKNOWLEDGMENTS

I'd like to thank my terrific agent, Sally Wofford-Girand, who loved this project the minute I told her about it. And about a minute later, she said, I know the right editor for it. She nailed it: thanks to Kathy Belden, who somehow completely understood me and my wild ideas.

My thanks to Pamela Holm, who can now add Sex Researcher Extraordinaire to her bio.

Thanks to the Ragdale Foundation for two wonderful weeks in Alice's Room.

Thanks to my remarkable contributors, who made this project a true joy. I've never had so much fun while sitting at my computer.

Thanks to Neal Rothman, my very in-house counsel (who took care of the one hundred contracts for this collection), my first reader, my last reader, my one-man band, my love.

EDITOR AND CONTRIBUTOR

ELLEN SUSSMAN is the editor of *Dirty Words: A Literary Encyclopedia of Sex*. Her anthology, *Bad Girls: 26 Writers Misbehave*, became a *New York Times* Editors' Choice and a *San Francisco Chronicle* Best Seller. She is the author of the novel *On a Night Like This*, also a *San Francisco Chronicle* Best Seller. Her Web site is www.ellensussman.com.

CONTRIBUTOR NOTES

ABIOLA ABRAMS is the host of BET's *The Best Short Films*. A writer and filmmaker who gives motivational talks, her empowerment movement and interactive site are called the Goddess Factory. Abiola's debut novel, *Dare*, a chick-lit *Faust*, was published by Simon & Schuster. She has a B.F.A. from Sarah Lawrence College and an M.F.A. from Vermont College of Fine Arts.

KIM ADDONIZIO has published two novels with Simon & Schuster: *Little Beauties* and *My Dreams Out in the Street*. She has also published four poetry collections, most recently *What Is This Thing Called Love*. She has been a National Book Award Finalist as well as a recipient of NEA and Guggenheim fellowships. She lives in Oakland, California. www.kimaddonizio.com

STEVE ALMOND is the author of two story collections, *My Life in Heavy Metal* and *The Evil B. B. Chow*. His new book is a collection of essays, *(Not That You Asked)*. He lives outside Boston with his wife and new baby daughter, whom he cannot stop kissing.

JONATHAN AMES is the author of *I Pass Like Night*, *The Extra Man*, *What's Not to Love?*, *My Less Than Secret Life*, *Wake Up, Sir!*, and *I Love You More Than You Know*. His graphic novel, *The Alcoholic*, will be published in 2008 by DC Comics.

NICK ARVIN has published two books, *In the Electric Eden: Stories* and *Articles of War: A Novel*, and his writing has won awards from the American Academy of Arts and Letters, the American Library Association, the Isherwood Foundation, and others. He is also an engineer, working in power plant design. He lives in Denver.

CRIS BEAM wrote *Transparent: Love, Family, and Living the T with Transgender Teenagers* (Harcourt, 2007). She teaches creative writing at Columbia University, New York University, the New School, and Bayview Women's Correctional Facility. She's currently working on a book about foster care in the United States. She lives in New York City.

THOMAS BELLER is the author of *Seduction Theory: Stories*, *The Sleep-Over Artist: A Novel*, and *How to Be a Man: Essays*. *The Sleep-Over Artist* was a *New York Times* Notable Book and an *LA Times* Best Book of 2000. His stories have appeared in the *New Yorker*, *Southwest Review*, *Ploughshares*, and *Best American Short Stories*. He coedits *Open City* magazine.

TONI BENTLEY danced with George Balanchine's New York City Ballet for ten years. She is the author of five books, including *Winter Season: A Dancer's Journal*, *Sisters of Salome*, and *The Surrender: An Erotic Memoir*, a *New York Times* Notable Book in 2004. She writes for numerous publications including the *New York Times Book Review*, the *New Republic*, and *Playboy*.

SARAH BIRD's last novel, *The Flamenco Academy*, a story of obsessive love, was named one of *People* magazine's Hottest Books of the Summer. Her latest, *Weightless*, a comic novel about a wannabe Texas princess surviving the Bush years, will be published by Knopf in May 2008. She is a columnist for *Texas Monthly* and writes for *O* and *Real Simple.*

JESSICA ANYA BLAU is a lecturer at the Writing Seminars at Johns Hopkins University. She is the author of the novel *The Summer of Naked Swim Parties* (HarperCollins).

ROBERT BOSWELL is the author of *Century's Son, American Owned Love, Mystery Ride, The Geography of Desire, Crooked Hearts, Living to Be 100, Dancing in the Movies, Virtual Death, Tongues*, and two forthcoming books, *The Half-Known World* and *Blood Follows: The Search for Treasure at Victorio Peak*. He teaches at New Mexico State University, the University of Houston, and in the Warren Wilson MFA Program.

BRIAN BOULDREY has written six books and edited six anthologies. His most recent book, *Honorable Bandit: A Walk Across Corsica*, was published in fall 2007 by the University of Wisconsin Press. He lives in Chicago and teaches creative writing at Northwestern University and the MFA Program in Writing at Lesley College.

DONOVAN BRIGHT is a pen name. The author lives in Los Angeles.

ADRIENNE BRODEUR's first novel, *Man Camp*, was published by Random House in 2005. She founded the literary magazine *Zoetrope: All-Story* with filmmaker Francis Ford Coppola and was its editor in chief from 1995 to 2002. Currently, she's a consulting editor for Harcourt and is at work on her second novel.

JASON BROWN grew up in Maine. His first book of short stories, *Driving the Heart and Other Stories*, was published by Norton in 1999. His second book of stories, *Why the Devil Chose New England for His Work* was published in November of 2007 by Open City/Grove Atlantic.

BLISS BROYARD is the author of the collection of stories *My Father, Dancing* (Knopf, 1999), a *New York Times* Notable Book of the Year, and *One Drop: My Father's Hidden Life—a Story of Race & Family Secrets* (Little, Brown, 2007). Her fiction and essays have appeared in *Best American Short Stories*, *The Pushcart Prize Anthology*, *Grand Street*, and *Elle* magazine.

SAM BRUMBAUGH is the author of the novel *Goodbye, Goodness*. His fiction has appeared in the *Southwest Review*, *Vice*, *Esquire.com*, and *Open City*. He produced the feature documentary *Be Here to Love Me: A Film about Townes Van Zandt* and is a music curator at the Guggenheim Museum. His novel *Restoration Ruin* will be published in 2008.

MAUD CASEY is the author of two novels, *The Shape of Things to Come* (William Morrow, 2001) and *Genealogy* (Harper Perennial, 2006), and a collection of stories, *Drastic* (William Morrow, 2002). She lives in Washington, D.C., and teaches at the University of Maryland.

NELL CASEY is the editor of the national bestseller *Unholy Ghost: Writers on Depression* (William Morrow), as well as the anthology *An Uncertain Inheritance: Writers on Caring for Family*. Her writing has appeared in *Slate*, *Salon*, the *New York Times*, and *Elle*, among other publications. She lives in Brooklyn with her husband and son.

TITA CHICO's research focuses on gender and sexuality in eighteenth-century English literature. She is the author of *Designing*

Women: The Dressing Room in Eighteenth-Century English Literature (2005), editor of *The Eighteenth Century: Theory and Interpretation*, and a faculty member of the University of Maryland–College Park English Department.

MARCELLE CLEMENTS's most recent book is a novel, *Midsummer.* Her journalism and essays have appeared in many national publications.

KAREN CONNELLY is the author of eight books, the most recent being *The Lizard Cage*, which won Britain's Orange Broadband Award for New Writers. She is also the recipient of numerous Canadian literary awards. She lives in Toronto, spends as much time as she can on Lesvos, and travels frequently in Southeast Asia. For news of her exploits, see www.karenconnelly.ca.

RAND RICHARDS COOPER is the author of a novel, *The Last to Go*, and a story collection, *Big as Life.* His fiction has appeared in *Harper's*, the *Atlantic*, and *Esquire.* A longtime writer for *Bon Appétit*, Rand lives in Hartford, Connecticut, with his wife, Molly, and daughter, Larkin, and writes a column about fatherhood, *Dad on a Lark*, for Wondertime.com.

T COOPER is the author of the novels *Lipshitz Six, or Two Angry Blondes* (Penguin/Plume, 2007) and *Some of the Parts* (Akashic, 2002) and editor of *A Fictional History of the United States with Huge Chunks Missing* (Akashic, 2006). Cooper's writing has appeared in the *New Yorker*, the *New York Times*, the *Believer*, *Poets & Writers*, and *Out*. www.t-cooper.com

When not exercising her animal impulses, **KARIN COPE** teaches writing at NSCAD (Nova Scotia College of Art and Design) University. She has published poetry, short stories, a play, a history, travelogues, and a study of Gertrude Stein entitled *Passionate Collaborations*. Her recent work includes a long documentary poem (*Falso*), an illustrated novel on the Korean War, and, naturally, a bestiary.

NATALIE DANFORD is the author of a novel, *Inheritance*, published by St. Martin's Press, and the coeditor of *Best New American Voices*, an annual anthology series that features fiction by emerging writers.

ALICE ELLIOTT DARK is the author of the novel *Think of England*; two collections of short stories, *In the Gloaming* and *Naked to the Waist*; *The Betty Book* under the pen name Elizabeth "Betty" Albright; and many nonfiction pieces.

LISA SELIN DAVIS is the author of the novel *Belly* and a freelance writer covering all things urban planning. She has written for the *New York Times*, *Salon*, *House & Garden*, and a zillion other publications and has written one other sex essay, about a pornography club, for *Nerve*. You can scrutinize her at www.lisaselindavis.com.

MELINDA DAVIS lives and writes in New York City and the Berkshires. Her fiction has appeared in the *Quarterly*, *Ploughshares*, and the *Pushcart Prize* collection. She is the author of *The New Culture of Desire*, published by the Free Press.

STACEY D'ERASMO is the author of the novels *Tea* (2000), *A Seahorse Year* (2004), and the forthcoming *The Sky Below* (2009). She is an assistant professor of writing at Columbia University.

LAWRENCE DOUGLAS is the James J. Grosfeld Professor of Law, Jurisprudence & Social Thought at Amherst College. He is the author of three books, *The Memory of Judgment* (Yale, 2001), a study of war crime trials; *Sense and Nonsensibility* (Simon &

Schuster, 2004), a collection of humor pieces; and *The Cat-astrophist* (Harcourt, 2007), a novel.

STEPHEN DUNN is the author of fourteen books of poetry and two of prose. His *Different Hours* won the 2001 Pulitzer Prize for poetry. He lives in Frostburg, Maryland.

HELENA ECHLIN is the author of the novel *Gone* (Secker & Warburg/Random House, UK, 2002), and she writes an advice column, *Table Manners*, for *Chow*, an online food magazine. She has written for UK newspapers such as the *Guardian*, the *Times*, and the *Sunday Telegraph*, as well as for U.S. publications such as *Yoga Journal* and the *San Francisco Chronicle*.

S. P. ELLEDGE has known few cicisbeos, but has had many short stories published in many magazines; a few of these stories have been collected in the volumes *Ensemble*, *Assemblage*, *Semblances*, and the latest, *And Other Stories*.

STEPHEN ELLIOTT is the author of six books including the novel *Happy Baby* and the sexual memoir *My Girlfriend Comes to the City and Beats Me Up*. His writing has been featured in *Best American Erotica*, *Best Sex Writing*, and *Best American Non-Required Reading*. He is the editor of the fiction anthology *Sex for America*. He lives in San Francisco.

The author of two novels, *The Loss of Leon Meed* (2005) and *The Prescription for a Superior Existence* (2008), **JOSH EMMONS** spent his formative years trying to emulate Don Juan, with predictable results. He is older and perhaps wiser now.

TIM FARRINGTON is the author of *The Monk Upstairs*, *Lizzie's War*, and *The Monk Downstairs*, a *New York Times* Notable

Book of 2002, as well *as The California Book of the Dead* and *Blues for Hannah*. His short stories have been published in the *Sun*, *Zyzzyva*, and *San Francisco* magazine. He lives in Virginia Beach.

MERRILL FEITELL is the author of the short-story collection *Here Beneath Low-Flying Planes*, which won the Iowa Award for Short Fiction. She is currently at work on a novel and new stories, and she teaches in the creative writing program at the University of Maryland. For more information, visit www.merrillfeitell.com.

LUCY FERRISS is the author of eight books, including the memoir *Unveiling the Prophet*. Her fiction collection *Leaving the Neighborhood* received the Mid-List First Series Award. Other work has recently appeared in the *New York Times* and elsewhere and been recognized by the National Endowment for the Arts and the Fulbright Commission, among others. She is Writer-in-Residence at Trinity College.

The fiction of **THAISA FRANK**, according to the *New York Times*, works "by a tantalizing sense of indirection." Among her books are *Desire, Sleeping in Velvet, A Brief History of Camouflage*, and *Finding Your Writer's Voice* (coauthored). Her work has been translated into Portuguese, Spanish, Finnish, and Polish.

JOSHUA FURST is the author of a novel, *The Sabotage Café*, and the book of stories *Short People*. He has received various awards for his writing, including a Nelson Algren Award and a Michener Fellowship.

ANTHONY GIARDINA is the author of four novels, including *Recent History* and *White Guys*, and a short story collection, *The Country of Marriage*. His short fiction and essays have appeared in

Harper's, the *New York Times Magazine, GQ,* and *Esquire,* and his plays have been produced at the Manhattan Theater Club and Playwrights Horizons. He lives in Northampton, Massachusetts.

ERIC GOODMAN has published four novels, most recently the award-winning *Child of My Right Hand.* He directs the creative writing program at Miami University. His short stories and food and travel writing are widely published. "Blue Balls" was written in Hang Dong, Thailand. Really.

MARIA DAHVANA HEADLEY is the author of *The Year of Yes: A Memoir.* Her prose has been seen in a variety of places, including the *New York Times, Elle,* the *Washington Post, Best American Erotica,* and the *Daily Telegraph.* She is a MacDowell Colony Fellow and a founding member of the Memoirists Collective.

KAUI HART HEMMINGS is the author of *House of Thieves* and *The Descendants,* a *New York Times* Editor's Choice. She is currently working on a book called *How to Party with an Infant.*

MICHAEL HICKINS is the author of a sexy collection of stories, *The Actual Adventures of Michael Missing* (Alfred A. Knopf, 1991; iUniverse, 2000). His most recent work includes *Blomqvist* (iUniverse, 2006), a picaresque novel about faithlessness set in eleventh-century Europe, and *The What Do You Know Contest.* He lives in New York City.

THORN KIEF HILLSBERY's most recent novel, *What We Do Is Secret,* was short-listed for the 2006 Lambda Literary Award. His other novels include *War Boy* and the forthcoming *King & Country.* He is a former columnist for *Outside* and has written for *Rolling Stone* and other magazines. He lives in Manhattan, where he teaches creative writing at Columbia University.

ANN HOOD is the author of seven novels, a collection of short stories, and a memoir. Her essays and stories have appeared in many publications, including the *New York Times*, the *Paris Review*, *More*, *Good Housekeeping*, *Tin House*, *Traveler*, and *Bon Appétit*. Her latest novel, *The Knitting Circle*, is in paperback from W. W. Norton.

BRET ANTHONY JOHNSTON is the author of the internationally acclaimed *Corpus Christi: Stories* and the editor of *Naming the World: And Other Exercises for the Creative Writer*. He can be reached at www.bretanthonyjohnston.com.

WHITNEY JOINER lives in Marfa, Texas. A former features editor at *Salon* and *Seventeen*, she now writes for the *New York Times*, *Seventeen*, *Glamour*, and other publications.

PAGAN KENNEDY has authored nine books (both novels and nonfiction), many of which have been optioned by Hollywood film studios. She also contributes to the *New York Times*, the *Boston Globe*, and other publications. Pagan also works as a writing coach and is proud of her private students, who have recently enjoyed some fantastic successes.

MICHAEL KIMBALL has published two novels, *The Way the Family Got Away* (2000) and *How Much of Us There Was* (2005), both of which have been translated (or are being translated) into many languages. His third novel, *Dear Everybody*, will be published in the United States, Canada, and the UK in the spring of 2008. He lives in Baltimore.

TOBIN LEVY is a freelance writer and editor, currently living in Marfa, Texas.

ELINOR LIPMAN is the author of nine wholesome novels including *The Inn at Lake Devine*, *Isabel's Bed*, *Then She Found Me*, and *My Latest Grievance*, which won the Poetry Center's 2007 Paterson Fiction Prize, awarded annually to the book judged to be the year's strongest work of fiction. She divides her time between Northampton, Massachusetts, and Manhattan.

PHILLIP LOPATE is the author of three personal essay collections (*Bachelorhood*, *Against Joie de Vivre*, *Portrait of My Body*), as well as *Waterfront*, *Being with Children*, and *Totally Tenderly Tragically* (film criticism). He lives in New York City and teaches at Hofstra, Columbia, and Bennington.

MICHAEL LOWENTHAL is the author of the novels *Charity Girl*, *Avoidance*, and *The Same Embrace*. His stories and essays have been widely anthologized, most recently in *Smut: Volume 1* (from Nerve.com) and *Do Me: Sex Tales from Tin House*. He teaches creative writing in the M.F.A. program at Lesley University and serves on the Executive Board of PEN New England. www .MichaelLowenthal.com

ALLISON LYNN is the author of the novel *Now You See It* (Touchstone/Simon & Schuster). Her work has appeared in magazines, newspapers, and anthologies, including the *New York Times Book Review*, the *Chicago Sun-Times*, and *People.* She lives in New York City.

FIONA MAAZEL's first novel, *Last Last Chance*, was published by Farrar, Straus and Giroux in March 2008. She lives in Brooklyn.

MEREDITH MARAN (www.meredithmaran.com) is the bestselling author of several nonfiction books and an award-winning journalist who writes for magazines and newspapers including *Salon, More, Health, Vibe, Family Circle, Parenting, Mother Jones,* and the *San Francisco Chronicle.* In keeping with her proclivity for crossing boundaries, she's currently slaving away at her first work of fiction, a novel starring a gorgeous bisexual.

PETER MARKUS is the author of three collections of short-short fiction, *Good, Brother, The Moon Is a Lighthouse,* and *The Singing Fish.* His latest book is the novel *Bob, or Man on Boat,* brought out by Dzanc Books.

PATRICIA MARX invented the word *mauve.*

STEPHEN MCCAULEY is the author of five novels, including *The Object of My Affection* and, most recently, *Alternatives to Sex.* He lives in Cambridge, Massachusetts.

JENNY MCPHEE is the author of the novels *The Center of Things, No Ordinary Matter,* and *A Man of No Moon.*

MARTHA MCPHEE is the author of the novels *Bright Angel Time, Gorgeous Lies,* and *L'America.* Her work has been honored with fellowships from the National Endowment of the Arts and the John Simon Guggenheim Memorial Foundation. In 2002 she was nominated for a National Book Award.

ANTONYA NELSON is the author of eight books of fiction, including *Some Fun* (Scribner, 2006). She is the recipient of the 2003 Rea Award for Short Fiction, as well as NEA and Guggenheim fellowships, and teaches in the University of Houston's Creative Writing Program. She lives in Telluride, Colorado, Las Cruces, New Mexico, and Houston, Texas.

KATHARINE NOEL's novel *Halfway House* was a *New York Times* Editor's Choice and the winner of the 2006 Kate Chopin Award for fiction, a Ken Book Award from the National Alliance on Mental Illness, and a Rona Jaffe award. She teaches at Stanford University, where she formerly held Wallace Stegner and Truman Capote fellowships.

ALIX OHLIN is the author of *The Missing Person*, a novel, and *Babylon and Other Stories*, both published by Knopf.

THOMAS O'MALLEY was raised in Ireland and England. He is the author of *In the Province of Saints* and has just completed his second novel, *This Magnificent Desolation*. When he's not updating his inventory of used panties and writing about it, he can be found with his three-year-old daughter, Colette Gráinne, swimming with gray seals in the North Atlantic.

T. J. PARSELL is a writer and human rights activist, dedicated to ending sexual violence against men, women, and children in all forms of detention. He is author of *Fish: A Memoir of a Boy in a Man's Prison* (Carrol & Graf, 2006). He lives in East Hampton, New York, with his long-term partner, Tom Wasik, and Dudley, their Golden-Doodle dog.

AMELIA PERKINS, a graduate of Harvard Divinity School, received a fellowship to study the revival of Eastern Orthodox monasticism in Greece. She is currently working on a documentary and a book about the year she spent living with nuns.

DAN POPE is the author of *In the Cherry Tree* (Picador). He has published short fiction in *Harvard Review*, *Crazyhorse*, *Post Road*, *Iowa Review*, *McSweeney's* (no. 4), *Shenandoah*, *Gettysburg Review*,

Night Train, Witness, and other magazines. He is a graduate of the Iowa Writers' Workshop.

CORNELIA READ's first novel, *A Field of Darkness,* has been nominated for the Edgar, Anthony, Audie, RT Bookclub Critics Choice, Barry, Gumshoe, and Macavity awards. A recovering debutante, she lives in Berkeley with her husband and twin daughters, the younger of whom has severe autism.

VICTORIA REDEL is the author of two books of poetry and three books of fiction: *The Border of Truth* was published on 2007. *Loverboy* was chosen in 2001 as a *Los Angeles Times* Best Book and adapted for feature film. *Swoon* was a finalist for the James Laughlin Award. She teaches at Sarah Lawrence College. victoriaredel.com

MICHELLE RICHMOND is the author of the novels *The Year of Fog* and *Dream of the Blue Room* and the story collection *The Girl in the Fall-Away Dress.* Her stories and essays have appeared in *Glimmer Train, Playboy,* the *Missouri Review,* the *Kenyon Review,* and elsewhere. She lives in San Francisco and publishes the online litmag *Fiction Attic.*

LEWIS ROBINSON is the author of *Officer Friendly and Other Stories.* He lives in Portland, Maine.

HEATHER ROSE is the author of two novels, *White Heart,* a tale of Tasmanian tigers and Native American ceremony, and the award-winning *The Butterfly Man,* about the disappearance of Britain's Lord Lucan in 1974. Heather lives on the remote island of Tasmania, south of the Australian continent. www.heatherrose .com.au

ZOË ROSENFELD is a writer and freelance book editor who lives in Brooklyn.

ELISSA SCHAPPELL is the author of the novel *Use Me* and coeditor with Jenny Offill of the anthologies *The Friend Who Got Away* and *Money Changes Everything*. She is a contributing editor of *Vanity Fair*, cofounder of the literary magazine *Tin House*, and a frequent contributor to the *New York Times Book Review*.

RAVI SHANKAR, founding editor of the international journal of the arts *Drunken Boat* (www.drunkenboat.com) and poet-in-residence at Central Connecticut State, has published a book of poems, *Instrumentality* (Cherry Grove), named a finalist for the 2005 Connecticut Book Awards. He has coedited an anthology of contemporary Asian and Arab poetry, *Language for a New Century* (W. W. Norton & Co.).

RACHEL SHERMAN is the author of the book of short stories *The First Hurt* (Open City Books, 2006), which was chosen as one of the 25 Books to Remember in 2006 by the New York Public Library. Her fiction has appeared in *McSweeney's*, *StoryQuarterly*, *n+1*, *Post Road*, and *The Best of Nerve Anthology* (Three Rivers Press, 2000), among other publications.

MARY-ANN TIRONE SMITH has written eight novels and most recently a memoir, *Girls of Tender Age*. Currently, she is working on a Civil War novel while at the same time collaborating with her son, Jere Smith, on a Major League Baseball mystery series. The first, to be published in fall 2008, is *Dirty Water: A Red Sox Mystery*.

JERRY STAHL is the author of the memoir *Permanent Midnight*, the novels *Perv*, *Plainclothes Naked*, and *I, Fatty*, and the short story collection *Love Without*.

LES STANDIFORD lives in Miami and is the author of ten novels, including *Havana Run*, and three works of nonfiction, including

Last Train to Paradise. If his mother knew he had even *typed* the word he writes about in this book, she would be spinning in her grave.

JONATHAN STRONG'S tenth book, *Drawn from Life* (Quale Press, 2008), traces the erotic and aesthetic development of a painter. Among his previous novels are *A Circle Around Her* (Zoland Books, 2000), *Elsewhere* (Ballantine Books, 1985), and *Ourselves* (Atlantic Monthly Press, 1971). He teaches at Tufts University, where he once had the pleasure of teaching the editor of this book.

KATHERINE TANNEY writes essays, fiction, and theater pieces from her home in Austin, Texas. She is also a radio announcer and worked in her twenties as an editor of mainstream porn for an adult video company. Learn more about her fascinating life at www.reallymotional.com.

DANIELLE TRUSSONI has written for the *New York Times Book Review*, *Tin House*, and the *New York Times Magazine*, among other publications. Her memoir, *Falling Through the Earth*, was awarded the 2006 Michener-Copernicus Society of America Award and was chosen as one of the *New York Times*'s best ten books of 2006. You can learn more about her at www.danielletrussoni.com.

KATHARINE WEBER (www.katharineweber.com) is the author of the novels *Objects in Mirror Are Closer Than They Appear*, *The Music Lesson*, *The Little Women* (all *New York Times* Notable Books) and *Triangle*, which was a Finalist for the Paterson Fiction Prize, the John Gardner Fiction Book Award, and the Connecticut Book Award. She is an M.F.A. thesis adviser at Columbia University.

MICHELLE WILDGEN is the author of a novel, *You're Not You*, and editor of an anthology, *Food & Booze*. Her work has appeared in publications and anthologies including the *New York Times, Best New American Voices, Best Food Writing, Death by Pad Thai,* and *Naming the World*. She is senior editor at *Tin House Magazine* and editor at Tin House Books.

ADAM WILSON is a candidate for an M.F.A. in fiction writing at Columbia University. He lives in New York City.

JONATHAN WILSON is the author of seven books, including the novel *A Palestine Affair* and, most recently *Marc Chagall*, a biography. His work has appeared in the *New Yorker*, the *New York Times Magazine*, and *Best American Short Stories*, and he has received a Guggenheim Fellowship. He is director of the Center for the Humanities and Arts at Tufts University.

Australian writer **DANIELLE WOOD**'s second book, *Rosie Little's Cautionary Tales for Girls*, begins with a riff on the word *fellatio*, contains important information about pubic hairstyling and penis size, and enables women and men to justify buying as many pairs of expensive shoes as they can wholeheartedly love at one time.